Correctional Case Management

Richard Enos, D.S.W.

Professor
Department of Criminal Justice
University of North Texas
Denton, Texas

Stephen Southern, Ed.D.

Clinical Consultant
Pine Grove
Forrest General Hospital
Hattiesburg, Mississippi

anderson publishing co.
p.o. box 1576
cincinnati, oh 45201-1576
(513) 421-4142

Correctional Case Management

ISBN 0-87084-164-5
Library of Congress Catalog Number 96-83689

The text of this book is printed on recycled paper.

Gail Eccleston *Editor*

Cover design by Edward Smith Design, Inc./New York, NY

Michael C. Braswell *Acquisitions Editor*

Kelly Grondin *Editor in Chief*

Acknowledgments

This book is dedicated to my parents, Manuel and Marie Furtado Enos. I also wish to thank Marnie E. Enos for her substantial assistance, including authorship of the *Instructor's Guide*, Michael Braswell, Ph.D., for his support, and Ann Reban, M.S.N., for her continuous encouragement. In addition, I wish to thank Patricia Van Voorhis, Ph.D., who reviewed the manuscript and Gail Eccleston, our editor at Anderson Publishing Co.

Richard Enos, D.S.W.

I want to thank my lovely wife, Donna, for all her patience and support. I also appreciate the children, Lauren, Molly and Charles, letting me "borrow" the time. I look forward to repaying them. I could not have completed my contribution without the support of Vicki Fernicola and the Pine Grove family.

Stephen Southern, Ed.D.

Foreword

Correctional case management has evolved from a more traditional counseling and rehabilitation model to a contemporary process that requires correctional helping professionals do much more with a lot less. Not only has the amount of work increased for today's correctional case managers, but the variety of tasks and responsibilities has dramatically increased as well. Their tasks include assessment, referral, intervention, evaluation and, on occasion, advocacy roles. As correctional case management approaches have become broader and more eclectic, the counselor/case manager has found himself or herself in the position of often being identified as a helping professional "for all seasons."

Corrections is essentially a context in which mental health, resource management, and problem-solving skills merge into a dynamic continuum—one that requires the case manager to recognize and utilize interdisciplinary insights and strategies. The family, social institutions such as schools and churches, and community and institutional criminal justice environments all contribute to the context within which the correctional case manager moves and works.

Richard Enos and Stephen Southern have written an excellent text that incorporates a comprehensive treatment of case management issues in corrections within a personal and reflective writing style. This combination of content and style offers the reader a look at the current state of correctional case management from an open-minded and inclusive perspective.

Chapters 1 and 2 provide a thorough introduction to the history and current state of the correctional case management process. Chapter 3 is concerned with the person in the profession, including the importance of communication skills, the nature of offender/counselor interactions, the uses of transference, and professional paradoxes.

Chapters 4 and 5 offer a substantive and coherent view of assessment, classification, and treatment planning strategies. Chapters 6 and 7 provide both the theoretical foundations for, and an overview of, counseling intervention techniques. Chapter 8 focuses on emerging group and family approaches that are particularly relevant to corrections. Chapter 9 addresses relapse prevention and provides specific insights and recommendations regarding how to reduce recidivism rates among certain types of offenders. In Chapter 10, Enos and Southern also offer a solid and thoughtful treatment of case-management issues with ethnic minorities, which is an area of growing concern in corrections. A chapter on ethical issues (Chapter 11) and one on the future of correctional case management (Chapter 12) rounds out the volume.

A noteworthy feature that these two authors have consistently employed throughout the text is the ample use of tables, examples, and case studies that effectively demonstrates the practice of correctional case management.

Too often, correctional helping professionals who find that they must work in a fragmented and repetitive justice system, themselves become fragmented, confused, and burned out. This book brings together the theory and practice of correctional case management in a way that is both realistic and hopeful; in a way that can encourage those who find themselves dazed and confused to become more creative and empowered in their quest to enable the offenders in their care to learn to manage themselves in more meaningful and responsible ways.

Michael Braswell
East Tennessee State University

Contents

Chapter 11
Ethical Issues   **217**

Chapter 12
The Future of Correctional Case Management   **237**

Chapter 1

An Overview of the Correctional Case Management Process

Introduction

Correctional case management is a systematic process by which identified needs and strengths of offenders are matched with selected services and resources in corrections. Case management was an integrative response to the myriad of biopsychosocial problems presented by chronically ill or disabled individuals. Many of these chronically ill clients were released from long-term care in state institutions and other restrictive environments to community settings. Their deinstitutionalization created promises and problems.

The case management model of treatment afforded enhanced protection of human rights and facilitation of growth. Case management provided more rehabilitation options than were typically available in the routine care of total institutions. However, deinstitutionalization produced challenges in individual treatment and service delivery, as well. Community treatment afforded more options and flexibility with less structure and supervision than provided by institutional programs. Case management evolved to bridge the gap between community and institutional care by organizing comprehensive, individually oriented services within a structured, stepwise model of treatment.

Offenders are similar to chronically ill clients of deinstitutionalized services. Offenders, like community mental health and social welfare recipients, have many severe and persistent biopsychosocial problems. In addition, offenders, who are usually treated in secure correctional settings, are increasingly referred to community-based programs. While the overall goals of corrections include deterrence of criminal behavior through punishment and rehabilitation of offender populations, the ultimate motivation for correctional case management may be considered deinstitutionalization from prison to community settings. Imprisonment is becoming prohibitively expensive in many states. Since the vast majority of offenders will eventually be released to the community, correctional case management provides a means for preventing relapse or reducing recidivism, while creating multiple treatment options for classes of offenders.

The correctional case management process insures adequate structure and supervision while pursuing the least-restrictive solutions to identified offender problems. There is opportunity to comprehensively address the many needs of an offender in an individually tailored treatment plan. Simultaneously, correctional case management requires careful planning for community-oriented treatment and overall accountability in service delivery. Therefore, the correctional case management process balances the needs for justice and rehabilitation, structure and innovation, and community protection and deinstitutionalization. The basic goals for correctional case management include:

1. Prevention of relapse or recidivism

2. Reintegration of offenders into their communities and society at large

3. Systematic monitoring of individual progress and program outcome to insure public safety, professional accountability, and offender behavior change. Attainment of the basic goals requires that the process of correctional case management be systematic and integrative.

The purpose of the present chapter is to introduce correctional case management as both a systematic model of offender behavior change and an integrative structure for service delivery. The process of correctional case management is composed of seven interrelated steps or stages, which apply to professional roles and functions in prison, community, and other correctional settings.

Stages in Correctional Case Management

There are seven basic stages in the correctional case management process. Each stage has corresponding tasks and activities as depicted in Table 1.1.

Some of the tasks associated with the seven stages of correctional case management focus on offender behavior change while other stage-specific activities address concerns in service delivery. Our model for correctional case management emphasizes the importance of integrating client needs and organizational requirements. The following sections explore the characteristics of each stage in correctional case management, as well as representative tasks and activities.

Advocacy

The correctional case manager engages in various tasks and activities, some of which form the basis for identified roles and functions. Advocacy is the first stage in our correctional case management model. It is directly related to intake, the next stage in the model, due to the logical necessity of securing clients to serve and preparing them to participate in the correctional intervention. Advocacy is also related to the other stages in that the tasks and activities of this stage are ongoing. Evaluation, the seventh stage of correctional case management, is linked significantly to advocacy because research and development efforts ultimately determine who can be served effectively.

Table 1.1
Tasks in Correctional Case Management by Stage

Stage	Service Delivery	Offender Behavior Change
1. Advocacy	Outreach Consulting	Information giving Pre-intervention training
2. Intake	Orientation Referral processing	Rapport building Intake interviewing
3. Assessment	Psychological evaluation Specialized evaluation	Psychosocial history Lifestyle assessment
4. Classification	Diagnosis Classification	Initial findings report Treatment planning
5. Referral	Resource brokering Liaison	Treatment assignment Tracking
6. Intervention	Relapse prevention Follow-up	Correctional counseling Supervision
7. Evaluation	Program evaluation Program evaluation	Process evaluation Outcome evaluation

Given the close connection between evaluation and advocacy, it is apparent that case management is not a simple linear process. Instead, there is the "looping phenomenon" that defines the existence of a system, which is a meaningful array of changing elements and the relationships among them (Watzlawick, Beavin, & Jackson, 1967). The process can be diagrammed thus:

Advocacy→Intake→Assessment→Classification→Referral→Intervention→Evaluation
Evaluation→Advocacy→Intake→Assessment→Classification→Referral→Intervention

Advocacy, as the first stage in the system, catalyzes the process of correctional case management by instigating changes in the individual offender and the service delivery. Each of the remaining stages in the model then impact upon the entire system. Advocacy prepares both offenders and service providers to have a stake in the correctional intervention. Specific roles, functions, and activities of the case manager converge on the intake process. Advocacy is delimited by evaluation findings, from single case studies to large-scale research and development efforts. In effect, evaluation establishes the classification categories and correctional interventions applied to future clients and whole classes of offenders. An example of the complex interrelationships among stages demonstrate how the correctional case management system operates.

Example 1.1
Family Violence and Correctional Case Management

Data secured from ongoing research, an expression of the evaluation stage of correctional case management, affects advocacy, intake, and other stages in the process. The following example from the family violence literature explores the relationships among stages in correctional case management.

Recent research on family violence (Buzawa & Buzawa, 1993) indicates that men who batter their partners differ in their response to law enforcement and correctional interventions. According to data from a large-scale national study, funded by the National Institute of Justice, there is no single, unequivocally effective approach to correcting the problem of battering (Binder & Meeker, 1988). An earlier study (Sherman & Berk, 1984) seemed to suggest that arresting and prosecuting batterers was effective in deterring future family violence. Therefore, many police departments and district attorney's offices adopted mandatory arrest and prosecution policies. Subsequent studies indicated that arrest works only with "good," low-risk perpetrators who have a stake in the community, such as being married and employed. Arrest and prosecution can actually increase future violence among "bad" prospects, who are unmarried, unemployed, and geographically mobile (Buzawa & Buzawa, 1993).

In this example, evaluation data refined a classification system for male batterers. In turn, changes in advocacy, intake, assessment, classification, referral, and intervention are indicated. According to the correctional case management model, corrections professionals, as consumers of evaluation data, are responsible for advocating changes in service delivery. One possible advocacy function in this case would be joining a local or regional task force on family violence and encouraging the criminal justice system to reconsider mandatory arrest and prosecution policies.

Similarly, the case manager may devise new intake and assessment strategies to reflect research advances and policy changes. For example, the corrections professional could be involved from the outset in differentiating among types of batterers, contributing to the evolution of a more effective, practical classification system. All of the aforementioned changes converge on new approaches to police calls, bail decisions, presentence investigation, and other criminal justice activities.

In the future, there may be an effective method for quickly assessing risk for battering and selecting the most appropriate interventions given an individual offender's characteristics and the collective features of known classifications of such offenders.

In the example of family violence, the advocacy effort focused upon changes in service delivery. Yet, advocacy can be directly related to offender behavior change. If the correctional case manager did become involved in task force membership, consultation, outreach, or the other innovations in service delivery, then there would be increased demand for assistance and strain in the intake system.

Therefore, the case manager could advocate offender change by increasing the efficiency of information giving and extending pre-intervention training. In this manner, new clients would be prepared for the demands of intake.

Intake

The intake stage of the system is the oldest and most familiar component of case management. In corrections, intake procedures can be as critical as processing patients in the hospital emergency room. Given the fact that criminal conduct produces the client base in corrections, there are acute crises and chronic psychosocial stressors among offenders and their families. Similarly, crisis and upheaval occur among victims, community members, and criminal justice professionals. Therefore, crisis intervention may be the first action in the intake stage of the correctional case management process.

Successful resolution of crises and ongoing adjustment to the correctional system require careful attention to rapport building. There are specific case manager behaviors that facilitate ongoing communication in the interview. Correctional professionals should learn the core conditions of facilitative communication. Rapport not only establishes a therapeutic basis for the case management relationship, but also encourages accurate and extensive disclosure in the monitoring of offender behavior.

The agency processing the offender also benefits from careful consideration of intake procedures. Many correctional and mental health agencies are understaffed. They must respond to the demands of increasing caseloads comprised primarily of involuntary clients. Offenders by their very nature have difficulty responding productively to stresses and the requests of authority figures. In addition, offenders and their families may lack education and experience with agencies, making access to services a threatening process. Therefore, service delivery is facilitated by orienting new clients and processing offenders in an efficient and empathic manner.

Orientation of new clients introduces individuals to the case management system as manifested in a particular setting. New clients need to know how to set and change appointments, prepare forms and reports, make requests and ask questions, and complete follow-up requirements and recommendations. Essentially, clients need to understand their rights and responsibilities. Well-informed clients are best prepared to comply with the correctional intervention regimen. Problems with orientation and communication contribute to missed opportunities, failure to report, lack of follow-up and other unnecessary complications, which can lead to case manager frustration and even probation/parole revocation in community corrections.

The orientation function in the case management process can take many forms. Frequently, agencies provide brochures or information sheets; however, some offenders and their families may have difficulty reading or remembering important details. Face-to-face orientation sessions are frequently ideal, but they consume scarce staff time. Videotaped programs and computer-assisted instruction represent innovations that blend interpersonal and informational components of orientation.

Client processing is another basic intake procedure. Throughout the correctional case management process, referrals are made by staff members and received by clients. The referral may be formal or informal, internal or external, casual or systematic. A correctional case manager can even make a "self-referral" in which the client will return to see him or her. The basis of any referral is recommending to a client, based on impressions of that person's need, some course of action. An informal referral may take the form of directing a client's family to the correct office for their appointment. A formal referral will normally be recorded on paper, perhaps in the case record.

Referrals may direct the client to pursue services inside the agency currently providing help or send the person to an external source or provider. During initial intake, offenders are often referred to community mental health professionals for specialized services, such as an assessment. Client families may receive referrals for crisis intervention and social welfare resources. Casual referrals take the form of indirect suggestions that clients may wish to explore. Systematic referrals, which are typically formal in nature, involve structured requests for particular behavior or action. A systematic referral involves a series of steps intended to facilitate the processing of clients through correctional case management. A systematic referral can include homework and contracting. Example 1.2 illustrates this process.

The formality and structure in the example will enhance compliance if the case manager uses facilitative communication and establishes rapport. The systematic nature of the homework helps the client to understand what is expected and to remember to follow up. The systematic homework assignment supports the intake requirements of the agency and moves the client into the next stage of the correctional case management process.

Assessment

The assessment stage of the correctional case management process answers questions raised during the intake process. The case manager develops sufficient rapport and provides enough information to bring the new client into the correctional system. There are initial impressions and recommendations based on the obvious and immediate needs of the offender and the client's family.

Much of the case management process will be concerned with matching available services and interventions to the identified needs of the offender. While initial impressions at intake will be sufficient to process the client within the agency, additional in-depth assessment is required in most cases to classify the offender.

Classification addresses client and service system concerns. The in-depth assessment is conducted by the correctional case manager and selected profes-

Example 1.2
Formal Referral Processing and
Systematic Homework Assignments

Correctional case management involves ongoing data collection from individual clients and collectively throughout the agency. In this manner, each stage of the case management system contributes to refinement of the process. Both client and service agency assume greater accountability.

During intake, many agencies require similar kinds of data in order to process the client. Therefore, the case manager may make routine requests for certain information that can be incorporated into systematic homework assignments. In addition, intake evolves into assessment as the correctional case manager becomes better acquainted with the needs and resources of the offender. Formal referrals to community service providers are common at intake and assessment.

The following example represents the case of a juvenile sex offender, recently released from a detention center to his father's custody. The 15-year-old boy and his father met with a family court counselor (i.e., the correctional case manager), who is processing the boy through juvenile probation. The case manager needs some additional information from the father and decides to refer the young man to a psychologist who specializes in psychosexual evaluation of sex offenders. In order to facilitate the processing of this case the counselor uses a systematic homework assignment (Shelton & Ackerman, 1974). The structure of the assignment and signing of names to the implied contract increase the likelihood that the father and son will comply with the identified requests. A facsimile of the homework is included below.

AGREEMENT

In order to complete the processing needed to arrange John's probation, we agree to perform the following tasks.

- Mr. Jones will contact Dr. Smith's office, making an appointment for John's psychosexual evaluation no later than 15 August. Dr. Smith's number is (504) 555-3333.

- Mr. Jones will secure and provide copies of previous school evaluation reports no later than the next appointment, scheduled on 22 August.

- John will complete and return his questionnaire by 22 August.

- Mr. Wilson will bring information on the Young Person's Weekend College Program to the 22 August appointment.

Tom Jones   John Jones   Ed Wilson

sional referral sources, depending upon the nature of the offender and the crime. In some cases, professionals from several agencies who have a stake in the client may complete various assessments, some of which probably overlap. In such cases, the correctional case manager assumes responsibility for securing, consuming, and organizing the available data into a coherent and meaningful classification of the individual.

Case management assessment typically includes some interviewing and history taking. Frequently, there are home visitations, contact with collateral sources (such as family members and employers), and communication with referral sources and other professional stake holders. The case manager must be proficient in interviewing to secure sufficient data for classification. The case manager conducts a psychosocial assessment, which takes into account at least the history of conduct disorder, delinquency, and criminality. In contemporary corrections, the psychosocial assessment probes various domains in the offender's life history including childhood, family life, schooling, substance abuse and chemical dependency, military service, and critical incidents in relationships.

At some level, the correctional case manager develops a portrait of the offender based on his or her lifestyle. This lifestyle assessment may reflect simply the cumulative impressions and judgment of the case manager. However, the lifestyle assessment, particularly in the counseling functions of the case manager, integrates data from the past, producing a portrait of current functioning, overall adjustment, present options, and future risk. The lifestyle assessment charts a trajectory from the past, through several present choices or options, into a foreseeable future. The medical model of evaluation would view the lifestyle assessment as the means by which risk and prognosis are determined. Risk factors and prognosis (i.e., the future course of a disease process) figure prominently in treatment selection according to the medical model.

Specialized assessment may be indicated given the initial impressions of the offender. Most juvenile and many adult offenders participate in at least some psychiatric or psychological evaluations. Frequently, jails, halfway houses, probation and parole departments, and other community correctional settings or agencies establish contracts with professionals in the area to provide psychological services. Psychological evaluations include paper-and-pencil testing of personality (e.g., the Minnesota Multiphasic Personality Inventory or MMPI); performance testing of intelligence, aptitudes, and abilities (e.g., the Wechsler Adult Intelligence Scale-Revised or WAIS-R); and differential diagnosis through problem-oriented interviews. Psychiatric, neurological, and other specialized medical evaluation are typically reserved for the most complicated cases in which there is a question of sanity or mental competency. Mental health services may be provided in prisons and institutional settings by psychiatrists and psychologists employed by the institution, public health doctors and community mental health professionals assigned an offender caseload, or contractors in private practice.

Mental health and specialized assessments in community corrections are usually provided by contractors, approved providers, or private practitioners chosen by the offender. Some offender behaviors demand specialized assessment, while other criminal cases involve routine evaluation. Burglary, motor vehicle theft, and property crimes can be addressed with relatively little data, such as the offender's criminal record. Sex offenses, arson, family violence, and other complex offenses without obvious financial motivations indicate need for specialized assessment. Given the close association of chemical dependency and crime, alcohol and drug usage are normally taken into account when compiling impressions into a classification.

Classification

Classification has been a focal point in corrections since Martinson (1974), sparked the "Nothing works" versus "What works?" debate. Traditionally, assessment in corrections addressed basic treatment amenability, whether or not a given offender, given the available assessment data, could be reasonably expected to benefit from a correctional intervention such as counseling. Amenability to treatment was a basic decision point in classification in that some offenders were viewed as good candidates for rehabilitation, while others were viewed as poor risks. Thus, basic treatment amenability was used to determine who should be treated in the community. Offenders who were viewed as not amenable to treatment were more likely to be incarcerated. Within institutions, amenability decisions effected referrals to available treatment programs. Overall, basic treatment amenability was used to limit services and clients or to invest resources in the best candidates for behavior change.

While it is generally true that the most psychopathic offenders have a poor prognosis for treatment and the highest risk for re-offending (Eysenck & Gudjonsson, 1989), even career criminals will benefit from some services. The concept of differential intervention (Beutler & Clarkin, 1990) has replaced basic treatment amenability in most correctional systems. Differential intervention addresses the question, "What offender will benefit from which service provided where and by whom?" The perspective of differential intervention best captures the matching model, which is a foundation of contemporary correctional case management. Treatment decisions, regarding community versus institutional placements, are made via consideration of a wide range of programs and services. This is a major step when using classification in the differential intervention model.

In classification, diagnostic impressions from all professionals involved in the case converge to typify or categorize the offender. In adult offender cases involving a minimum of assessment, classification decisions may be made by completing checklists, based on data already available in the criminal record. In complex cases, having some mental health implications, the correctional case manager receives reports from the professionals who completed the assessments. Data from the reports are compiled into some meaningful classification. The accuracy of the resulting classification depends upon the technical merits of the underlying assessments and the competency of the case manager in inte-

Example 1.3
Presentence Investigation of a Chemically Dependent Offender

William Street is a 23-year-old white, single male who was arrested and charged with auto theft valued at under $750.00, after breaking into a neighbor's home and stealing a VCR. He impulsively decided to commit the crime after bingeing for a week on alcohol and prescription medications and realizing he had no money left from his unemployment check. While he had committed several petty crimes since adolescence, he was never detained or arrested. Therefore, he had no criminal record. Mr. Street was legally intoxicated when he was arrested at his apartment, at which he resided for three years. He was not in possession of any drugs or controlled substances.

The County Adult Probation Department interviewed Mr. Street while he remained in the community on bail. He completed a presentence investigation form with the assistance of an intake officer. The questionnaire addressed specific details related to the present offense, criminal history, family history, alcohol and drug use, education, military service, employment background, financial status, future plans, and references. Collateral contacts were made with selected references and Mr. Street was referred to Dr. Robert Smith, a psychiatrist who specializes in the evaluation and treatment of addictive disorders.

The results of the interview and questionnaire substantiated the correctional case manager's initial impression that Mr. Street was chemically dependent. The lack of criminal history and Mr. Street's openness during the interview suggested that he would benefit from correctional intervention. The burglary offense reflected "bottoming out" or serious deterioration in the client's adjustment due to emergent problems with alcoholism and chemical dependency (marijuana).

Collateral contacts established that Mr. Street had been a good high school student and an employee in retail trade. He was involved in organizations and sometimes attended church during his high school years. However, he began to associate with the "wrong crowd" and to drink excessively. Binge drinking resulted in blackouts, hangovers, and increasing tolerance. Marijuana use contributed to lack of motivation. Mr. Street lost a good job in the year before the offense due to his chemical dependency.

Dr. Smith established that Mr. Street had an extensive family history of alcoholism and depression. Biologically predisposed to alcoholism, Mr. Street also grew up in a dysfunctional, alcoholic home. His father, a housepainter, was an alcoholic who struggled to make a living for his family. Mr. Street failed to identify with his father, and therefore, he did not learn how to structure his efforts to become a productive individual. Mr. Street's mother was a co-alcoholic who had recently become involved in Al-Anon.

Mr. Street left home at age 18 following high school graduation. He rarely communicated with his family due to the pain and shame of his youth. Dr. Smith identified some significant developmental and family issues in addition to the obvious problem with chemical dependency. He recommended that the patient become involved in an intensive outpatient chemical dependency program, meeting three nights weekly for 10 weeks, as well as individual and family therapy at the community mental health center.

*Example 1.3—*continued

> The correctional case manager integrated the data from psychiatric evaluation, interviewing, questionnaire, and collateral contacts. The resulting classification of chemically dependent offender indicated that Mr. Street should receive treatment for chemical dependency and delayed adjudication of his case. As long as Mr. Street complied with the terms of his intensive supervision probation agreement and received no other charges during the next five years, he would be treated in the community. Mr. Street met weekly with his probation officer, completed the chemical dependency treatment program, entered Alcoholics Anonymous, and attended weekly therapy sessions.

grating the data. A key classification system that is often used to describe, code, and classify mental disorders of all types is the *Diagnostic and Statistical Manual of Mental Disorders* (DSM-IV), published by the American Psychiatric Association (1994).

The correctional case manager integrates assessments data into a meaningful classification from which interventions are selected. The case manager completes a report of the initial evaluation and makes treatment recommendations. The presentence investigation (PS) in probation work is a good example of a classification stage activity (Example 1.3).

In the example, the presentence investigation combined information gained from the probation department's questionnaire, the evaluation and diagnosis of a psychiatrist/addictionologist, and findings from interviews with collateral contacts. In addition, the criminal history revealed a pattern of alcohol-related offenses. His classification as a chemically dependent offender resulted in referral to an intensive outpatient chemical dependency treatment program. Given his family of origin issues, he was also referred for outpatient individual therapy at the community mental health (MH) center. The classification phase of the correctional case management process organized decisionmaking from several service providers. Classification in this case resulted in assignment to community treatment and supervision.

Treatment plans are devised for different classes of offenders in jails, prisons, and other secure settings. Institutional treatment plans may simply reflect the rules and privileges of the unit to which an offender is assigned. However, sophisticated classification and treatment planning can occur depending upon the nature of the diagnostic service in the jail or penitentiary. Most prisons offer academic assistance, vocational education, and related remedial services. Some innovative systems include adjunct services, ranging from crisis intervention to individual and group counseling. Willingness to accept referral to some correctional intervention is a consideration in parole decisions.

Classification is a very important component in the success of the correctional case management process. Treatment planning, service assignment, and integration of findings in an initial report or referral reflect the convergence of case management functions. Convergence results in pinpointing of offender needs and available services in preparation for referral. Convergence begins with classification. Classification may be envisioned as the apex of a funnel resulting from first recruiting potential clients (Advocacy), taking them into the correctional system (Intake), determining client characteristics (Assessment), and planning a course of treatment or custody (Classification). The remaining components of correctional case management reflect a gradual divergence from the pinpointing of classification to an increasingly broad array of activities from referral to intervention and evaluation. Evaluation of treatment process and outcome finally produces feedback data that correct advocacy efforts.

Referral

Referral is the means by which classification recommendations are implemented. Correctional case managers are involved in the decision to treat an offender in the community versus incarceration in a secure facility. Subsequently, the case manager is involved in resource brokering and liaison with service providers and with other interested persons in the community. The correctional professional also is involved with monitoring compliance with the treatment plan and with tracking the progress of offenders.

Resource brokering is essential because no one professional can meet all of the needs of an offender. Like the advocacy activities in case management, resource brokering requires knowledge of available services in the community or institution, as well as the willingness to network and otherwise form linkages with various agencies and service providers.

Similarly, liaison requires that the correctional case manager maintain good communication and working relationships with all those involved in the custody or care of the offender. Telephone and personal contacts, written reports and case record-keeping are typical means for accomplishing resource brokering and liaison.

When there are gaps or inadequacies in the referral process, the offender may fail to comply with the terms of the treatment contract or agreement. In a reciprocal manner, adequate monitoring and tracking are usually needed to help the offender achieve behavioral change. Monitoring service delivery is a requirement for effective correctional case management.

Ongoing communication with referral sources and providers maintains the network by which services are brokered. Careful communication with an offender, the family, his or her employer, and other relevant collateral sources affords the opportunity to monitor compliance and behavior in general in the least obtrusive manner. Lack of communication with the client disrupts rapport building, collaboration, and the correctional intervention.

Intervention

When one thinks about corrections in the United States, punishment and rehabilitation inevitably come to mind. Most criminal justice models emphasize the value of punishment in the deterrence of crime. Efforts to rehabilitate offenders vary in worth and acceptability according to the prevalent political climate. Regardless of the underlying ideology, punishment and rehabilitation have the same goal: relapse prevention. The means by which the goal of reducing recidivism is accomplished vary depending upon the model of helping applied to the offender behavior.

Brickman and Associates (1982) devised a schema for comparing and contrasting models of helping in community service. Their model of helping reflects combinations of attributions about responsibility concerning: (1) Who is responsible for the problem? and, (2) who is responsible for the solution? This model of helping can be instructive for individual case managers, service agencies, and community interest groups. In fact, this model may mirror, to some extent, the prevailing problem-solving views of society as a whole.

The medical model of helping emphasizes that a person in need must consult an expert professional (e.g., a doctor) who will diagnose and treat a problem, typically viewed as a disease. Lombroso (1917) and others developed theories of innate criminality based on physical and biological factors. Today, we know many physical and mental health problems, including predisposition to aggression (Eysenck & Gudjonsson, 1989), are based on genetic inheritance, neurological defects, and chemical imbalances. Therefore, when crime is perceived to be a function of an offender's basic constitution, medical interventions, such as taking anti-seizure medication, may be indicated.

The moral model of helping is the opposite of the medical model. In this approach to service delivery, the client is perceived as responsible for both the problem and the solution. Individual choice and commitment to change problem behavior are emphasized rather than intervention by an expert. This model of helping includes a wide range of professional and lay opinions about social problems from those who advocate people "picking themselves up by their bootstraps" to others who believe people "manifest" (or cause by believing) the lifestyles they deserve. The moral model may confuse causal and moral responsibility, resulting in the perception that persons choose to be victims. Some addicts and offenders may be blamed for the real-life social deprivation that contributed to the emergence of their problems.

The enlightenment model holds a person responsible for the problem, but not for the solution. The enlightenment model has been associated with addictionology, the study and treatment of addictive behavior based on the Twelve Steps Program of Alcoholics Anonymous. An important variation derived from that program uses destigmatization processes to achieve change in behavior. This was the Seven Step Program developed by Sands (1964) for treatment of addicted offenders. In addictionology, the root cause of chemical dependency is a disease process, possibly inherited and essentially emerging as a chronic illness with high risk for death. This component of the addictionology viewpoint fits the medical model. However, the field of addictions also emphasizes how the alcoholic or addict maintains his or her suffering by relying upon distorted beliefs, self-will, and self-sabotaging character defects, rather than seeking help outside oneself. The second step in the Alcoholics Anonymous program states: "We came to believe a power greater than oneself could restore us to sanity." This statement captures the essence of finding solutions for personal problems outside oneself, and is consistent with the enlightenment model of helping.

The compensatory model is the major professional perspective in rehabilitation and contemporary corrections. The model acknowledges that most offenders are products of dysfunctional family backgrounds and social disadvantages, perhaps from birth onward. However, the compensatory model charges clients to plan and act responsibly in order to resolve their problems. The perspective associated with the compensatory model would not fit the cognitive distortions of an offender who tries to justify a criminal lifestyle by perceiving inequity in life. Rather, this perspective reflects an action-oriented matching of client needs and available resources in order to overcome disadvantage and chronic lifestyle problems.

The compensatory model has been expressed eloquently by Reverend Jesse Jackson who said, "Tears and sweat are equally salty but they yield a different result. Tears will get you sympathy and sweat will get you change" (cited in Brickman et al., 1982). In keeping with this model, we believe that correctional case management should focus on alleviating chronic problems of offenders through matching available resources to their identified needs. The client is held accountable for individual behavior change while the correctional case management system is responsible for identifying and providing selected resources.

Various models of helping afford an opportunity to refine thinking about correctional case management interventions. While a particular case manager or service provider may emphasize parts of all four models or primarily one perspective on helping, the compensatory model best fits the comprehensive correctional case management system described herein. Later in this book, this approach to the treatment of offenders will be discussed in more detail as the "cognitive-behavioral approach."

Intervention in this type of case management system is an attempt to match services and resources in the institution or community setting to the needs of offenders, who have been adequately assessed and classified. Specific interventions with particular offenders are intended to address his or her problems in living such that a relapse or reoffense is prevented. Similarly, the correctional case manager intervenes with classes or groups of offenders, brokering and providing reasonable services with the long-term goal of protecting the public by reducing recidivism.

Intervention in criminal lifestyles to prevent individual relapse and reduce overall recidivism is very similar to intervention in addictive disorders. For most practical purposes, criminal conduct may be considered "addictive." Addicts and offenders possess many of the same cognitive distortions and character defects. They engage in similar boundary violations and offending behaviors. Offenders and addicts are "cut off" or isolated from corrective, nutritional life experiences. Instead, they organize their entire lifestyles around having access to drugs or opportunities to commit crime. Both criminals and addicts share traumatic life experiences and difficulties in adjustment. The two groups may share common underlying neurological defects that lead them to be sensation-seeking risk takers, who have trouble concentrating, learning from experience, and adjusting to demands of school, work, and other societal institutions. There is a tremendous overlap or concordance between the offender and addict subpopulations, as well. Therefore, correctional case management typically addresses the individual and family needs of offenders who rely upon addictive behavior in daily life.

Correctional case management reflects two major perspectives concerning relapse prevention. On the one hand, corrections professionals take responsibility for structuring the environments of delinquents and offenders through rules and surveillance. On the other hand, correctional case managers encourage individual offenders, that is, probationers or parolees in the community, to take responsibility for developing their educational, vocational, psychological, and interpersonal resources in order to cope better with life's demands. The aims or objectives of correctional case management imply that the correctional officer or agency is responsible for change and that the client is also responsible for change. The apparent tension or conflict between the two perspectives can be resolved by synthesizing them within a larger, more inclusive framework.

In truth, corrections provides structure to offenders who have demonstrated an inability to organize their lifestyles and assume personal responsibility for citizenship. Over the course of a correctional intervention, one goal is to shift from intensive supervision and external structure toward increasing freedom of choice and responsibility on the part of the offender. Thus, professional or agency responsibility for change applies most in the early stages of a correctional intervention. Later, the individual offender assumes greater personal responsibility by demonstrating self-control. Fading from high structure, professional monitoring of compliance, and environmental control toward natural consequences and self-regulation is a major, contemporary approach in maintenance of treatment gains and relapse prevention. The process of fading from professional to personal responsibility in correctional case management consists of three basic interventional phases. The first phase involves high external or environmental control of the individual offender in order to avoid relapse. The offender is perceived as having few self-regulating mechanisms; therefore, in accordance with an addictionology or enlightenment framework, the offender turns to a power greater than oneself, which can be viewed collectively as the recovery program itself. During this initial phase, the correctional intervention includes not only high structure and surveillance, but also the dual focus of correctional case management is fulfilled by extensive brokering of resources by the professional to meet needs of vulnerable, relapse-prone offenders.

The second or middle phase of correctional treatment involves gradual decreases in professional or agency control and increases in personal responsibility for maintaining behavior change. Less structure and surveillance are required as individual offenders demonstrate compliance with the correctional case management plan. Frequent office and home visits of the initial phase may begin to lessen. Drug testing and other intensive forms of monitoring, such as electronic monitoring, may be suspended in favor of self-reports, collateral contacts, and service provider reports. The middle phase of intervention still requires careful professional attention. However, the focus is shifting responsibility for behavior change to the offender, moving the entire correctional effort toward the compensatory model of helping. If the offender is able to assume personal responsibility, then he or she will be afforded access to less restrictive correctional environments. For example, an inmate who demonstrates good behavior in the prison setting may first reach trustee status, in which there is greater mobility and access to programs. Then, the trustee prepares for early release to parole or community supervision by successfully completing educational and therapeutic programs selected to match the inmate's needs. The end of the middle phase of the correctional intervention is signified by the balance of personal and professional control.

The third or final phase of intervention involves transferring institutional structure and professional control to offender decisionmaking and self-control. In this manner, the offender is best prepared to adjust to typical life responsibilities in the community. Without adequate transfer or fading of structure and control, there is higher risk for relapse or recidivism. In the past, some offenders were abruptly moved from total institutions, in which there were few opportunities for exercising problem-solving and coping skills, to their typical communities, in which there were all of the temptations to reoffend, as well as criminal associates. The motivation to engage in law-abiding, prosocial behavior is quickly overwhelmed by environmental triggers and stressors. Maintenance of gains realized in earlier phases of treatment requires careful, well-planned transitions. The final intervention phase is concluded by termination of professional or agency control, which could include cessation of community supervision, and restoration of individual freedom of choice. At this point, the client may exit the correctional case management system.

The conclusion of a correctional intervention affords a transition to the last stage in the correctional case management process: evaluation. Like the intervention stage, evaluation involves activities to promote individual offender behavior change and efficient service delivery. The intervention component concludes logically with follow-up of an individual offender, as structure and control are shifted from the service delivery system to the client. Follow-up of groups or classes of offenders provides the means by which a correctional intervention may be evaluated.

Evaluation

The evaluation stage of the correctional case management process returns the focus from individual behavior change to the collective characteristics of groups of offenders. There is an ongoing emphasis upon reducing individual relapse and offender recidivism on the whole. During the evaluation phase, the correctional case manager has the opportunity and responsibility to assess the efficacy of the entire process. However, most evaluation efforts determine the effectiveness of correctional interventions. The results of evaluation provide data and direction for the advocacy phase in the correctional case management system.

The final stage of correctional case management addresses program and offender changes. When the case manager is concerned primarily with offender behavior change, there is an emphasis upon outcome evaluation. The evaluation activity somehow establishes that beneficial behavior change has occurred by virtue of the offender's participation in a correctional intervention. The focus on offender change may be facilitated also by evaluating the process of a particular program evaluation and innovation in service delivery. Outcome evaluation may be targeted at single cases as well as identified groups of offenders.

The professional practice of correctional case management must be founded on demonstrable results. While classification efforts determine basic treatment amenability versus differential intervention, outcome evaluation is at the heart of the whole issue of effectiveness and professional accountability. Differential treatment selection is the key means by which effectiveness is demonstrated (Beutler & Clarkin, 1990). Paul (1969) has challenged counselors concerning the effectiveness of treatment by raising questions concerning the relationship of differential intervention and effectiveness with respect to the type of treatment, the type of problems the client presents, the circumstances of the treatment, the course of the treatment, and how it comes about.

Responses to Paul's challenge sparked much integrative research on the particular outcomes of psychotherapy. A similar focus is needed in corrections. Outcome evaluation initiates the process of research by observing systematically the results of participation in an intervention of interest.

The basic form of outcome evaluation involves the single case study. Single case experimental methodologies, which are types of quasi-experimental research designs, have been used historically to evaluate behavior change, using interventions as widely discrepant as Freudian psychoanalysis and behavior therapy. By focusing on the individual case, it is possible to determine if an offender changed in a significant, relevant way in response to the "treatment package" he or she received in the correctional intervention.

Case managers have considerable data available from the offender, as well as from collateral sources such as the family or employer, regarding meaningful behavior change. Correctional case managers may have access to available data sources, such as: urine drug screen results, treatment attendance reports, and arrest data from which to directly establish offender status with respect to compliance and recidivism. Various ratings, checklists, and impressions can be used to indirectly measure offender outcome. Although there are sophisticated single case experimental designs (Hersen & Barlow, 1976), the basic requirements for single case studies involve carefully describing the offender's characteristics, the behavior targeted for behavior change, and the steps in the correctional intervention. Target behaviors can be measured throughout the treatment process; however, the most important measures are secured before and after the intervention (pre-test to post-test). It is possible to determine that the intervention is associated with behavior change by measuring target behavior before any intervention (i.e., determine baseline levels of the behavior), during the intervention or treatment package, and after discontinuing the intervention. In this manner, some control is exerted over the experimental conditions, but there are ethical and scientific limitations of this form of evaluation (Kazdin & Wilson, 1978).

Modern psychotherapy research is based on large-scale, carefully controlled group studies in which offender characteristics, treatment conditions, and target behaviors are specified. Outcome evaluation may involve comparisons of behavior change realized by several groups of offenders over selected periods of time. For example, the correctional case manager may be concerned with the efficacy of intensive supervision for high-risk offenders. The case manager compares recidivism and target behavioral data of probationers who receive intensive supervision with data collected from probationers participating in traditional supervision and those who receive minimal supervision. Group studies of outcomes increase the power and impact of evaluation, as well as the generalizability of results to offenders who do not participate in the study.

While there are significant similarities across various interventions (Goldfried, 1982), outcome evaluation is improved when there is significant attention to matching subjects amenable to treatment with particular treatment packages that address their problems and concerns.

Process evaluations address the effects of particular components of treatment packages upon behaviors relevant to change. Target behaviors may be less specific or less directly related to recidivism than behaviors selected for outcome evaluations. Perceptions, feelings, impressions, and a host of relationship variables may be included in the evaluation of the treatment process. Frequently, process evaluation involves attention to rapport, intervention structure, motivation to comply, requisite knowledge and skills, and other targets related to the means for attaining beneficial outcomes from correctional interventions. By focusing on the process of offender behavior change, the case manager addresses needs in service delivery.

Changes in service delivery follow program evaluation. Program evaluation emphasizes not only data on process and outcome, but also efficiency and cost-effectiveness in producing such results. It is possible to produce beneficial offender outcomes in an intensive correctional program, which cannot be justified based upon time, expense, or other service delivery criteria. When programs are evaluated, some innovation is indicated generally. Programs develop over time, becoming increasingly effective and efficient. Community stakeholders in the correctional system demand accountability in terms of basic efficacy and efficiency. Administrators of correctional case management services are involved primarily in program evaluation and innovation. Nevertheless, each case manager has some important contribution to make to program development and change. Correctional case managers may represent their client's interests in advocating changes in service delivery. Thus, correctional case management cycles through a system of increasing sophistication: from advocacy; through intake, assessment, classification, referral, intervention, and evaluation; to the next level of advocacy.

Conclusions

The correctional case management process reflects an increasingly sophisticated attempt by empirically minded corrections professionals to match identified needs and strengths of offenders with selected services and resources. The case management process functions as a system in which there are complementary service delivery and offender behavior change activities in each of seven stages. While several of the stages converge on problems and needs of individual offenders, overall accountability demands the demonstration of efficacy in interventions with identified groups of offenders and efficiency in program design and administration. Correctional case management balances the need for structure and change, supervision and rehabilitation, and community treatment and deinstitutionalization by focusing on three interrelated goals:

1. Prevention of relapse or recidivism

2. Reintegration of offenders into the community

3. Systematic monitoring of individual progress and program outcome.

The correctional case manager engages in various tasks and activities, performing professional roles and functions throughout the seven steps of the process. The seven basic steps in the correctional case management process provide a systematic structure for conceptualizing offender behavior change and service delivery. In practice, there are many relationships between and among the stages. One stage leads to another in a linear sequence, yet all stages may be affected by activities of a particular phase. The stages are:

1. Advocacy

2. Intake

3. Assessment

4.   Classification

5.   Referral

6.   Intervention

7.   Evaluation

Changes in advocacy efforts affect intake procedures, which in turn require modifications in assessment protocols. However, advocacy efforts are influenced by evaluation results, particularly outcome studies and program innovation. Thus, the correctional case management system functions as a complex process having multiple inputs and impacts.

Interventions constitute the backbone of correctional case management. Advances throughout the case management process attempt to answer the question which has often been raised about correctional counseling concerning what works. While interventions vary according to the extent of focus on structure or relationship, professional control or self-regulations, the aim of correctional case management is to prepare individuals who can function adequately at home and at work, and control their behavior when assuming typical adult responsibilities. Since most offenders and their families have serious deficits in their backgrounds, they develop criminal lifestyles that are fundamentally addictive, given the prevalence of cognitive distortions limiting growth and change. In our model of correctional case management, we view the process as moving from an addictionology perspective to a compensatory model of helping as an offender demonstrates readiness to assume additional responsibility. The systematic nature of correctional case management is designed to reduce individual risk of relapse and recidivism for known groups of offenders.

References

American Psychiatric Association (1994). *Diagnostic and Statistical Manual of Mental Disorders* (Fourth Edition). Washington, DC: Author.

Binder, A. & J. Meeker (1988). "Experiments as Reforms." *Journal of Criminal Justice,* 16:347-358.

Beutler, L.E. & J.F. Clarkin (1990). *Systematic Treatment Selection: Toward Targeted Therapeutic Interventions*. New York, NY: Brunner/Mazel.

Brickman, P., V.C. Rabinowitz, J. Karuza, D. Coates, E. Cohn & L. Kidder (1982). "Models of Helping and Coping." *American Psychologist,* 37:368-384.

Buzawa, E.S. & C.G. Buzawa (1993). "The Scientific Evidence is Not Conclusive: Arrest is No Panacea." In R.J. Gelles & D.R. Loseke (eds.) *Current Controversies on Family Violence* (pp. 337-356). Newbury Park, CA: Sage Publications.

Eysenck, H.J. & G.H. Gudjonsson (1989). *The Causes and Cures of Criminality*. New York, NY: Plenum Press.

Goldfried, M.R. (ed.) (1982). *Converging Themes in Psychotherapy: Trends in Psychodynamic, Humanistic, and Behavioral Practice*. New York, NY: Springer.

Hersen, M. & D.H. Barlow (1976). *Single-Case Experimental Designs: Strategies for Studying Behavior Change*. New York, NY: Pergamon.

Kazdin, A.E. & G.T. Wilson (1978). *Evaluation of Behavior Therapy: Issues, Evidence, and Research Strategies*. Cambridge, MA: Ballinger.

Lombroso, C. (1917). *Crime, Its Causes and Remedies*. Boston, MA: Little, Brown.

Martinson, R. (1974). "What Works? Questions and Answers about Prison Reform." *The Public Interest*, 35:22-54.

Paul, G.L. (1969). "Behavior Modification Research: Design and Tactics." In C.M. Franks (ed.) *Behavior Therapy: Appraisal and Status* (pp. 29-62). New York, NY: McGraw-Hill.

Sands, B. (1964). *My Shadow Ran Fast*. Englewood Cliffs, NJ: Prentice-Hall.

Shelton, J.L. & J.M. Ackerman (1974). *Homework in Counseling and Psychotherapy* (Second Edition). Springfield, IL: Charles C Thomas.

Sherman, L.W. & R.A. Berk (1984). "The Specific Deterrent Effects of Arrest for Domestic Assault." *American Sociological Review*, 49:261-271.

Watzlawick, P., J.H. Beavin & D.D. Jackson (1967). *Pragmatics of Human Communication: A Study of Interactional Patterns, Pathologies, and Paradoxes*. New York, NY: W.W. Norton.

Chapter 2

Development of the
Case Management Perspective

Introduction

The term "case management" began to appear in the clinical and counseling literature about two decades ago. Although the term is of recent origin, the concept is not new. A review of historical and current theories about biopsychosocial determinants of criminal behavior will bring the reader into contact with assorted notions about how to rehabilitate the offender. Many of the ideas about rehabilitation encompass methods that one could clearly associate with today's case management method. Moreover, some of the key elements of case management, such as the ideas of self help and support networks, have always been a part of Western cultural history when one examines how our society has dealt with social problems. This has been true from Biblical times through the Middle Ages; during the period of the Enlightenment, and through the history of scientific thought and progress encompassing the twentieth century. Froland, Pancoast, and Parker (1983) make this point very clearly. For them, we are only now discovering what they call "helping networks." They remind us that natural support networks have always existed in human society.

Helping networks consisted of families, friends, kinship systems of various sorts, as well as persons from other social groups, from which an individual could receive support and help. These kinds of helping networks comprise what Wilensky and Lebeaux (1958), in their monumental work about social welfare, refer to as the "residual" conception of social welfare. The residual conception of social welfare refers to networks consisting of formal and informal support systems that emphasize the nature of private and charitable approaches to problem solving. Families, churches, schools, labor unions, and, ultimately, the economy and the market system, drive and determine the conditions of eligibility for help, types of help, and limits of help available.

In 1935, with the passage of the Social Security Act, and with subsequent issues of federal legislation that followed, we saw the beginnings of what Wilensky and Lebeaux would call the "institutional" conception of social welfare. This conceptualization rests on the assumption that in modern industrial and technological societies, a certain number of social and economic casualties will be produced. This is based on the notion that there are all sorts of vagaries associated with the rise of industrial societies: deteriorated and marginalized inner-city environments; dysfunctional families; and various health, economic, and educational fatalities. Since 1935, the term "helping networks" has come to include all of the informal and formal support systems in society. Thus, it includes all of the family and privately based charitable systems, as well as the formal (institutionalized) or governmental programs and services. This melding reflects our social welfare system today.

The most specific connection between the terms "helping networks" and "case management" can be seen in the research of Froland, Pancoast, Chapman, and Kimboko (1981). For them, informal helping activities needed to be vitalized and intensified so that they could serve as links between formal and informal systems of giving and receiving help and support. This notion provides an accurate definition of how the term case management is generally thought of today: as a bridge and as a system of networks resulting in the coordination and distribution of informal and formal services on behalf of someone in need.

In the remainder of this chapter, the writers will describe the evolution of the case management perspective by: describing its development in parallel with revolutionary ideas about humanizing mental health treatment; describing how it is conceptualized today; discussing the issue of case management as a sociotherapy versus case management as a psychotherapy; and, by describing a variety of applications of the case management approach across a range of social problem areas.

Evolution of the Case Management Perspective

Clearly, the case management perspective developed from ideas about the importance of formal and informal systems of support. With respect to the historical literature about psychotherapy and counseling, the notion of the "therapeutic community" or "therapeutic milieu" was well established early on in the writings and research of the major theorists in the field. For example, Susser (1968) noted that Freud suggested that psychotic symptoms could be understood from the standpoint of the patient's experiences. Susser also noted that Bleuler believed that secondary symptoms associated with psychoses derived from past and present events, including the hospital setting and not the disease. In addition, Richmond (1917) who is considered to be the founder of professional social work, noted that social evidence, consisting of facts about the client's personal and family history, would serve to identify the kinds of social problems that a person has, and will contain the means by which these problems could be solved.

The development of case management can also be traced to the work of Sullivan (1931) concerning differences between non-schizophrenics and schizophrenics. His working hypothesis was that non-schizophrenics, in their interactions with other individuals, act and think in concordance with their cultural milieu. Schizophrenics, by contrast, think and behave in contradiction to their cultural milieu. In short, for Sullivan, the personality developed through interactions with other persons. These other persons were "significant others." In his view, the personality structure could be understood by observing individuals interacting with other individuals in community settings. The logical extension of Sullivan's thinking is that care of the mentally ill was best accomplished through community care.

Pitts (1963) interpreted Sullivan's ideas most clearly by declaring that Sullivan meant that if we are interested in understanding the socialization of children, then we need to study the structure of various institutions which help to socialize the child. Chief among these was the nuclear and extended family, peer groups, the church, and other sorts of institutions in the neighborhood and the community that provided opportunities for socialization and acculturation. Much of this kind of thinking, of course, mirrored the historical ideas contained in the fields of cultural and social anthropology; particularly, the idea that people could principally be understood in the context of their cultural and social settings.

Erickson (1963) is the key proponent of the anthropological view as applied to the medical model of psychotherapy. In his seminal work, *Childhood and Society*, he presented a number of case studies, reminiscent of anthropological field studies, to illustrate the point that clinical pathologies are closely related to social and cultural events. He refers to these kinds of events as "psychic stimulus." There are, of course, many other historical precedents in the clinical literature which were harbingers of the case management ideology.

Currently, the evolution of the case management perspective, in the opinion of the writers, can be principally traced to the work of Jones (1953), Stanton and Schwartz (1954), Goffman (1961), and Cumming and Cumming (1962). Their concerns about the treatment and status of patients in mental hospitals set the stage for deinstitutionalization, and helped to define the nature of the treatment of patients within therapeutic milieux. However, since the end of World War II, the popular literature had contained many portrayals of abuse of mental patients which tended to inflame public opinions about the care of the mentally ill. A principal example could be found in Ward's (1946) novel, *The Snake Pit.*

For Goffman (1961), mental hospitals were basically antitherapeutic. He helped bring awareness to the fact that these kinds of settings, in general, were primarily custodial in nature and relied heavily upon physical and medical methods for managing and controlling the behavior of patients. These methods often took the form of electroconvulsive (shock) therapies, and later, insulin therapy, and even in some cases, lobotomies (psychosurgeries). Furthermore, most of the work in mental hospitals was carried out by poorly trained staff members. In fact, in most mental hospitals in the 1950s, there existed an inverse relationship between the amount of education and training compared with the amount of time spent in therapeutic encounters with the patients. For example, the most highly trained persons, such as psychiatrists and clinical psychologists, spent the least amount of time with the clients, while the custodial personnel, who were the least educated and trained, spent the most amount of time with patients. This pattern was altered, somewhat, with the advent of the

1960s, during which the use of tranquilizing drugs to manage and control behavior became widespread.

Jones (1953) is the founder of the community psychiatry approach. His work is often referred to as the notion of the "therapeutic milieu." He felt that all service elements in the mental hospital setting could be brought to bear and focused on the treatment of the patients. Jones believed that the hospital setting could be transformed into a therapeutic treatment milieu if all of the staff members, and the actual physical environment of the hospital, were oriented toward psychotherapeutic treatment. Principally, Jones meant that the hospital setting needed to become transformed into a humanistic and democratically oriented setting in which the patients could try out new behaviors and skills in order to learn how to come to grips with reality. This led to the reconfiguration of the physical environments of hospitals in order to make them more user-friendly to the patient, for example, by giving them free access to most areas, or by changing the color of the paint on the walls. It also meant changing the attitudes of the staff so that they would appear to be more friendly and supportive. It also led to the introduction of a wider variety of psychotherapies, instead of just psychoanalysis. Behavioral approaches, for example, began to be introduced, as well as various group approaches. In addition, educational, recreational, and vocational training services became emphasized.

Cumming and Cumming (1962) pioneered the use of group methods to achieve therapeutic gain. The interaction between and among members of the mental hospital community were thought to be the primary process in bringing about change. The use of group processes to bring about change was certainly well known before this time. However, Cumming and Cumming stressed the importance of placing the responsibility and authority for the therapeutic group processes with the staff person who appeared to have the most important and significant contacts with the clients, as well as the best potential and ability to bring about change. This was a kind of democratization of treatment because, quite often, a paraprofessional staff member, for example, might be determined to be the most important person in the client's life space. The reality of the inverse correlation between increasing levels of training and experience, and the amount of contact with clients, could be exploited in order to increase the efficiency of therapeutic services by increasing the training of the paraprofessional staff, and by utilizing them as primary therapists rather than as custodial services personnel.

A study by Stanton and Schwartz in 1954 titled *The Mental Hospital—A Study of Institutional Participation in Psychiatric Illness and Treatment*, had an explosive impact upon the mental health community, and, ultimately, contributed to the emergence of the case management perspective as well. Their book was based upon a three-year social-psychological study of a ward in a psychiatric hospital. They concluded that the mental hospital was a type of social system in which social as well as mental health interactions took place. They felt that the environment of the mental hospital was anti-therapeutic. In essence, mentally ill persons became more mentally ill as a consequence of their being institutionalized. The problem resided in the nature of the structure, organization, and functions of the mental hospital. The mental hospital appeared to have a kind of antitherapeutic culture characterized by problems of staff morale, and intra-staff conflicts, resulting in an impaired ability to deliver therapeutic services, while having a detrimental effect upon patients. They suggested that in order for mental hospitals to become therapeutic, patients needed to be involved as active participants in their treatment.

In the 1960s, the use of tranquilizing drugs with mental health patients in institutionalized settings was widespread, and perhaps rampant. The 1960s also witnessed the growth and development of community-based mental health clinics. Many of these clinics were specifically centered in cities and counties, but others covered large geographical areas across county and regional geopolitical jurisdictions. Multistate cooperation with respect to mental health programs and services also developed.

By the late 1960s, the trend was apparent: a movement away from institutionalized (hospital-based) mental health treatment settings and toward community-based mental health settings. And, in the community-based settings, the trend was increasingly away from inpatient mental health treatment programs toward outpatient or day-care centered approaches. Deinstitutionalization then, especially with its emphasis upon outpatient treatment approaches, called for a new treatment methodology, hence the rise of the case management perspective to accommodate that change.

Current Perspectives about Case Management

To understand current conceptualizations and applications of the case management approach, one must first begin by exploring the push for deinstitutionalized mental health services beginning with the federal government's role in that history. The current history of federal government involvement in deinstitutionalized mental health services can be traced to 1963. In 1963, the 88th Congress passed Public Law 88-164. This Act authorized funding for the construction of mental retardation and mental health centers. A later amendment to the act provided for staffing of these centers. This was followed in the 89th Congress by Public Law 89-749. This Act authorized grants to states in order to help them develop comprehensive plans of service for persons with health, mental health, and environmental problems.

Of singular importance for correctional counselors was Public Law 89-793. This piece of legislation allowed for the rehabilitation of narcotics addicts. The Act stressed care instead of imprisonment of substance abusers. Furthermore, it emphasized an holistic approach to treatment. Finally, Public Law 91-211 was issued. It amended previous legislation in the mental health field by expanding the funding for staff, and provided for funding for a wider array of mental health services, including treatment of alcoholics and narcotics addicts as well as to provide for mental health services for children.

The case management perspective, as we know it today, had its beginnings in Public Law 94-63: "The Public Health Service Act Amendments and Special Revenue Sharing Act of 1975." This piece of federal legislation was developed in order to amend the previous Public Health Service Act, as well as other related public health laws, by revising and extending certain features of the previous act. These features were:

1.   The health revenue sharing program.

2.   The family planning programs.

3.   The community mental health centers program.

4.   The program for migrant health centers and community health centers.

5.   The National Health Service Corps.

6.   And, various programs of assistance for the education and training of nurses.

The sections of Public Law 94-63 that were directed at community mental health centers, and the migrant health centers and community health centers programs, are the genesis of the current case management perspective. Specifically, the legislative language called for the development of outreach programs to identify health problems among migrant laborers, and to foster cooperation and coordination between various federal, state, and local agencies. The legislative language also specified that the intention of the outreach effort and coordination was to help bring comprehensive community mental health and health care services to all. The purpose was to develop a system of comprehensive care and to insure a continuity of care. This legislation established the ideology of deinstitutionalized care since it specified that community-based mental health centers were to provide outpatient services for mental health clients as a preferable alternative to the current norm of inpatient hospital services.

The second major piece of federal legislation that contributed to the specific evolution of the case management perspective was Public Law 100-485, "The Family Support Act of 1988." This legislation is often referred to as the "Welfare Reform Act." The Act set up a new employment program to replace the previous Work Incentive Program. The new program would be called the Job Opportunities and Training Program (JOBS). The purpose of the Act was to make sure that families on welfare would have an opportunity to obtain the necessary training, education, and employment that would assist them in avoiding long-term dependency upon public welfare. Specifically, the Act was designed to help states establish and operate programs designed to help provide job opportunities and basic skills training in order to enhance the employability of welfare recipients, as well as to increase their chances of becoming economically self-sufficient. This Act also mandated that the states conduct assessments and reviews of the needs and skills of welfare recipients so that viable employability plans could be developed.

However, what is especially interesting in this legislation is its language when it addresses the operationalization of the employability plan. It declared that the state agencies may assign a case manager to each client participating in the program, as well as to the family of the participant. Furthermore, the case manager would be responsible for helping the family secure any of the programs or services that would be necessary in order to assure that the clients would be able to effectively participate in the program.

In the opinion of the authors, the best federal clarification of the case management perspective was provided by the National Institute of Mental Health (NIMH). In 1977, the NIMH, through its Community Support Program (CSP), began to sponsor a number of pilot projects in order to explore the effectiveness of federal and state partnerships in the implementation of case management treatment approaches. The CSP identified several kinds of essential activities within the CSP case manager role. Goldstrom and Manderscheid (1983) presented a descriptive analysis of the use of these activities in a community-based mental health facility serving the chronically mentally ill. These activities included:

1. Identifying the client base and providing outreach services to them.

2. Helping the clients apply for various types of social welfare and medical entitlement.

3. Providing for a crisis oriented, 24-hour quick response mental health services component.

4. Providing for psychosocial and other types of supportive or relationship-centered services.

5. Providing for health services, to include medical, dental, and mental health services.

6. Arranging for transportation services for the clients.

7. Providing for respite and other types of supportive services for their families and others.

8. Providing a mechanism for the expression and arbitration of their grievances, as well as a mechanism to guard their rights.

In the non-governmental sector, the case management perspective as we use it today began to emerge as mental health agencies began exploring the use of paraprofessionals. This activity started in the early 1960s. For example,

Rioch et al. (1963) were among the first to explore the use of paraprofessional mental health counselors. They conducted a qualitative study, sponsored as a pilot project by the National Institute of Mental Health, to determine if non-medically trained personnel, with aptitudes for mental health work, could effectively conduct short-term psychotherapy. Although the results were mixed, they generally felt that these types of personnel could be successful in some areas of work. Similarly, Reiff and Reissman (1965) examined the activities of what they called the indigenous nonprofessional. These persons were inhabitants of high poverty neighborhoods. Their report contained a description of some strategies and suggestions for training these types of personnel to work in "War on Poverty" neighborhood service centers. They discovered that the greatest difficulty experienced by these personnel was role ambiguity. However, they felt that indigenous personnel could develop new identifications as staff members, while still maintaining their traditional roles and relationships with the neighborhood. Additional impetus in this direction was provided by Lief (1966). He commented in an editorial article in an influential journal, the *Archives of General Psychiatry,* that what was needed to deal with rising patient loads and diminishing professional personnel was not a new mental health professional trained in the traditional ways, but a subprofession of mental health psychotherapists who would be trained in several short-term and crisis-oriented psychotherapies. He further suggested that they especially needed to be trained to recognize severe symptomatology so that they would be able to make referrals to appropriately trained professional psychotherapists.

What seemed to emerge from the work in the 1960s was the idea of paraprofessional mental health staff as "mental health expediters." Hansell, Worarczyk, and Visotsky (1968) presented an excellent description of the role responsibilities of the mental health expediter. They felt that the expediter must be able to interpret his or her roles to the agencies and institutions in the community. Following this, they would be primarily responsible for linking the patient with resources and services in the community. Several other tasks were subsumed within the expediter role. These included keeping a data base about the array and extent of services in the community, and establishing and maintaining contacts with various service providers in order to facilitate the referral process. The expediter was responsible for giving the professional treatment team information about the nature and quality of the services available in the community in order to help them in their patient planning, staffing, and referral activities. Much of this information was obtained from the clients. The expeditor was also required to follow up on the referrals so as to make certain that the client was utilizing the services. The expediter also had a role in determining the quality of the services that the client received.

The mental health expediter roles are illustrated in current perspectives about case management. For example, very little has been done to improve on the perspective that the expediter should do everything possible to facilitate the implementation of the treatment plan in order to achieve a successful client treatment outcome. However, some recent theorists have expanded upon these roles. Johnson (1986), for example, saw the main task as that of coordination so that the services were not fragmented. She also emphasized the point that the case manager should work toward creating interdisciplinary respect and coop- eration among the service providers. For Sheafor, Horejsi, and Horejsi (1988), case management roles and activities were derived from the theoretical per- spective of the client in relation to various social systems. They reiterated what had been the long-standing position of the National Association of Social Workers (1981), that social work practice is based upon an understanding of the client within the twin perspectives of human behavior and the social envi- ronment. The social work case manager, among other distinctions, must make sure that the treatment plan meets the needs of the client and his or her family. These guidelines also added another important element: the idea of advocating on behalf of the client, or of his or her family, in order to obtain necessary ser- vices. Heffernan, Shuttlesworth, and Ambrosino (1992) described an addition- ally important role for case managers. They felt that the case manager should be responsible for monitoring clients who were previously institutionalized, but were now placed in residential treatment centers in the community such as in group homes, halfway houses, respite centers, and so forth. This activity would also include working with the agencies in the community to be sure that the clients were getting necessary services, communicating with family members, and meeting with other persons who impacted on the client, in order to main- tain a viable, effective, and efficient community placement.

With respect to criminal justice, Enos, Black, Quinn, and Holman (1992) have applied the case management concept to the field of correctional counsel- ing. They differentiated between the case management "generalist" and the case manager "counselor" functions. The generalist roles are directed at provid- ing the offender with services in order to effect change in their social and phys- ical environmental situations. They define these roles as:

1. Case finding or social epidemiology.

2. Networking, or promoting interagency collaboration and moni- toring of services to offenders.

3. Advocacy, or promoting the development of program and ser- vice resources for offenders.

4. Enabling, or helping offenders make maximum use of appropri- ate programs and services in the community. They also described the case manager as a counselor who works with the offender in order to achieve psychotherapeutic change.

Today, although there are various conceptualizations about case manage- ment activities, some clear themes have emerged. Consensus seems to have evolved around these activities of case managers, whether they operate inde- pendently or as a part of an interdisciplinary team:

1. The case manager is responsible for outreach activities in order to identify community social problems, and in order to bring at-risk individuals into helping services systems.

2. The case manager conducts assessments of the client and of his or her problematic situation.

3. The case manager develops a plan for remediation of the problems in social or psychological functioning.

4. The case manager is responsible for identifying and keeping a record of programs and services in the community.

5. The case manager is responsible for linking the client to the needed service providers in the community.

6. The case manager monitors and evaluates the client's participation in the programs and services.

7. The case manager maintains liaison with other professionals and with other agencies in the community, and works collaboratively with them on behalf of the client.

8. The case manager provides supportive counseling services to the client's family and to other persons in the community who may have an impact on the client.

9. The case manager advocates on behalf of the client with respect to the development of needed resources in the community.

10. The case manager provides supportive counseling services to the clients, including crisis-oriented services.

Case Management: Sociotherapy or Psychotherapy?

Originally, case management personnel, as we know them today, were variously labeled as subprofessionals, nonprofessionals, indigenous personnel, paraprofessionals, or mental health expediters. Their role responsibilities changed over time from serving as assistants to the professional staff, to professionals in their own right.

The kinds of roles and activities assigned to them generally had to do with sociotherapies, that is, services directed at bringing about changes in the social and physical environments of the clients or patients. To reiterate, these services included: outreach to at-risk persons, early identification of social problems, development and maintenance of resource and service databanks, maintaining linkages and brokering between and among service providers, networking among service providers on behalf of the client, monitoring the progress of the clients' treatment, liaison work with other professionals and other agencies; and, advocating on behalf of the client in order to develop needed resources, or to gain access to services for the client.

Over time, additional activities, which were commonly thought of as being exclusively the responsibility of highly trained professional staff, became identified as case management activities as well. For example, case managers became responsible for assessments and diagnoses of client problems in social functioning, and for developing a plan for remediation or treatment. Rioch et al. (1963) felt that certain types of nonprofessional staff could do general, short-term psychotherapy, providing that they had appropriate training, competencies, and attitudes. Others, such as Lief (1966), believed that nonprofessionals, with appropriate training and supervision, could provide certain types of short-term therapies. Goldstrom and Manderscheid (1983) noted that the National Institute of Mental Health, in its guidelines for Community Support Programs, described one activity of the case manager as that of directing the client toward, or personally providing, psychosocial, rehabilitative, and support services. Although it was not clear that nonprofessionals could provide psychotherapies per se, the literature seems to be clear that they could provide short-term, crisis-oriented, relationship and other forms of client-support centered therapies. In other words, by the late 1960s and early 1970s, a pattern emerged that seemed to suggest that nonprofessionals could provide not just sociotherapies, but psychosocial therapies as well. These psychosocial therapies included treatment or counseling that was directed at the social and environmental aspects of the clients' problematic functioning, as well as upon the nature of the clients' personality system and his or her perception and feelings about the problems in social functioning. Much of this kind of activity was often managed and controlled since the activities of many paraprofessionals were often subsumed within the interdisciplinary mental health team model of treatment. In this type of model, nonprofessional staff would be limited to their areas of competence and expertise. But, with appropriate supervision, they could provide psychosocial therapies.

Others, however, felt that paraprofessionals/case managers were, in reality, providing therapy. For Rueveni (1979), the issue was clear. In his model for using support systems on behalf of families experiencing stress, he stated that terms such as intervenor, networker, and so forth, characterized the therapist. Weil, Karls, and Associates (1985) view case management as an extension of the therapeutic interview. While Greene (1992), in defining social work case management, lists clinical interventions to ameliorate emotional problems associated with illness or loss of physical functioning as a case management practice technique. In fact, some clinicians (Carkhuff, 1969; Schwartz & Zalba, 1971; Schulman, 1984), have developed models of supportive and/or relationship therapies that contain core skills and activities that can underpin psychotherapeutic work by paraprofessionals.

In a realistic sense, trying to distinguish between and among sociotherapies and psychotherapies is quite impossible. Some differentiations can be made on the basis of levels of education, training, theoretical orientation, credentialing, and licensing. More often than not, in the real world of counseling, these distinctions appear to be artificial. It is probably more accurate to assume that the differences between the two approaches or methods have more to do with the ideological orientation of the counselor or clinician concerning the nature of client change and how to achieve it. The attitudes, values, feelings, and other personal characteristics of the counselor may largely influence chosen approaches or methods. The research of Rapp and Chamberlain (1985) is very instructive concerning the core of the problem of trying to make such a differentiation. In their study, they placed senior level bachelor's degree social work students and master's level social work students in an internship in an agency that served chronically mentally ill patients. The services of the agency were designed to prevent re-institutionalization. The students were to function as case managers. It was envisioned that they would provide case management services that fell somewhere between the roles of therapist and broker. It was specifically intended that they not act as therapists with the clients. What Rapp and Chamberlain found, however, was very telling. They discovered that even though the students did not act as therapists, they engaged in therapeutic activities when they provided traditional case management services such as companionship, support, and advice to their clients. In other words, it was not possible to accurately determine the point at which the margins of sociotherapies vanished and psychotherapies began. They noted that when social problems started to diminish, mental health symptoms decreased, resulting in a therapeutic effect. In effect, a secondary gain.

The fact of the matter is that case managers are engaged in activities that range from identifying social problems to clinical activities. Some clinicians argue that case management is poorly defined if we limit the definition only to a set of activities carried out by case managers. They believe that case management should be viewed as a part of a system. That system is the interdisciplinary mental health team. Supporters of the systems perspective tend to limit the activities of case managers to traditional nonprofessional roles (Miller, 1983). Proponents of the systems approach argue that federal legislation supporting a comprehensive approach to community mental health envisioned case management as a part of a comprehensive mental health system. This inference may be correct, however, a number of contingencies served to create a case management approach. Conditions, such as rapid deinstitutionalization of facilities serving the mentally ill, the aged, and the mentally retarded; litigation as a response to neglect and abuse of patients in institutional settings; the development of numerous alternatives to sentencing of offenders; the development of community college associate of science mental health paraprofessional programs, as well as the development of baccalaureate-level professional programs in social work, counseling, correctional counseling, and rehabilitation services at colleges and universities; coupled with a shrinkage of the availability of more highly trained mental health personnel beginning in the mid 1960s and becoming more pronounced as more and more of these kinds of personnel entered private practice, coalesced to form a case management approach rather than an organized, interdisciplinary mental health team-centered case management system.

The outcome is that case management today is not a system but is instead a set of activities and intervention strategies along a continuum of sociotherapy to psychotherapy. Case managers work in a variety of human service systems across a number of social and psychological problem areas. Its practitioners have a variety of educational backgrounds and have varying levels of expertise and experience. They approach treatment from a variety of clinical and counseling theoretical perspectives. The genie is out of the bottle, case management is not confined to mental health settings alone.

Some Applications of the Case Management Approach

A review of the clinical and counseling literature will reveal numerous examples of the use of the case management approach across a variety of social problem areas. Vourlekis and Greene's work (1992) contains a wide range of studies about the use of case management with: teenage parents, the elderly, disabled infants and toddlers, children with AIDS, the developmentally disabled, the chronically mentally ill, in employee assistance programs, in conjunction with child welfare services, and with military families. In a similar vein, Sanborn (1983) presents some important case studies about the use of case management with the developmentally disabled, in mental health programs, and with welfare programs.

Other important applications can be found with additional types of clients. For example, it has been used with psychotic clients (Kanter, 1990); with the families of developmentally disabled children (Feine & Taylor, 1991); by nurses with at-risk elders (Reban, 1994); with AIDS patients (Magee & Senizaiz, 1987), (Sousel, Paradise & Stroup, 1988); and, of particular interest to correctional counselors, with substance abusers (Godlay, Godlay, Pratt & Wallace, 1994), (Sullivan, Hartmann, Dillon & Wolk, 1994).

The literature reveals the increasing use of case management with different types of clients, by many types of agencies and service systems, and by a variety of service providers. It is just beginning to become utilized in criminal justice settings. It appears as though its use in criminal justice settings will be increasingly favorable. Although the nature and types of research studies about the use of case management vary greatly from empirical studies to case studies, in general, the literature seems to suggest that the case management approach is effective in helping to bring about social and psychological rehabilitation for a wide range of clients.

Conclusions

The development of the case management perspective, as we view it today, has many historical antecedents. To begin with, Western culture, as least since Biblical times, has held to the notion of self-help as the primary vehicle for dealing with social and psychological problems. The chief elements of self-help were to be found in certain systems, such as the family, the kinship and extended family network, and other support systems including friends, churches, and other types of private, charitable resources. As society became increasingly industrialized and complex, and as kinship systems yielded to nuclear families, it became apparent that private systems of support alone were inadequate to the task of social and psychological problem solving. This point was clearly demonstrated in this country during the Great Depression of 1929 when, as a consequence of massive unemployment and concomitant social and psychological problems, families and private charitable sources became overwhelmed. Although previously scattered examples existed, by 1935 it was clear that what was needed was a combination of private and governmental services or social insurances, to deal with social problems that were sui generis to industrial and technological societies. Eventually, a melding took place between and among private and governmental services. The belief in the importance of having both private and governmental services, and ideas of blending and coordinating these services on behalf of the clients, comprises the social welfare ideology of this country.

In addition, theorists in the mental health areas, at least since the time of Freud, maintained that the individual was influenced, in the developmental sense, by psychological factors as well as by social and environmental factors. It had become quite clear that certain constructs of the personality, such as values, attitudes, feelings, and behavior were often influenced by the cultural milieu. It had also become increasingly clear that the social and cultural environment not only had an effect in shaping behavior, but could also be influential in helping to change non-conforming behavior.

Following World War II, several researchers raised the issue concerning the usefulness of hospitalization in treating mentally ill persons. Beginning in the 1950s, much popular literature, as well as social science literature, was directed at examining and depicting these institutions. They were found to be anti-therapeutic. Chiefly, the reasons had to do with the structure, functions, personnel, programs, and services of the hospitals. Their primary treatment approaches seemed to focus on the management and control of behavior, often through the use of highly coercive and stringent methods. Staff with the least amount of education and training appeared to exercise primary treatment responsibilities for the patients. There were problems in staff morale, inter-staff rivalries, and conflicts. It seemed that patients became more mentally ill as a result of their hospitalization.

The development of the notion of the therapeutic community or therapeutic milieu in mental hospital settings was a response to the problems of institutionalization. It was thought that if patients could be treated in a more humane and democratic way, and if they could be involved in their treatment in a meaningful way, then hospitals would become more therapeutic and patients would achieve higher levels of mental health functioning. In these new types of hospitals as therapeutic communities, nonprofessional staff persons were given more professional tasks. They became members of the interdisciplinary treatment team. Sometimes, they were in direct charge of client treatment. Eventually, the notion of the therapeutic community was extended into the community. By the 1960s, community-based, outpatient treatment settings became the therapeutic mode of choice.

Beginning in 1963, federal legislation in the health and mental health areas emphasized the importance of treatment in the community. Federal legislation provided for funding for community-based centers as well as for staffing patterns that included nonprofessional staff. These kinds of nonprofessionals eventually were called case managers. By the mid 1960s, deinstitutionalization was in full swing. Meanwhile, in the nongovernmental sector, many mental health agencies were exploring the use of nonprofessional persons primarily as support staff to the professional staff. Many of the initiatives to explore the use of nonprofessional staff as case managers in mental health and War on Poverty agencies came from federal government initiatives, particularly from pilot projects funded by the National Institute of Mental Health. The use of nonprofessional staff members in many agencies also can be traced to an occupational void that came about because of the severe shortage of highly trained mental health personnel by the mid 1960s, as well as the increasing movement of highly trained mental health personnel into private practice.

Initially, case managers were limited to activities or interventions that were directed at resolving problems in the social and physical environment of the clients and their families that impinged on their ability to function appropriately. This was in keeping with the role of sociotherapist that had historically been assigned to nonprofessionals. Later, case managers were given responsibilities for working with problematic aspects of clients' functioning with respect to their attitudes, behaviors, and values. Thus, their role expanded to include supportive and relationship-based client-centered, or psychosocial therapies. Eventually, they were given responsibilities, with appropriate supervision, to be a direct therapist, or psychotherapist, with certain types of clients.

In any case, today case management can be best described as a perspective or approach, rather than as a system contained within an interdisciplinary mental health team. Nowadays, depending upon their levels of education, training, and experience, as well as their personal values, attitudes, and beliefs about the viability of various theoretical approaches to planned change with clients, case managers perform a variety of activities or interventions. These activities and interventions range from traditional sociotherapeutic techniques, such as a networking and brokering on behalf of their clients, to psychosocial therapies that use supportive and client-centered relationship techniques to bring about behavioral and attitudinal change; and to the practice of psychotherapies that involve the client in a reflective process in order to achieve insight about the genesis of his or her problems in social and psychological functioning.

Although most of the applications of the case management approach have been directed at persons who have problems in mental health functioning, particularly the chronically mentally ill, increasingly case management has become a method of choice for treating many other types of clients. The literature contains numerous examples of the use of case management with adults with disabilities, people with AIDS, the elderly, the mentally retarded and their families, military families, disabled infants, school children, and with impaired employees in employee assistance programs. Although fewer examples exist concerning the application of case management techniques to offender populations, some work has been noted with respect to its use with parolees and probationers on electronic monitoring, with substance abusers, with alcoholics, and with delinquents. Reports of the use of case management range from case studies to empirical types of studies. In general, the research seems to suggest that case management is an effective method for working with many different types of clients, who have a range of social and psychological problems, and who seek services from a variety of agencies and settings. The trend seems to favor its increasing use in the field of criminal justice by correctional counselors.

References

Charkuff, R. (1969). *Helping and Human Relations: Practice and Research.* New York, NY: Holt, Rinehart & Winston.

Community Mental Health Centers Amendment of 1970, Pub. L. 91-211.

Comprehensive Health Planning and Public Health Service Amendment of 1966, Pub. L. 89-749.

Cumming, J. & E. Cumming (1962). *Ego and Milieu.* New York, NY: Atherton Press.

Enos, R., C.M. Black, J.F. Quinn & J.E. Holman (1992). *Alternative Sentencing: Electronically Monitored Correctional Supervision.* Bristol, IN: Wyndham Hall Press.

Erickson, E. (1963). *Childhood and Society.* New York, NY: W.W. Norton & Company.

Family Support Act of 1988, Pub. L. 100-485.

Feine, J.I. & P.A. Taylor (1991). "Serving Rural Families of Developmentally Disabled Children: A Case Management Model." *Social Work*, 36:323-327.

Froland, C., D.L. Pancoast, N.J. Chapman & P.J. Kimboko (1981). *Helping Networks and Human Services.* Beverly Hills, CA: Sage Publications.

Froland, C., D.L. Pancoast & P. Parker (1983). "Introduction." In D.L. Pancoast, P. Parker & C. Froland (eds.) *Rediscovering Self-Help* (pp. 17-30). Beverly Hills, CA: Sage Publications.

Godlay, S., M. Godlay, A. Pratt & J. Wallace (1994). "Case-Management Services for Adolescent Substance Abusers—A Program Description." *Journal of Substance Abuse Treatment*, 11: 309-317.

Goffman, E. (1961). *Asylums: Essays on the Social Situation of Mental Patients and Other Inmates.* Garden City, NY: Anchor Books.

Goldstrom, I.D. & R.W. Manderscheid (1983). "A Descriptive Analysis of Community Support Program Case Managers Serving the Chronically Mentally Ill." *Community Mental Health Journal*, 19:17-26.

Greene, R.R. (1992). "Case Management: An Arena for Social Work Practice." In B.S. Vourlekis & R.R. Greene (eds.) *Social Work Case Management* (pp. 11-25). New York, NY: Aldine De Gruyter.

Hansell, N., M. Wodarczyk & H.M. Visotsky (1968). "The Mental Health Expediter." *Archives of General Psychiatry*, 18:392-399.

Heffernan, J., G. Shuttlesworth & R. Ambrosino (1992). *Social Work and Social Welfare–An Introduction* (Second Edition). St. Paul, MN: West Publishing Co.

Johnson, L.C. (1968). *Social Work Practice* (Second Edition). Boston, MA: Allyn & Bacon.

Jones, M. (1953). *The Therapeutic Community.* New York, NY: Basic Books.

Kanter, J. (1990). "Community-Based Management of Psychotic Clients: The Contributions of D.W. and Clare Winnicott." *Clinical Social Work Journal*, 18:223-241.

Lief, H.I. (1966). "Subprofessional Training in Mental Health." *Archives of General Psychiatry*, 15:660-664.

Magee, P. & F.L. Senizaiz (1987). "AIDS: A Case Management Approach, the Illinois Experience." *Child and Adolescent Social Work Journal*, 4:278-289.

Mental Retardation Facilities and Community Mental Health Centers Construction Act of 1963, Pub. L. 88-164.

Miller, G. (1983). "Case Management: The Essential Service." In C.J. Sanborn (ed.) *Case Management in Mental Health Services* (pp. 3-15). New York, NY: The Haworth Press.

Narcotics Addiction Rehabilitation Act of 1966, Pub. L. 89-793.

National Association of Social Workers (1981). *Guidelines for the Selection and Use of Social Workers*. Silver Spring, MD: Author.

Pitts, J.R. (1963). " Introduction." In T.L. Parsons, E. Shils, K.D. Naegele & J.R. Pitts (eds.) *Theories of Society* (pp. 685-716). Glencoe, IL: The Free Press.

Public Health Service Act, Amendments. Special Health Revenue Sharing Act of 1975, Pub. L. 94-63.

Rapp, C.A. & R. Chamberlain (1985). Case Management Services for the Chronically Mentally Ill. *Social Work*, 30:417-422.

Reban, A. (1994). "Nurses as Case Managers for At-Risk Elders." In M. Stanley & P.G. Beare (eds.) *Gerontological Nursing* (pp. 122-132). Philadelphia, PA: F.A. Davis.

Reiff, R. & F. Reissman (1965). "The Indigenous Nonprofessional. *Community Mental Health Journal,* Monograph Series No. 1.

Richmond, M.E. (1917). *Social Diagnosis.* New York, NY: Russell Sage Foundation.

Rioch, M.J., C. Elkes, A.A. Flint, B.S. Usdonsky, R.G. Newman & E. Silber (1963). "National Institute of Mental Health Pilot Study in Training Mental Health Counselors." *American Journal of Orthopsychiatry,* 33:678-689.

Rueveni, U.R. (1979). *Networking Families in Crisis.* New York, NY: Human Sciences Press.

Sanborn, C.J. (ed.) (1983). *Case Management in Mental Health Services.* New York, NY: The Haworth Press.

Schwartz, W. & S.R. Zalba (eds.) (1971). *The Practice of Group Work.* New York, NY: Columbia University Press.

Schulman, L. (1984). *The Skills of Helping Individuals and Groups* (Second Edition). Itasca, IL: F.E. Peacock Publishers.

Sheafor, B.W., C.R. Horejsi & G.A Horejsi (1988). *Techniques and Guidelines for Social Work Practice.* Boston, MA: Allyn & Bacon.

Sousel, G.E., F. Paradise & S. Stroup (1988). "Case Management Practice in an AIDS Service Organization." *Social Casework*, 69:388-392.

Stanton, A.H. & M. Schwartz (1954). *The Mental Hospital—A Study of Institutional Participation in Psychiatric Illness and Treatment.* New York, NY: Basic Books.

Sullivan, H.S. (1931). "The Modified Psychoanalytic Treatment of Schizophrenia." *American Journal of Psychiatry*, 11:519-540.

Sullivan, W., D. Hartmann, D. Dillon & J. Wolk (1994). "Implementing Case Management in Alcohol and Drug Treatment." *Families in Society—The Journal of Contemporary Human Services*, 75:67-73.

Susser, M. (1968). *Community Psychiatry: Epidemiologic and Social Themes.* New York, NY: Random House.

Vourlekis, B.S. & R.R. Greene (eds.) (1992). *Social Work Case Management.* New York, NY: Aldine De Gruyter.

Ward, M.J. (1946). *The Snake Pit.* New York, NY: Random House.

Weil, M., J.M. Karls & Associates (1985). *Case Management in Human Services.* San Francisco, CA: Jossey-Bass.

Wilensky, H.L. & C.N. Lebeaux (1958). *Industrial Society and Social Welfare.* New York, NY: Russell Sage Foundation.

Chapter 3

Personal and Professional Issues

Introduction

The nature of the relationship between the correctional case manager and the offender is the key factor in terms of achieving successful counseling outcomes. "Relationship" may be defined as the development of trust and confidence between the correctional case manager and the offender. The relationship develops via the process of the professional encounter and interplay between them. Through the process of the encounter, the offender comes to understand the nature of the offense, acknowledges his or her role in the offense, and understands the personal and legal consequences that flow from the offense.

The process starts with the correctional case manager describing and clarifying for the offender the specific dimensions of the offense. In the case of a probationer, the rules regarding the conditions of probation must be understood. With respect to offenders on intermediate sanctions, such as intensive probation supervision, home confinement, and various forms of alternatives to sentencing, the conditions concerning those sanctions must be clearly understood. Concerning parolees, they must clearly understand the conditions of their supervision in the community. These conditions are generally set forth in a court order that describes the behavior or circumstances that may cause parole to be revoked. Following this step, the offender and the correctional case manager develop a contract regarding the nature and structure of the counseling relationship. This might be referred to as the "who, what, and why" of the counseling encounter. After this, they meet for regular counseling sessions. During these sessions, problems are discussed in a systematic way, and the counseling goals and behavioral outcomes are described and evaluated.

The viability of the counseling relationship is always dependent upon the offender's understanding and acceptance of the goals and outcomes that were defined in the counseling contract. The acceptance has to be genuine, and the goals and outcomes must be mutually agreed to by both parties. However, it is important for the correctional case manager to understand and to become aware of a number of personal and professional issues that may impact upon his or her counseling efforts. These will be discussed in the following pages of this chapter.

Core Conditions of Facilitative Communications

Probably the most important personal and professional issue for correctional case managers is the issue of facilitative communications. Facilitative communications are communications, both verbally and nonverbally, that tend to further the attainment of the purposes and goals of the counseling relationship. Any examination of facilitative communications must begin with a look at the contributions of Carl Rogers, a preeminent American psychologist and the "father" of client-centered therapy. He is generally acknowledged to have been the seminal researcher with respect to identifying and examining personal and professional characteristics of counselors, and the relationship of these characteristics to successful counseling outcomes. Although Rogers (1951, 1957), and others who built on his work (Truax & Mitchell, 1971), identified a number of core conditions that they believed to be associated with positive therapeutic outcomes in therapy, in the opinion of the writers, three, in particular, are most useful for correctional case managers. These conditions are: genuineness, congruence, and unconditional positive regard.

Genuineness

Genuineness has to do with the nature of self disclosure and, specifically, refers to the ability of the counselor to be an open, direct, and candid communicator. "Real" counselors are those who are not pedantic, pedagogical, or "phony." To be a successful correctional case manager, one must communicate with offenders clearly and unambiguously. Hepworth and Larsen (1986) characterized it as "authenticity." For them, it meant that the counselor needed to be able to self disclose. This meant being able to share with the client bits and pieces of one's personal self or life history. This must be done in a genuine, sincere, open, and spontaneous way. It is not a premeditated or staged performance. It must be a natural and genuine disclosing. There are some very important reasons for the use of self disclosure. It can be a very powerful therapeutic tool. Self disclosure, when it is natural and genuine, is a powerful force that can be used to establish an interpersonal and empathetic link or connection with the offender. The personal material that is shared with them helps humanize the counseling encounter by making it less bureaucratic, impersonal, and antiseptic. It also helps to universalize the problem. In universalization, the offender comes to see that other people also have had problems in life as well. This can be accomplished, for example, when self disclosure reveals that the correctional case manager and the offender once confronted a similar problem in life. In using universalization, the case manager must always use the historical incident to describe how he or she used normative, socially acceptable, ways of dealing with a problem.

The material that is shared is intended to give the offender a piece of the personal history of the case manager so that he or she can identify with the humanness of the other person. However, there are limits to self disclosure. Personal history that does not promote the psychological or mental health capacity of the client is not shared. Similarly, sharing a piece of personal history which may encourage socially unacceptable behavior is also never shared. And, certainly, sharing a bit of personal history which, even indirectly, may encourage criminal behavior, is never acceptable. Finally, the case manager should never share personal feelings that might cause the case manager/client relationship to become reversed. This means that the purpose of the relationship is to meet the needs of the offender, not the needs of the case manager.

Congruence

It is also very important for case management correctional counselors to understand the nature of congruence. Congruence refers to the degree of interface or match between the case manager's thoughts, feelings, expressions, affect, and body language, and his or her outward expressions or verbalizations to the client. For example, the parent, with his arms crossed, who is saying emotionally reassuring things to his child while facing the child is conveying a mixed message that is ambiguous and paradoxical. As two prominent clinicians and researchers in the field of therapeutic communications noted, we need to "say it straight" (Englander-Golden & Satir, 1990).

The successful correctional case manager must project a singular message to the offender, both verbally and nonverbally. His or her verbalizations should not be paradoxical or confused or negated by conflicting nonverbal messages (such as inconsistent body language or facial expressions) which implicitly convey a contrary message. Keefe and Maypole (1983) provided some important clarifications about this construct. From their research, they concluded that certain nonverbal ways of communicating empathy to the client may be related to positive outcomes in counseling when the nonverbal behaviors match the corresponding verbal responses by the counselor. This would occur when the counselor's thoughts and feelings were matched (congruent) with their words, their facial expressions, their tone of voice, physical movements, and gestures.

For the writers, congruence also has to do with the manner in which we listen to our clients as they share their problems with us. In essence, there are types of "healthy" and "neurotic" ways of listening. Barbara's (1958) work about listening to ourselves, listening to others, and listening to the essence of things, is most instructive about this point. In healthy listening, the case manager listens for the important statements that the offender is making, and listens for what is being said as well as for what is not being said. Healthy listening means asking questions, asking for clarifications, and challenging assertions and allegations when necessary. Healthy listening also means observing the various manifestations of the client's nonverbal behaviors, such as body language, facial movements, degree of eye contact, and so forth.

An additional point about healthy listening is of great importance to correctional case managers. That is, healthy listening also means trying to understand what the offender is implying, and whether or not his or her story is internally consistent with the reality of the experience, as the case manager perceives it, that the offender is sharing.

Neurotic listening, by contrast, refers to a kind of listening that it influenced by our own fears. It can take the form of listening in a superficial manner so that we obtain only bits and pieces of what the client is saying. It can also be noted as a kind of listening which is very passive in nature so that the counselor rarely participates in the process of verbal interaction. Neurotic listening means listening without having care or concern for what the client is disclosing. This is listening without empathy. Neurotic listening can also mean listening only for the sound of our own voice, while we manipulate the client by expressing our opinions about what he or she ought to do when we have not listened sufficiently in order to have enough information to make a proper determination about what needs to be done.

In summary, healthy listening is effective listening. It is a skill that is attained by participation and practice. It is acquired. For Reik (1949), it meant developing the capacity to listen with the "third ear;" that is, to listen in an intuitive manner in order to determine what the other person is not saying, but is probably thinking and feeling. At the same time, it means not letting our own cognitive processes screen out what is being said. It is not a passive, non-directive activity; rather, it is an active and engaging process. It is important for a correctional case manager to become an active listener because this helps him or her in dealing with the mass of anxieties about speaking and interacting that often flood in when we engage our clients. Healthy listening can be fostered by having effective supervision of one's work.

Unconditional Positive Regard

Unconditional positive regard is another important characteristic of a successful correctional case manager. Unconditional positive regard may be defined as the ability to understand the behavior of the offender, while not rejecting the offender in the personal or humanistic sense. Meador, in interpreting Rogers (Meador & Rogers, 1974) believed that unconditional positive regard was manifested by the counselor's nonpossessive caring or acceptance of the client as an individual. She felt that in order to be able to do this, the counselor must be able to trust that clients possessed an ability to act in such a way as to achieve self-actualization. Self-actualization means that clients, and, indeed, all rational persons, possess a psychological self-wisdom that can cause them to discover for themselves their inner strengths and resources, as well as the directions that their life should take. That is, they have the inner psychological ability to understand and act on normative or socially acceptable choices. The role of the counselor is to act in a caring but non-directive way in order to help them make these kinds of choices.

Consistent with Rogers' theoretical formulations, then, unconditional positive regard means acceptance of the person. It is an acceptance of what the Quakers refer to as "that of God in every man." For some clinicians, acceptance of the person in the therapeutic relationship means acceptance of the person but not necessarily approval of the behavior. A therapeutic mid-course would be the stance of a non-judgmental view of the behavior. This is a condition that may consciously be supportable but which is difficult to maintain in the unconscious sense because, for example, it is difficult not to both dislike the murder and the murderer. In terms of the correctional case manager in criminal justice settings, perhaps Biestek's (1957) clarification of the term "acceptance" comes closest to being a realistic commandment for successful case management. For him, acceptance meant that the counselor should not be sanguine about the client. The counselor needed to see the client as he or she really is. It is a kind of accounting system in which the strengths and weaknesses, positive and negative attitudes, and constructive and destructive behaviors of the offender, would be tallied. While doing this, the counselor must simultaneously maintain an appreciation for the innate dignity and personal value of the client. But (and this is a key point for correctional counselors), acceptance did not, for Biestek, mean acceptance or approval of deviant behaviors or attitudes. The focus has to be upon the behaviors and attitudes, not upon good intentions.

With respect to the issue of counseling with offenders, the writers believe that the conditions of empathetic counseling include acceptance of the person but not acceptance of the behavior, nor approval of the behavior. This point must be clearly noted since offenders, by contrast with most types of traditional, that is to say, voluntary clients seeking counseling services, are persons who have violated criminal laws. This is the over-arching personal and situational dynamic with respect to offenders that must be understood.

In many ways, correctional clients mirror the universe of mental health patients. And, correctional counseling strategies often mirror traditional mental health counseling approaches as well. However, what is unique about this population is the fact that they have entered the criminal justice system because they have committed criminal offenses, or because they have a high probability of committing such offenses. Therefore, boundaries must be set to circumscribe aberrant behavior.

Empathetic Functioning

Empathetic functioning is another matter of keen importance for case management correctional counselors. This construct refers to the degree to which the counselor can achieve an empathetic understanding of the client's personal frame of reference. It is a very difficult ideal to achieve.

For Rogers (1957), "empathy," as he called it, represented a principal core condition that successful counselors needed to have in order to bring about therapeutic personality change for the client. Rogers believed that a counselor needed to develop the ability to understand the client's awareness, or phenome-nological understanding, of his own life and situational experiences. It meant that the counselor should strive to develop the ability to sense a client's private and intimate world, and attempt to understand what this world means to them. It also meant that the counselor should consciously develop the capacity to iden-tify or empathize with the client's feelings, and to attempt to experience these feelings as though they were the counselor's feelings, without becoming caught up in or emotionally involved in these experiences. As Rogers put it: "To sense the client's private world as if it were your own, but without ever losing the 'as if' quality" (1957:99).

Therefore, to be successful, the correctional case manager must try to tune in and become aware of the problems offenders bring to the counseling encounter. The tuning in must be done in a sensitive manner by not trampling on the meanings for the clients that are contained within their problems, and in their expressions of feelings about their problems. The antithesis of empathetic functioning is to tell the clients that you "understand how they feel." One can never truly understand how another person feels, but we can try to enter anoth-er person's psychosocial world in a sensitive and unobtrusive manner. Other-wise, our attempts to understand will only be naive and superficial.

Empathetic functioning also means that the case manager must respond in an appropriate professional manner by not playing into or getting caught up in the problems of the client. Correctional case managers, since they work with many types of offenders who are manipulative and controlling, must become aware of their "emotional softspots," that is to say, their needs, wishes, desires, and insecurities. This is important because often offenders try to exploit these softspots in an attempt to manipulate or control the case manager. The "con game" is a good example of this problem (Berne, 1964). In short, it means that the case manager tries to understand what it must be like to "walk in the shoes of the probationer or parolee" but, at the same time, he or she must be able to establish appropriate professional, that is to say, social and psychological dis-tance or space, between the clients and their problems, and the case manager's own needs, wishes, desires, and insecurities.

Metaphorically speaking, when his or her clients hurt emotionally, the case manager must not cry. An essential question to ask here is: "Whose needs are being met?" It is all too easy to take the less conflictive course and say yes when we should say no; or to give an overly optimistic evaluation when we could more effectively promote social and psychological growth in offenders by giving them a realistic evaluation. The successful case manager, in responding appropriately to his or her clients' feelings and problems, demonstrates the capacity to have both a hard head and a soft heart. In the opinion of the writers, this last point is at the core of professionalism in criminal justice.

Understanding Your Reactions to Offenders and Their Reactions to You

In many instances, the nature of the offenses committed by clients of correctional case managers may create emotional stress for the case managers. In spite of the admonition that an empathetic counselor should be able to intellectually compartmentalize or isolate his or her feelings and attitudes about the behavior of the client from the client as a person, it is often very difficult to hate the crime but understand the criminal. Offenders who murder, rape, or commit other types of sexual assaults, particularly upon children, can test the empathetic elasticity of case managers. Similarly, offenders who come to the case manager for treatment arrive with a whole carload of psychological and emotional baggage that is often a residue of their history of contacts with significant others and authority figures in their developmental past. With respect to most forms of psychotherapy, these issues are termed "transference" and "countertransference."

Theoretical Considerations

Freud (1962) is considered to be the original formulator of the term "transference." For Freud, transference referred to the transfer of unconscious feelings from the client onto the physician. This transfer was a phenomena that was external to the arena of the physician's treatment of the patient. The treatment context provided an opportunity for the patient to transfer feelings onto the person of the physician.

In the psychoanalytical literature the best exposition of this construct can probably be found in the work of Freud's daughter, Anna (1965). For her, transference consisted of all those impulses experienced by the patient during his or her relationship with the analyst. These feelings were not newly created by the analytic situation but, instead, had their origins in early object relationships with people in their past. These feelings came out during the psychotherapy encounter as the patient interacted with the therapist. Transference, like many psychological ideas, is a theoretical abstraction that can only be really understood by a process of mental assembly called inference. For example, for Menninger (1958) transference can be inferred as being one of four parts, phases, or moments that commonly occur during psychotherapeutic encounters. For him, these movements are labeled as "regressions," namely: regression in the object, regression in the subject, regression in the verb, and regression in the indirect object.

Menninger's notion of transference as regression in the indirect object is of most interest for correctional case managers. Transference as regression in the indirect object occurs as the psychoanalyst involuntarily participates in the treatment. This form of transference is seen as a type of displacement in that successive alternations in the indirect object of the conscious-unconscious wish of the client takes place so that a change occurs from the wish that "I want help from the psychotherapist" to "I want something from someone." In this type of indirect object association, the psychotherapist or counselor often becomes, in the mind of the client, various "someones," such as brother, father, mother, teacher, in the fantasies and formulations of the client. To fully understand this construct, is becomes necessary to differentiate it from the term "transference neurosis."

Transference neurosis is a type of psychotherapeutic treatment relationship in which the client plays out his or her wishes or fantasies, via a rigid transference with the psychotherapist, which allows the client to project and displace unconscious feelings. Transference neurosis, then, is in reality a relationship between the psychoanalyst and the patient which is characterized by fantasy and not by a real (conscious or reality-level) interplay between the two. In transference neurosis, the psychotherapist refuses to become a real object to the client and thus pushes him or her back into his or her inner fantasy life with the intention of having the client replay that fantasy life in order to expose it vicariously and relive it, while directly or indirectly influencing a corrective for those parts of the fantasy that are aberrant.

Dramaturgical approaches to psychotherapy, which can range from role-playing to sociodrama to psychodrama, are examples of treatment approaches that are transference-based. Moreno (1946) was the founder of this school of psychotherapy. Psychodrama is a method that allows individuals or groups to come to grips with problems that they have repressed or suppressed by the use of dramatic images, symbolisms, and representations. Role-playing and drama and other types of script-playing are techniques that are used in psychodrama to enable the client to act out the neurosis or deviant behavior. Lester and Van Voorhis (1992) have described the theory and applications of psychodrama to correctional counseling with a great deal of detail. Prendergast (1991) has described some very effective ways to use psychodrama with sexual offenders. In his approach, role-playing is used for behavioral rehearsal in order to recondition sexual offenders to deal with sexual images, dreams, and fantasies. An example is the use of masturbatory reconditioning techniques wherein a psychotherapist or clinically advanced correctional counselor reconditions a sexual offender by having him learn to fantasize about a pleasurable and normal sexual contact and to masturbate to orgasm to it. Or, by contrast, to recondition by aversion a sexual offender's deviant fantasies, for example, pedophilic fantasies, by having the offender masturbate to the pre-ejaculatory phase but never masturbating to an orgasm based on deviant fantasies.

It is also important to also understand transference as a dichotomy: negative and positive transference. Positive and negative transference refers to how the client identifies the therapist or correctional counselor. If in his or her background the client had parents or friends or others who were friendly and tried to be helpful, or who had his or her best interests at heart, or who functioned as conventional persons (Hirschi, 1969), then the client may be apt to transfer a desire for help in changing behavior onto the therapist or correctional counselor in a positive way. On the other hand, if during their psychosocial developmental history or process of socialization clients primarily encountered significant persons who were not helpful, or who were socially or psychologically dysfunctional, or who abused and neglected them, or who presented inappropriate models of socialization to them, then they may be inclined to view the opportunity for help via counseling in a distrustful or negative manner.

Since transference "cuts both ways," it is important for the correctional case manager to develop the ability to identify and understand his or her reactions to the offender as well. Sometimes, a case manager may transfer unconscious thoughts and feelings onto the offender. These thoughts and feelings represent positive or negative reactions growing out of the case manager's own life experiences, principally with other persons, but also influenced by his or her social class, value, religious, or moral orientations. This phenomena is called "countertransference." These reactions need to become psychologically isolated from the counseling context so that they will not influence the counseling process, either in a positive or negative direction. This is important because countertransference reactions often contain strong irrational and unconscious elements, particularly with respect to the type of offense committed by the client. It is also important for the case manager to become aware of these types of reactions since these feelings can also impact his or her professional conduct with clients. Opportunities for case consultation, as well as good clinical supervision of the work of the case manager, particularly a method of supervision that allows the case manager to share his or her thoughts and feelings about their counseling efforts with offenders, can help to achieve this goal.

In a related vein, the experience of the writers suggests that often students enter counseling professions in order to perhaps exorcise their own personal psychological demons. Becoming aware of this dynamic is, of course, emotionally healthy and can cause one to become a more effective counselor. It is an appropriate use of an ego defense mechanism: sublimation. However, it can be a negative in the counseling process if the case manager brings into the counseling relationship with the offender distorted ways of dealing with people that are a part of the case manager's developmental history that were not worked through. The offender may react to these tendencies in the case manager in a number of ways. For example, if the offender is highly manipulative (and, typically many offenders who are sociopathic fall into this category) it allows the offender, as previously noted, an opportunity to play many types of "con" games with the case manager.

How Transference and Countertransference Should Be Used in Correctional Counseling

One should understand that there are limitations to the correctional case manager's use of transference. These limitations are associated with the levels of clinical training and experience in psychotherapy possessed by the case manager. The discussion that follows is predicated upon the authors' belief that most experienced correctional counselors who are ideologically oriented toward the rehabilitation ethic in criminal justice can make effective use of transference and countertransference in their everyday work with offenders.

For this to happen, case managers need to develop the ability to recognize and identify transference phenomena both within themselves and in their clients. This will have the effect of making the unconscious conscious. It will also enhance their ability to manage, direct, and focus the counseling process upon the attainment of the rehabilitation goals. For most case managers this probably means that they need to manage the counseling relationship in such a way as to allow only a minimum amount of transference to emerge. However, there are some ways in which the case manager can use transference phenomena for the betterment of the offender.

One such way involves directing a transference reaction received from the offender toward a pattern of adaption. It involves a kind of moral re-education or value clarification. It may be used, for example, with an offender who has the kind of conscience or superego disturbance that Redl and Wineman (1965) term "model rigidity." Juvenile offenders can often be characterized this way. Redl and Wineman define the term thus: "by 'model rigidity' we mean inability of a person to experience guilt unless the situation is directly tied up with the original persons who made the first value demands, usually the parents" (1965:242). In this kind of situation, the case manager may role-play for the offender "good mother" and "bad mother" themes. This will present the offender with a therapeutic opportunity to identify with and appraise both the functional and dysfunctional aspects of his or her developmental history. In this process, the case manager emphasizes the positive and functional aspects of the mothering role in an attempt to reeducate the conscience of the offender. At this point, the case manager may also make a link of insight for the offender between their current problems in social functioning and their "bad mothering" experiences. This technique can be very therapeutically productive with an offender who, for example, as a consequence of his own childhood physical abuse, repeats this pattern with his children or with his spouse.

Transference may be used by correctional case managers in other ways as well, such as when they attempt to "straighten out" the relationship between themselves and offenders. For example, this can be done by telling an offender that they are trying to urge the offender to do something just as his or her mother, for example, tried to urge them to do something. This helps to clarify the relationship between the case manager and the offender. It is only used when the offender has some understanding of his or her feelings towards his or her parents and has generally had positive feelings about them. Transference, when used in this way, gives reassurance to the offender in order to encourage or promote a positive adaptation or a positive course of action. This happens if the case manager is viewed, via the transference, as a positive parental figure.

Countertransference can be used in correctional counseling as well. Indirectly, it can be used as the case manager develops an awareness of the ways in which he or she may be responding to the offender that may be irrational with respect to the sex, race, or ethnicity of the offender, or to some other characteristic of the offender. One relatively easy way to chart this is for the case manager to systematically review his or her encounters with the offender depicted in various materials about the offender, such as case recordings, reports, and summaries, and then examine these for the purpose of identifying areas of bias or insensitivity.

Countertransference reactions are important for correctional case managers because knowledge of these kinds of reactions provides a key to self-awareness. When appropriate, countertransference reactions can be shared with the offender. Sometimes this kind of sharing may facilitate the treatment relationship. This is in keeping with Rogers' notion of "genuineness" as previously discussed, or with Jourad's (1964) notion of "transparency."

Since self-awareness is an essential component in successful counseling, it becomes important for the correctional case manager to continually monitor his or her feelings about the offender as the counseling relationship progresses. Sometimes case managers want to work only with certain types of offenders, or they may try to alter or modify the counseling relationship in some way. Often, a case manager may describe an offender as being "unworkable." These reactions to offenders may be symptomatic of countertransference problems because they may be resistances, on the part of case managers, to dealing with their own psychological baggage. Case managers sometimes need to take an introspective look at their own feelings before deciding that they cannot work effectively with a particular offender or with offenders who commit particular types of offenses. A good guide to remember here is the thought that oftentimes when we are resistant to dealing with some issue or with someone, the resistance is usually an important indication of the need to deal with the issue or the person. This kind of psychological signaling is a part of the wisdom of the human psyche.

Dealing with Some Professional Paradoxes

Correctional case managers also have to learn to deal with paradoxes. This is a more complicated concept. Paradoxes come about for correctional case managers when they perceive that they are acting against what appears to be the general opinion or broad societal consensus. Often, what appears to be the general opinion or societal consensus is, instead, ideologically driven, and represents a particular political viewpoint. Dealing with paradoxes means that we have to have the capacity to resist the common consensus and to go with what our experience, common sense, intuition, or "case work" wisdom tells us to be true. Several descriptions will make this point.

To begin with, there is the widely held notion, originating with Martinson (1974), that "nothing seems to work." The basis of his research suggests that rehabilitative efforts generally, and psychologically based strategies specifically, do not work in terms of rehabilitating offenders. When placed in the "strum und drang" of correctional work, it often seems to correctional case managers that they are swimming against a professional and public opinion tide. This can be illustrated, for example, when at a party, someone asks you about what you do for a living. When you share the information with them, they proceed to demean what you do. You get tarred with the same brush as the offender. If one gets caught up in this, the net result can be a feeling of hopelessness and despair.

However, with some professional experience we begin to see that some things work, and that some offenders attain their treatment goals and objectives and do not become recidivists. We also become chary about "research studies." We know from the clinical literature that there are just too many unresolvable methodological difficulties in doing empirical human services research. Attempts to measure the outcomes of therapeutic interventions, with any significant degree of validity and reliability, are simply not feasible given the nature of social science research. The difficulties in doing this kind of research are mathematical, methodological, and substantive in nature. This was pointed out by Pierce and von Vorys (1962) in their notable critique about the use of mathematical modeling in the social sciences. Or, perhaps we need to recall Disraeli's statement (via Mark Twain): "There are three kinds of lies: lies, damned lies, and statistics" (Andrews, 1993:870). Out of our experiences of working with offenders, we simply begin to understand that there are no simple solutions to complex problems, and that there may not even be complicated solutions to simple problems.

An additional area of concern has to do with falling into the mea culpa trap. Correctional case managers should not personalize the successes or the failures of their clients. They need to remember that most offenders have a long history of social and psychological problems. These problems existed before they came into counseling. We are not responsible for that history. We are not guilty. It cannot be expected that levels of micro intervention, such as in correctional counseling, will "fix up" everyone. We are often rowing against a tide of social, environmental, and psychological pathology of long standing. A correctional case manager must develop the ability to enjoy and savor the small victories, because if he or she is conscientious, these will follow. On the other hand, we must not personalize our counseling failures. We must avoid "conning" ourselves via the game that some professionals play: "I'm only trying to help you" (Berne, 1964).

Another paradox is also worth noting. General uninformed opinion often holds that in order to be a good counselor, one has to be almost perfect, psychologically speaking. It would be wonderful if counselors were always in tune with their inner feelings, and genuine, and empathetic, and insightful. However, most of us who come to counseling are not perfect. Often, people seek out human service careers because of their own traumatic developmental experiences. The fields of psychology, counseling, and social work, in particular, are filled with people who, in the course of their own professional work, are also working through and resolving some of their own history. This may seem paradoxical, but often some of the most effective correctional counselors are persons who are working on or who have worked out their own personal demons. As Nietzsche stated it: "What does not destroy me makes me stronger" (Levinson, 1971:287).

But, there are some caveats concerning this issue. First, the case manager must become aware of why he or she entered into a correctional counseling career. Case managers need to develop a link of insight and awareness of their motivation for this type of profession. This connection of insight can be a plus because it may allow them to more sensitively enter the emotional world of their clients, and understand that world more emphatically. Second, case managers should understand that their choice of this kind of career probably represents a healthy type of sublimation by which the emotional energy from previous traumatic encounters has become redirected in a positive direction. This point can be illustrated by the story, commonly noted, of the traumatized war veteran who later becomes a priest.

Conclusions

In this chapter, the authors described a number of personal and professional issues that impact upon correctional case managers. First among these issues is that of relationship. They maintain that the key element in case management correctional counseling is the nature of the relationship between the case manager and the offender. The nature of the relationship is the vehicle by which the offender comes to understand and acknowledge his or her problems, comprehend the personal and legal consequences of his or her actions, understand the goals and objectives of the counseling encounter, enter into a treatment contract, and, understand the roles and responsibilities of the counselor and of the offender.

The research-based literature about the effectiveness of counseling identifies several core conditions that seemed to facilitate the communications process between the counselor and the client. These core conditions were thought to be related to successful counseling outcomes, irrespective of the level of training and experience of the counselor, or their academic field or theoretical orientation. In terms of correctional case management, three particular core conditions were identified: genuineness, congruence, and unconditional positive regard.

Correctional case managers should realize that acceptance of the offender is a critical variable in the correctional counseling process. However, there are boundaries around this construct. Acceptance is directed toward the offender as a person. His or her humanness is accepted. The aberrant behavior is never accepted nor legitimized in correctional counseling, either directly, or by indirect actions or behaviors which seem to imply acceptance. Furthermore, socially unacceptable behavior should always be linked to the reality of the legal consequences of the behavior, and the terms of the judicial order that circumscribes the behavior of the offender in community-based correctional settings.

Case managers also need to note the importance of understanding the phenomena of transference and countertransference in counseling. Most of us tend to have initial and ongoing reactions to others based upon our consciously realized or unconsciously felt impulses. Some of these reactions are rational and some are irrational. These impulses have their genesis in early object relationships. The reactions are either negative or positive, and they are experienced by the client toward the counselor and by the counselor toward the client. They are thus reciprocal and symmetrical if positive, or asymmetrical if negative. An understanding of the interplay of these dynamics is important for the correctional case manager. This is true because this helps to explain why offenders may react to case managers in certain ways. It is also important for case managers to recognize these reactions so that they have a means for evaluating whether the way they are reacting to the offender is rational or irrational. For example, if one has an understanding of the nature of the transference that is being played out by the offender, one can use those reactions as a therapeutic corrective. It can be redirected in a positive way. This is what Satir (1968) refers to as "model analysis," that is to say, the counselor helps the offender discover how past parental models influence their behavior and helps determine what they expect from other people. An example of a communication from the therapist to the patient using Satir's technique illustrates this point: "Your mother handled money that way. How *could* you have learned other ways?" (1968:173). A communication of this sort, when shared with an offender, can help them gain insight about their behavior, and can influence them to change the behavior.

Finally, a description of some common paradoxes that correctional case managers face were discussed. Paradoxes come about when general, uninformed societal opinion (sometimes politically driven) about issues in criminal justice is contradictory, divergent, inconsistent, or ambiguous in terms of the face validity of what we know to be true by experience, intuition, or common sense. Paradoxes of many kinds are encountered by correctional counselors.

A major paradox that is often encountered has to do with a general consensus of opinion that correctional counseling does not work, and that nothing works in relation to rehabilitating offenders. The reality of our own experiences and our own professional judgment tells us that some things work. While some politicians may deride what they refer to as "midnight basketball" programs, many correctional counselors know that basketball is the lure to get gang members off the street and into a more socially constructive milieu wherein they can have an opportunity to make use of education and job training programs. In short, there are often small victories. Even though correctional case managers are, metaphorically speaking, climbing up a mountain of social pathology, they are finding some footholds.

There is also something of a common myth that correctional counselors have to be perfect people. It seems paradoxical that people who have experienced various social or psychological problems could be of much usefulness in counseling. The reality is that many persons seek counseling careers in order to help them work through some of their own problems. This is not necessarily a problem as long as they have gained some insight about what has happened to them in the past, and how they are working out the problems of the past through their choice of a career. Armed with this, correctional counselors can experience a healthy sublimation by directing their emotional impulses in a constructive way toward helping their clients resolve problems; problems with which they can usually empathize.

References

Andrews, R. (1993). *The Columbia Dictionary of Quotations*. New York, NY: Columbia University Press.

Barbara, D. (1958). *The Art of Listening*. Springfield, IL: Charles C Thomas.

Berne, E. (1964). *Games People Play*. New York, NY: Grove Press.

Biestek, F. (1957). *The Casework Relationship*. Chicago, IL: Loyola University Press.

Englander-Golden, P. & V. Satir (1990). *Say it Straight*. Palo Alto, CA: Science and Behavior Books.

Freud, A. (1965) *Normality and Pathology in Childhood*. New York, NY: International Universities Press.

Freud, S. (1962). "Analytic Therapy and Transference." In D. Parsons, E. Shils, K.D. Naegele & J.R. Pitts (eds.) *Theories of Society*, Vol. 110 (pp. 896-903). Glencoe, IL: Free Press.

Hepworth, D. & J. Larson (1986). *Direct Social Work Practice* (Second Edition). Chicago, IL: The Dorsey Press.

Hirschi, T. (1969). *Causes of Delinquency*. Berkeley, CA: University of California Press.

Jourard, S. (1964). *The Transparent Self*. New York, NY: Van Nostrand & Reinhold.

Keefe, T. & D. Maypole (1983). *Relationships in Social Services Practice*. Monterey, CA: Brooks/Cole.

Lester, D. & P. Van Voorhis (1992). "Group and Milieu Therapy." In D. Lester, M. Braswell & P. Van Voorhis (eds.) (Second Edition) *Correctional Counseling* (pp.175-191). Cincinnati, OH: Anderson Publishing Co.

Levinson, L. (1971). *Bartlett's Unfamiliar Quotations*. Chicago, IL: Cowles Book Co.

Martinson, R. (1974). "What Works? Questions and Answers about Prison Reform." *The Public Interest*, 35:22-54.

Meador, B.D. & C. Rogers (1974). "Client-Centered Therapy." In R. Corsini (ed.) *Current Psychotherapies* (pp. 119-155). Itasca, IL: F.E. Peacock.

Menninger, K. (1958). *Theory of Psychoanalytic Technique*. New York, NY: Basic Books.

Moreno, J.L. (1946). *Psychodrama*. New York, NY: Beacon House.

Pierce, A. & K. von Vorys (1962). "The Concept of Functional Relationship of Mutually Interdependent Variables: A Comment on Mathematical Models in Social Sciences." *Social Science*, 37:78-84.

Prendergast, W. (1991). *Treating Sex Offenders in Correctional Institutions and Outpatient Clinics*. New York, NY: Springer Publishing Co.

Redl, F. & D. Wineman (1965). *Children Who Hate*. New York, NY: Free Press.

Reik, T. (1949). *Listening with the Third Ear*. New York, NY: Ferrar & Straus.

Rogers, C.R. (1951). *Client-Centered Therapy*. Boston, MA: Houghton Mifflin.

Rogers, C.R. (1957). "The Necessary and Sufficient Conditions of Therapeutic Personality Change." *Journal of Consulting Psychology*, 21:95-103.

Satir, V. (1968). *Conjoint Family Therapy*. Palo Alto, CA: Science and Behavior Books.

Truax, C.B. & K.M. Mitchell (1971). "Research on Certain Therapist Interpersonal Skills in Relation to Process and Outcome." In A.A. Bergin & S.L. Bergin (eds.) *Handbook of Psychotherapy and Behavior Change: An Empirical Analysis* (pp. 299-344). New York, NY: John Wiley & Sons.

Chapter 4

Assessment and Diagnosis

Introduction

This chapter contains a description and examples of the assessment and diagnostic phases in case management correctional counseling. The assessment phase of case management continues the process of bringing a new client into the correctional system. Assessment answers questions raised during intake, resulting in meaningful classification and subsequent referral to correctional services.

In terms of correctional case management, during the assessment phase, data is gathered through interview methods, by home visits, from collateral contacts, and by interviews with significant others in the offender's life span. This is usually followed by the diagnostic phase. During the diagnostic phase, three activities occur: development of the psychosocial history, the psychiatric examination, and the psychosocial evaluation. These three processes, along with the material obtained from the assessment, are then formulated into a clinical diagnosis. This diagnosis represents the "best case" hypothesis concerning the offender's problems in functioning.

In a sense, the diagnosis is a type of classification of the offender. However, most classification systems in criminal justice, whether they are risk assessment systems, needs assessment systems, or psychological classification systems, are designed to respond to institutional concerns about matching an offender with appropriate programs and services, staff and correctional resources, and security arrangements within a correctional institution. The diagnosis, as used in correctional case management, is principally directed toward the treatment needs of the offender. This is the case because most offenders, as clients of correctional case management, are located in non-institutional, community-based correctional settings.

Assessment

Assessment refers to intentional activities of a professional to describe characteristics, motivations, and needs of clients requiring correctional interventions. Assessment, like the other stages in correctional case management, is a process, rather than a discrete event. Some approaches to assessment attempt to describe basic features of a client, while other methods concentrate on underlying dimensions or variables relevant to the assessment question. The assessment question is the statement of the reason or purpose of data gathering in a specific case. Assessment ranges from simple description, such as recording behavioral observations gathered in an intake interview, to complex analysis involving investigation of potential causes of criminality.

The descriptive approaches to assessment include some systematic, linear methods of summarizing major features of the client. Analytical approaches to assessment incorporate abstract methods of investigating underlying traits or variables of some theoretical interest. Therefore, assessment may emphasize description of current status or focus on remote causation of dimensions of criminality. Descriptive methods tend to secure data that translate readily to decisions in a selected classification system, especially if the resulting classes or categories contribute to decisionmaking in custody or supervision. Analytical approaches, often derived from theories of individual differences, result typically in some form of diagnosis, which may be related only indirectly to existing classification. However, analytical assessment may be applicable to decisions regarding rehabilitation and treatment.

Data gathering begins with reviewing existing information, continues through interviewing, and concludes with some basic description or impression of the client's current status. As assessment questions evolve, specific evaluation techniques are indicated. There is a formulation of the client's case, resulting in classification and matching of individual needs with available community resources.

Data Gathering

Basic data gathering involves the systematic collection of available information in order to describe the client's current status. Data gathering methods include review of extant documentation, interviewing, home visitation, and collateral contacts. Much information may be available from intake. Initial impressions from the intake process guide the data gathering effort.

Review of Documentation

There are many forms of data already available for the majority of correctional clients. Most adult offenders have previous contact with the criminal justice system. Even juveniles have some relevant history. Therefore, it is important to review existing documentation in refining the focus of assessment.

Extant documentation includes cumulative records, statistical data, case files, and various reports. In the United States, records accrue over time in such domains as schooling, health, financial status, employment, and especially offender behavior. Cumulative records in schools provide useful data about academic performance and aptitude, conduct, and extracurricular activities. Naturally, such records are confidential, released only with the permission of the student, the parents (if the subject is a juvenile), or a judge, by appropriate court order. Cumulative health records include medical charts, which are extensive in such settings as military service, prescription and insurance computerized data bases, and hospital statements. While there are restrictions placed on release of these cumulative records, clients can authorize release of medical, legal, and other specialized professional records. Therefore, correctional case managers can gather medical data under some circumstances.

Other cumulative records relate to finances and employment history. Such data may be accumulated for specific purposes (e.g., processing a mortgage loan application) or limited to internal agency uses (e.g., case records in public welfare agencies). Law enforcement agencies and certified officers may have access to financial records, particularly in the midst of a criminal investigation. However, financial and employment records can be released voluntarily to the correctional case manager. Employment history, such as documentation of promotions, adverse personnel actions, salary changes, and transfers, could be very relevant to correctional classification and decisionmaking.

Cumulative record-keeping is obviously essential in the investigation and adjudication of crime behavior. Although juvenile justice records may be sealed to protect vulnerable youth, information regarding juvenile offenses are increasingly available to criminal justice professionals. The adult offender's "rap sheet" is useful in determining extent of criminality, risk of reoffense, and need for supervision. Similarly, records from previous incarceration, probation, and parole assist the correctional case manager in assessing the need for structure and potential for rehabilitation.

Some criminal justice records reflect statistical data such as the number of arrests, days in detention, and other information related to criminal history. Attendance records at school or employment settings may "objectify" subjective constructs related to motivation or commitment to change, both of which are important in the evaluation of the correctional case management process. Other statistical data, including number of sick days and duration of employment, may be useful, as well. Frequently, incidence data are stored in a computer-managed, aggregate data base, maintained by a branch of government. States and counties are jurisdictions charged with the responsibility of maintaining such data bases.

Case files and reports are common in review of extant documentation. If a correctional client has participated previously in any counseling or therapy, there will be a file or chart, which can be obtained with an appropriate Authorization to Release Confidential Information form, signed by the client or guardian. Health and human services agencies also keep files that could be relevant to some assessment questions. Professional service providers in community and institutional settings produce reports of investigation, evaluation, findings, progress, outcome, and other important determinations. It is useful to obtain reports from other professionals because a large amount of information may be condensed in a brief, readable format. In addition, the correctional case manager will benefit from reading the impressions, opinions, and perspectives of other professionals. Securing material from extant files and reports is essential if the sources of documentation contain results from previous assessments of the client. Existing assessment results form a baseline with which one can compare current findings.

Review of extant documentation is a typical first step in the assessment process. The correctional case manager will usually be the recipient of various reports, files, statistical data, and cumulative records. Each of these sources of data address particular client concerns, standards of the professional or agency maintaining the data, and many situational factors. The correctional case manager makes sense of the data gathered through the review of documentation by abstracting recurrent and significant findings and converging the extant data with current information in the emerging portrait of the client. The assessment continues by refining the case formulation as additional data are gathered.

Interviewing

Although there are many methods and increasingly sophisticated technologies in assessment, the interview remains the basic tool in data gathering. Interviewing for assessment purposes incorporates the core conditions of facilitative communication described in Chapter 3. Given the lack of trust and problems in honest self-disclosure presented by most correctional clients, it is essential to establish rapport. Rapport is established by communicating, at least to a minimal degree, the core dimensions of genuineness, congruence, unconditional positive regard, and empathy. Encouraging concreteness, through direct requests for clarification and both open- and closed-ended questions, is necessary to pinpoint material when interviewing an evasive, anxious, or confused client. In most cases, the use of self-disclosure, immediacy, confrontation, and interpretation are best reserved for ongoing counseling or psychotherapy. However, data gathering is a cumulative process in correctional case management, requiring increasingly deeper and more sophisticated interviewing methods as the relationship with the correctional client progresses.

There are at least three sources of power or influence associated with the role of the interviewer: expert power, relational power, and coercive power. The first, *expert power,* establishes the special knowledge and position of the professional, which elicits respect and cooperation among clients in general. Since correctional clients frequently have unresolved issues with authority figures and tend to struggle with experts who seem to be controlling or dominating, another source of power is needed.

Relational power refers to the beneficial influence that accrues in a developing relationship. Rapport and familiarity contribute to the emergence of relational power. Addressing the common goals of the data gathering effort (i.e., the interviewer needs information, while the client needs services) and fostering teamwork contribute to relational power. The interviewer can shift from expert to relational power through verbal and nonverbal communication. For example, moving from behind a desk and sitting in a chair next to the client may foster relational power or overcome obstacles created by expert power. Addressing a client as "Mr." or "Ms." and otherwise demonstrating respect tends to equalize power, reducing the likelihood that the client feels "one-down" or inferior to the interviewer. The final source of power in interviewing is coercive power.

Coercive power is a reality in correctional case management. The majority of clients are somehow mandated to participate in the process. The correctional client probably feels coerced in the initial interviewing. Real or perceived coercion mobilizes defenses, such as resistance to providing sensitive information, because the client feels threatened. Correctional interviewers must address the barrier to communication imposed by the fact of coercive power.

The first step in neutralizing coercive power is acknowledging its presence and potential harmful effects. The interviewer observes and states in tentative fashion some version of the obvious, "You probably don't want to be here today." Next, the interviewer outlines what information is needed and ways in which the interview can be conducted. This approach permits the client to choose from among several options for the process of the interview. Encouraging choice is a major means for overcoming perceived coercion and creating a collaborative environment for the interview. The correctional interviewer may ask if the client wishes to answer an existing set of questions (e.g., contained in a presentence investigation form), describe his or her background in a conversational manner, review possible questions and take time to formulate responses, guide the interviewer's questioning, or otherwise exert some control over the potentially coercive or threatening interview process.

The interviewer uses empathy to reflect the feelings of the client during the data gathering to reduce coercive power and enhance relational power. Respect is also helpful in overcoming the initial barriers. The interviewer may ask permission to write notes or tape-record the interview. If the client seems curious or suspicious, the skillful interviewer will be prepared to read back responses or show the written remarks to the client, asking and accepting correction or clarification. Neutralizing coercive power next involves discussion of the limits of confidentiality and establishment of the relevant domain for the interview.

A recurrent issue in correctional case management is the protection of confidentiality. Inmates of total institutions, subjected to extensive surveillance, still have the right to some privacy and confidentiality. For example, prison inmates can visit their attorneys and communicate confidential information without monitoring by correctional staff members. In community supervision, probation and parole officers need to scrutinize carefully many aspects of their clients' lives. However, offenders enjoying the privilege of probation or parole require some confidentiality in interactions with their physicians, pastors, therapists, and other helping professionals. Thus, a parole officer may need verification of an offender's ongoing participation in therapy, while the content of the communication between the client and therapist is confidential. As mentioned previously, a client or guardian may choose to release confidential information to the correctional case manager by signing an authorization form. An example of an authorization to release information form is included below.

Example 4.1
Authorization to Release Information

I authorize

Name of Person/Organization _____

Mailing Address/Telephone _____

to release materials or information from my case record to

Name of Person/Organization _____

Mailing Address/Telephone _____

Dates of Care _____

Records/Information to be Released _____

Purpose for Release of Information _____

_____

I understand that I am not required to authorize the release of information to any person or agency. I may revoke this consent at any time. It shall expire 90 days from the date I sign the form, unless earlier revoked, but not retroactive to the release of information made in good faith. Consent will automatically expire without express revocation upon fulfillment of the above stated purpose. Disclosure of this information to another party without the specific written consent of the person to whom it pertains may violate Federal Law 42 CFR Part 2 or other regulations or statutes.

Name _____

SSN/Date of Birth _____

Signature _____ Date _____

Witness _____

Signature _____ Date _____

This form specifically addresses the limits of confidentiality, including stating the purpose and duration of the authorization. Confidentiality must be protected in order to advance the process of data gathering. Breeches of confidentiality threaten the foundations of assessment and intervention among typically suspicious correctional clients.

When adequate trust and rapport have been established by neutralizing coercive power and insuring confidentiality, the interviewing process begins in earnest. The interviewer has in mind the assessment question, clarifying the domain in the client's life which requires additional exploration. The interviewer may have extant documentation and initial impressions from the intake process, as well. The professional continuing the assessment process initiates an interview that has at least three phases: beginning, middle, and end.

Beginning the correctional case management interview involves establishing roles and responsibilities, addressing confidentiality and power issues, encouraging rapport and client choice, and initiating questioning or some other method of data gathering. The interviewer may provide information about the requirements of the correctional agency, especially those related to the assessment effort. The major focus of the beginning phase of the interview is matching the needs and expectations of the correctional case manager and client, thus instigating a process that will result in differential intervention. There is progress toward openness and teamwork which will facilitate the second phase of interviewing.

The middle phase of the interview is the longest in duration and most directly related to data gathering. In the middle phase, the interviewer is asking questions, listening actively to client responses, taking mental or written notes, and organizing the incoming information. Many correctional case management interviews are highly structured because specific data must be gathered (often by court or legislative mandate) in the most efficient, cost-effective manner. As previously discussed, the formality of the interview and expert status of the interviewer can actually inhibit the assessment process and reduce the beneficial outcomes. Therefore, the transition from the beginning to the middle phase of interviewing should be as natural and conversational as possible. Regardless of how well the interviewer has established rapport and relational power, direct questioning will predictably elicit some client resistance or defensiveness.

Questioning during the middle phase of interviewing may be direct or indirect, open- or closed-ended, and time-limited or ongoing. Direct questioning may involve the use of pre-selected questions, which are usually printed on some form or protocol. The interviewer may complete the form during the course of the interview. Indirect questioning refers to the more conversational style in which the interviewer intersperses questions in the ongoing conversation, perhaps abstracting necessary information from the client's remarks with little or no follow-up questioning. Note-taking is essential in indirect questioning because it will be necessary to record direct quotes from the client and otherwise recall important data gathered in the less structured, more conversational process. Indirect questioning, while optimal in many correctional case management situations, requires considerable time and extensive agency resources.

The middle phase of interviewing involves open- and closed-ended questions. If the indirect, conversational style of interviewing encourages client divergence, association, and exploration (e.g., "Tell me more about your relationship with your wife"), open- and closed-ended questioning attempts to converge on some topic of interest or importance. Open-ended questions clarify broadly the domain and suggest direction for responses, while encouraging client reflection. Closed-ended questions delimit sharply the client's response, trading potential exploration for specific, targeted responses. Closed-ended questions increase accuracy and client responsibility. However, correctional clients can hide behind closed-ended questions, providing as little information as possible. Open-ended questions present opportunities for clients to say more than they intended, even more than they know as the process deepens. Yet, open-ended questions may sacrifice some precision or specificity.

Questioning about factors related to relapse or recidivism, such as interpersonal conflict and substance abuse, usually elicits client defenses. The goal of the middle phase of interviewing is securing enough data to answer the assessment question, such as estimating the offender's risk of relapse in the community setting. Open-ended questions help to explore important domains, including the current marriage and family life. Thus, the interviewer may secure some interesting, relevant information when he or she asks: "How do you feel about your marriage?" Use of closed-ended questions focuses upon some specific concerns, frequently contained in a direct interview format. For example, the interviewer may need to gather particular responses associated with some risk assessment protocol used by the correctional agency. In the aforementioned case of marital exploration, closed-ended questions could secure specific responses. The interviewer asks "How often do you and your wife argue?" or focuses even more narrowly: "Have you been questioned or arrested for a family violence offense?"

The most direct forms of interviewing, using series of closed-ended questions, frequently involve printed questionnaires and checklists. Much of the data is gathered and organized during the structured interview process. Often, the results of such interviews translate directly into some classification or decision-making system used by the correctional agency. Since the process is highly structured, the average time required to complete the interview is known. Interviewers and agencies can plan their schedules and make effective use of resources. The middle stage of case management interviewing can be quite time-limited, being restricted to a single visit in some cases. The more indirect and open-ended the approach to questioning, the greater the likelihood that the interview process will span several sessions.

In correctional counseling and psychotherapy in general, interviewing is ongoing. The counselor or therapist collaborates with the client or patient in facilitating self-exploration and securing more information about patterns of behavior and general functioning. Correctional case management interviewing tends to be structured and time-limited. Similarly, behavioral interviewing emphasizes structure and precision in data gathering. However, some approaches to diagnostic interviewing, focusing upon remote causes of current behavior and underlying psychodynamics, are very open and ongoing.

The end of the interview, whatever the goals of the process or the professional perspective of the interviewer, eventually addresses the obvious problem of reducing a large amount of data to some meaningful terms. When a probation officer completes a presentence investigation form during an hour-long interview and transfers the responses to a risk assessment checklist, it is possible to describe the interview outcomes in a precise manner. Some assessment systems link interview and diagnosis or classification, resulting in a score for the case. Frequently, the interviewer must organize and interpret the mass of data resulting from even a brief interview. Efforts in the end phase are invested in reducing the data to a format that is useful in answering the explicit or implied assessment question.

Reducing and organizing the interview data is a mental process that may include careful reading of notes, selecting quotes and making behavioral observations; recognizing recurrent themes and patterns across client responses; abstracting from the data a few relevant generalizations; and, occasionally, inferring underlying motives or speculating about ambiguous or equivocal data. The interviewer must have some relevant knowledge base, based on training and experience, that helps to organize the data into meaningful impressions and recommendations. The interviewer must also be sufficiently analytical in cognitive style or personality to approximate the role of a scientist in interpreting the interview results.

The end of the interview process involves some kind of debriefing of the client who supplied the data. Such debriefing is an ethical requirement in research and professional practice. The debriefing may involve only the casual sharing of a few impressions. When time permits, it is useful to the ongoing correctional case management process to provide in-depth explanation of the results, especially any relevant diagnoses or classification decisions arising from the interview and other components of the assessment. The results usually give direction to subsequent assessment and intervention. Therefore, the debriefing can include formal and informal referrals to services and providers. Given the severity of offender problems and the importance of efficacy in service delivery, the assessment of most correctional clients will involve referrals beyond the interview.

Overall, the interview is an essential tool in data gathering, linking intake information and extant documentation to subsequent referrals for follow-up assessment and intervention services. Data gathered during the middle of the interview process form the basis for much correctional classification and decisionmaking. Depending upon how well initial needs and expectations of professional and client have been met by the end of interviewing, the offender may be defiant and oppositional, evasive and dishonest, wary and suspicious, or open and hopeful. The goal of any interview is to prepare the client for the next interview. When rapport building leads to effective debriefing, the interviewing process has been a success. Ideally, the interview answers or refines the assessment question that created the need for data gathering in its various forms. Effective interviewing lays the foundation for additional data gathering, such as home visitation and collateral contact, and referral for other evaluation methods, including the psychosocial history.

Home Visitation

Interviewing affords an opportunity to examine a client in an agency or professional setting, while home visitation makes possible observations of the offender and his or her family in their natural environment. Behavioral assessment (Bellack & Hersen, 1988), a technical, yet practical approach to data gathering, emphasizes the utility of behavioral observations in settings as close to the natural environment of the client as possible. Interviewing the client in the home facilitates data gathering in which the content and process can be related to the individual's real life situation.

Home visitation is a common practice among a diverse group of helping professionals. Law enforcement officers investigate complaints through home visits. Nurses and other health care professionals provide services in the patient's residence. Public welfare workers make home visits to verify eligibility requirements. Home visitation could be viewed as a service, a convenience, or an intrusion, depending upon the perceptions of client. Therefore, it is especially important to demonstrate respect for the client's home and family life.

The home visit is primarily a tool of supervision in community corrections. However, in the related field of child welfare, home visits are conducted to investigate allegations, conduct studies, and offer family sustaining resources. This model for home visitation is quite relevant for correctional case management in juvenile justice. However, home visitation has merit for enlarging the scope of adult community corrections beyond the obvious surveillance and custody functions.

The probation or parole officer may make home visits to establish residence, observe behavior in typical living conditions, estimate need for community resources, verify terms of the community supervision agreement (e.g., not drinking alcohol), and provide counseling in the privacy and comfort of the client's own home. Periodic unannounced visits may be needed to investigate allegations or verify compliance with the agreement. Regularly scheduled visits could be important adjuncts to intensive, office-based supervision.

Data gathering in the home visit extends the parameters of the interview to include a vast array of relevant client behaviors. The interviewer can detect health and hygiene problems, poverty and disadvantage, lifestyle disorders such as compulsive overeating, violations involving chemical dependency, family communication patterns, and overall organization of the home. Chaos and conflict are serious psychosocial stressors that contribute to risk of relapse or reoffense. Similarly, alcohol and drug use, by the client or friends and family members, markedly increases risk of recidivism.

When the client is a juvenile, the interviewer in the home can gather essential data regarding parenting and discipline, adult supervision, homework and chores, friends and associates, leisure activities, and other domains relevant to a particular case. Sex offender supervision is facilitated by home visits in that significant information about boundary violation (e.g., the stipulation of no contact with children, exposure to pornography, and involvement in effective coping and problem-solving techniques) can be gathered. In general, home visitation dramatically expands the range of lifestyle assessment, enhancing the capacity to predict and reduce risk of recidivism.

Home visitation is a generally useful approach to data gathering in the client's natural environment. Since chaos and conflict in the home increase recidivism, the lifestyle and relapse potential of the offender can be evaluated through random and planned visits. Home visitation can be used to conduct interviews, observe living conditions, monitor compliance with community supervision terms, investigate allegations, and provide resources and counseling services in a setting that is more comfortable for many clients. Home visits also afford opportunities to interview family members and follow-up collateral contacts with people who have important information about the client's current status.

Collateral Contacts

Since it is very common for offenders to be deceptive and dishonest, it is important to check client self-report data against information provided by persons who know and have regular contact with the offender. Collateral contact refers to the intentional effort of the interviewer to secure information directly from a person who has intimate knowledge of the client's lifestyle and behavior. Collateral contacts are made frequently with family members, friends, employers, co-workers, and service providers. However, neighbors, schoolmates, and other individuals who have some stake in the client's progress or well-being could be contacted.

Making collateral contacts bears resemblance to checking the references of applicants for employment or schooling. At a fundamental level, every collateral contact is a form of character reference. The interviewer may be checking the accuracy of a particular client self-report or evaluating the overall consistency of the client's presentation. On another level, the collateral contact may provide new information about the client's lifestyle or natural environment, which may be even outside the awareness of the client.

Collateral contacts are used regularly to estimate risk. However, well-timed and adequately explained contacts can actually facilitate teamwork and resource brokering. In institutional corrections, the walls of the facility and the surveillance of the correctional officers afford the structure necessary for an inmate's rehabilitation. Collateral contacts and home visits are tools by which the correctional professional in the field can vary the amount of structure in community supervision. Such contacts create opportunities for early problem identification and relapse prevention.

Collateral contacts, home visitation, interviewing, and extant document review are means for gathering and organizing data concerning the correctional client's current status, past history, and near future behavior. Collectively, the data gathering methods connect the perceptions and impressions of various professionals to the empirical realities in the daily life of the client referred for correctional services. Data gathering techniques address ongoing concerns with relapse risk and prevention, as well as opportunities to improve the coping capacity and quality of life of the client and family members.

Data gathering moves the correctional case management process from tentative impressions formed in the intake process toward a more sophisticated understanding of the characteristics, needs, and psychosocial dimensions of the correctional client. Data gathering involves refinement of the initial assessment question through review of extant documentation to the various forms of interviewing. By the end of the data gathering phase of the assessment process, the correctional case manager is aware of what information is needed to advance services to clients.

Diagnosis

In retrospect, the assessment phase can be thought of as a type of social study. In the assessment, the case manager is interested in obtaining information about the biopsychosocial condition and situation of the offender. Data obtained from various assessment activities are generally factual or empirical in nature. By contrast, the diagnosis is a series of related statements that are really hypotheses about the offender's problems in biopsychosocial functioning. The diagnosis is formulated from data derived from a psychosocial history, a psychiatric examination, and a psychological evaluation, after it has been integrated with the information from the assessment. Information derived from the psychosocial history, the psychiatric examination, and the psychological evaluation is generally considered to be subjective or impressionistic in nature (qualitative), although such information is often presented in quantitative forms. By contrast, information derived from data-gathering is more often in quantitative form, (e.g., an arrest record).

A diagnosis generally consists of four parts:

1. An hypothesis concerning the nature of the offender's personality, and particularly his or her psychological functioning.

2. An hypothesis about the genesis of the offender's problems in biopsychosocial functioning as a consequence of his or her developmental history.

3. An hypothesis concerning the importance of the problems in biopsychosocial functioning for the offender.

4. A type of category, classification, or specific clinical diagnosis about the problem in biopsychosocial functioning, for example, "Antisocial personality disorder;" "Cocaine-induced disorders: Cocaine dependence."

Psychosocial History

Most correctional clients will complete a psychosocial history with some attention to the current lifestyle. The psychosocial history may be initiated during the intake process and extend to interviews in diagnostic centers in institutional corrections and presentence investigations in community corrections.

The psychosocial history, sometimes called the social, family, or life history, is a standard feature in social casework and mental health agencies. In correctional case management, the psychosocial history is a major tool for collecting past information that is believed to be related to current status and functioning. The history-taking actually involves more fundamental methods for gathering data: reviewing extant documentation, interviewing, and contacting collateral sources. Synthesizing information about past events into a clinical portrait of the client is essentially based on the theoretical assumption that one's history causes or determines important features of personality. That is, there is an implicit bias built into taking stock of one's past in order to understand the present and possible future.

Generally, psychodynamic theories of human development, for example Bowlby (1969), emphasize the importance of remote causes to current functioning. Recent cognitive and behavioral approaches to assessing human behavior (Merluzzi & Boltwood, 1989), discount the influence of historical factors in the etiology of current problems in living. Instead, the cognitive-behavioral approaches focus on the recent learning history, consisting of contingent consequences (e.g., reward and punishment) and confirmation or refutation of key expectations or schemata (cognitive structures) that filter input from the natural environment. Psychodynamic and cognitive-behavioral theorists would agree that children acquire enduring behavioral predispositions that are expressed in adolescence and adulthood as recurrent patterns of behavior (e.g., Chess & Thomas, 1984; Millon, 1981).

The psychosocial history provides a structured means for rapidly gaining information about lifespan development. It is possible to discern recurrent patterns and general trends that have shaped the individual, constructing barriers and pitfalls, as well as aptitudes and opportunities. Factors in the evolution of offender behavior are increasingly well-known (Chess & Thomas, 1984; Peters, McMahon & Quinsey, 1992; Wilson & Herrnstein, 1985). Therefore, it is possible to match characteristics of the client, garnered from the psychosocial history, to known features of conduct-disordered youth, juvenile delinquents, and adult offenders. Features in the evolution of offender behavior may be grouped according to whether they are contributing factors or symptoms.

Table 4.1
Features in the Evolution of Offender Behavior

Contributing Factors

Having a father or stepfather who has criminal or masculine history
Being born prematurely or having low birth weight (less than five pounds)
Having a young (early adolescent) mother
Having a chemically dependent parent
Living in poverty
Living without a parent (i.e., broken home)
Lacking an attachment or bond to the mother
Lacking a father with whom to identify
Experiencing neglect and lack of clear, consistent discipline
Being physically or sexually abused by a parent or another adult
Wandering or lacking adult supervision, especially after age 8
Associating with delinquent or antisocial individuals
Failing to adjust in transition to school
Dropping out or being expelled from school
Using alcohol or drugs
Engaging in delinquent conduct

Symptoms

Mesomorphy or masculine body type
Attention deficit disorder and hyperactivity
Affectionless psychopathy
Shame or low self-esteem
Disadvantage or perceived inequity
Sense of loss and unresolved grief issues
Problems with anger and conflict with authorities
Lack of self-control
Post-traumatic stress and lack of ego strength
Poor boundaries and time consciousness
Peer influence
Modeling, and increasing rewards for offender behavior
Learning disabilities and failure identity
Escape and avoidance
Deviant role and status
Lacking stability in residence and employment
Crime opportunity

As depicted in Table 4.1, childhood experiences impact on conduct disorder of youth, delinquency, and, indirectly, adult criminality. A general theory of crime (Wilson & Herrnstein, 1985), asserts that constitutional (i.e., within the person), family, and schooling variables account for the majority of unresolved variance in criminality over the lifespan. Similarly, unresolved trauma arising from childhood neglect and abuse figures prominently in the development of aggressive and antisocial behavior (Bowlby, 1969; Peters, McMahon & Quinsey, 1992). Thus, information obtained from the psychosocial history would be important in estimating the chronicity and severity of offender behavior, as well as predicting the future course, or prognosis.

The psychosocial history typically includes information about birth and infancy, childhood health and accidents, family environment and relations with parents and siblings, physical and cognitive development, school adjustment and academic performance, social adjustment and relations with peers, extracurricular activities and leisure preferences, alcohol and drug use, spiritual development and religious observance, military service, advanced training and education, employment and career development, dating and relations with intimates, marriage and family life, and current residence and status. In correctional case management, criminal history and evidence of youthful conduct disorder would be quite relevant. Case management with special correctional populations may result in particular emphases in the psychosocial history, as well.

In the Masters and Johnson Sex Offender Treatment Program (Southern & Schwartz, 1994), the "life history" involves an extensive review of factors that affect the development of intimacy from birth onward. The life history assignment in this treatment program requires the client to answer 364 questions presented in outline form. Typically, the client writes responses, records on audiotape the responses to facilitate additional recollection, and discusses critical incidents from the life history according to six critical developmental periods: 0-3 years of age, 4-6 years of age, 7-9 years of age, 10-12 years of age, 13-15 years of age, and 16-18 years of age. The therapist or interviewer may summarize the results of the life history review in a verbal or written report. Nevertheless, primary responsibility for gathering, organizing, and interpreting data rests with the patient at this stage in the treatment process. Later, the sex offender will present to the group his or her life history, noting harmful patterns of behavior arising primarily from childhood physical and sexual abuse. Throughout the life history review for sex offenders, there is extensive exploration of sexual development, emergence of perversion or paraphilia, and patterns of sexual acting-out behavior.

The psychosocial history is an omnibus approach for securing background and developmental data related to the evolution of offender behavior. Since criminologists and other professionals have identified some of the etiological factors associated with conduct disorder of youth, juvenile delinquency, and adult criminality, it is possible to compare characteristics of clients with features of criminals. One can identify learning strengths, family resources, and other factors that shape the individual away from crime as well.

Psychiatric Examination

A true psychiatric examination is rarely available in correctional case management. If there is a question of competence to stand trial or an insanity defense is presented, it is likely that a psychiatric examination was conducted.

Thus, the psychiatric examination is most common in forensic settings. However, psychiatrists or other medical doctors may complete some parts of the examination in order to diagnose mental illness or prescribe medication in such settings as the county jail, the youth detention center, or the diagnostic unit of a penal system. Clients in community corrections may complete a psychiatric examination during a hospital stay or in the course of outpatient care. While a comprehensive psychiatric examination would be optimal in most cases, the time and cost requirements limit its application.

A comprehensive psychiatric examination consists of a history and physical evaluation, a mental status examination, a structured clinical interview, and specialized medical tests, such as neurological examinations. Since psychiatric diagnoses may change over time, follow-up examination is indicated in most cases. Information gained from the psychiatric examination addresses not only competence and criminal responsibility issues (e.g., mens rea or the intention to offend arising from the criminal mind), but also such constructs as mental disorder, risk of harm, prognosis, and diagnostic impression.

The history and physical (H & P) is a standard feature in clinical medicine. Taking a complete medical history and conducting a physical examination are essential in psychiatry because numerous physical problems, such as endocrine dysfunction, produce symptoms of some mental disorders (American Psychiatric Association, 1994). In addition, the history reveals patterns over time and constellations of symptoms related to disease process. The H & P also addresses family history of illness, relevant to such psychiatric concerns as depression, thought disorder (i.e., schizophrenia), suicidal tendency, and chemical dependency. Since criminality itself may reflect substantial genetic predisposition (Blackburn, 1993; Ellis, 1988; Mednick & Christiansen, 1977; Mednick, Gabrielli & Hutchings, 1984), intergenerational transmission of such features as minor physical anomaly, body type, neurological dysfunction, mental retardation, and temperament can be assessed through the history and physical examination.

The mental status examination (MSE) is a cornerstone of psychiatric examination. While other medical doctors and allied health professionals, especially psychologists, conduct the MSE as a component of their assessments, the examination is closely linked to psychiatric diagnosis. The mental status examination can be completed quickly and indirectly to obtain an estimate of current mental functioning. A formal mental status examination is indicated when there are questions of severe disruption of perception, mood, and memory. The examination addresses signs and symptoms that may be related to mental illness and organic problems.

The formal mental status examination is a systematic process in which an interviewer asks standard questions and makes careful behavioral observations. Underlying problems are inferred from the patient's responses and examination behavior. Attire, posture, grooming, gesture, and other aspects of appearance are taken into consideration. The process and content of thought, as manifested in verbal production, are examined. The clinician examines the patient as though the MSE were producing a photograph or X-ray of mental functioning.

The formal mental status examination includes some standard features. The MSE may be conducted according to an outline or protocol. Using standard features or a protocol facilitates communication among professionals on the treatment team. The MSE addresses issues related to offender behavior. The appearance and overall behavior of the patient often reflects underlying mental functioning. Eccentric or unusual appearance may indicate some form of psychosis, such as impulse control disorder, mania, or any of the various personality disorders. It may also indicate membership in a subcultural group. Wearing certain colors, having particular tattoos, and making symbolic gestures could indicate gang or group membership. Poor hygiene and dress could indicate lower socioeconomic status, disadvantage, or mental confusion. Humans naturally form first impressions and begin relating to the individual as though these hypotheses or expectations were true. Professional interviewing requires a delicate balance between impressions formed through specialized knowledge and previous experience, and neutrality or suspension of ordinary biases and personal opinions.

The attitude of the client toward the examiner is important in setting the tone of the MSE. The interviewer may address anger, anxiety, and other negative affective states that could interfere with the progress of the MSE, even in the formally structured examination. The initial response of the patient to the examiner presents some valuable information about how he or she relates and presents himself or herself to the world.

Psychomotor activity, affect, and mood components of the MSE explore possible depression or affective disorder, thought disorder (including subtypes of psychosis, e.g., schizophrenia), and anxiety disorders. These clinical syndromes are commonly associated with mental illness, as described in the *Diagnostic and Statistical Manual of Mental Disorders,* (American Psychiatric Association, 1994). Similarly, questions addressing the process and content of thought and speech, as well as perceptual disturbances, help in diagnosing mental disorders. However, some responses associated with major clinical syndromes, such as thought disorder, can be related to organic conditions (e.g., closed head injury) or substance abuse. Chronic abuse of such drugs as PCP, amphetamines, hallucinogens (LCD), and cocaine can produce symptoms of mental illness (Mirin, Weiss & Greenfield, 1991).

Mental status examination items concerned with orientation, attention, concentration, and memory measure not only chronic mental disorders, organic dysfunction, and substance abuse, but also, short-term and recurrent interference with information processing due to major psychosocial stressors. Frequently, correctional clients become involved in assessment during periods of peak stress and life upheaval. Therefore, the results of the MSE may be affected by situational and temporal factors that change over relatively short periods. The MSE and other relevant assessments should be repeated over time to gain an accurate picture of the patient's mental functioning. The skilled examiner takes into account situational factors in rendering diagnoses.

Questions concerned with intelligence, judgment, and insight address the basic information processing capacities of the individual. Typically, the psychiatric examiner administering the MSE uses items derived from intelligence tests, such as the Wechsler Adult Intelligence Scale (Wechsler, 1981), to complete these components. Correctional clients are generally predisposed to rule breaking and offender behavior because they are deficient in verbal and social intelligence (Herrnstein & Murray, 1994). They act before they think, failing to adequately consider potential consequences or to learn from their experiences. The MSE and other assessments explore the reasons for offender impulsivity and antisocial conduct. However, the accumulating evidence indicates that lack of intelligence is a major constitutional factor in criminality (Herrnstein & Murray, 1994; Wilson & Herrnstein, 1985).

The formal or comprehensive mental status examination is a fundamental tool in psychiatric evaluation. The skilled psychiatrist (or other mental health professional), who has several years of experience with offender populations, is best prepared to render a diagnosis. Impressions and recommendations informed by the MSE could have far-reaching effects upon the correctional client and the community at large. Most psychiatrists employ other methods to refine the clinical portrait or diagnosis before making recommendations. The structured clinical interview can be considered a special case of the MSE that better integrates interview data with psychiatric diagnosis.

The structured clinical interview focuses upon particular mental functions or problems reported by the patient or referral source and suggested by intake interview and MSE results. The structured interview method facilitates a close, progressive examination of focal concerns such that subtle differences among related syndromes can be discerned. In order to enhance the reliability, validity, and utility of psychiatric diagnostic categories (e.g., American Psychiatric Association, 1987; 1994), decision trees, capitalizing upon gains in systems science, enable the clinician to rule out related syndromes, arriving at an eventual classification in which there is adequate confidence or certainty. The process of forming an accurate psychiatric classification through application of decision trees is called differential diagnosis. Structured clinical interviews apply similar logic to compare and contrast, delimit and rule out related categories in order to enhance diagnostic certainty.

Structured clinical interview protocols may be constructed by a skilled examiner, produced by a health care institution, or purchased commercially. With the rise of managed mental health care, structured interview formats are frequently used to converge on a diagnostic impression in the most cost-effective manner. The clinical interview may address any domain in mental functioning. However, since specificity and efficiency are goals of structured clinical interviews, they tend to address some limited aspect of mental disorder, which is difficult to diagnose through indirect and informal means and critical in terms of clinical relevance and significance. Several domains of structured clinical interviews are relevant to correctional case management.

Some offenders report they have little or no recollection of crime incidents or that they have no feelings about their offender behavior. When such reports go beyond the stereotypical avoidance of responsibility associated with antisocial traits, important questions are raised about the individual's functioning. The "affectionless psychopathy" (Millon, 1981), of an offender may represent well-developed antisocial personality disorder or some other mental dysfunction. The dissociative disorders include some unusual features, arising primarily from unresolved childhood trauma, that could be associated with delinquency and adult criminality (Ross, 1989). Dissociation involves mechanisms for forgetting or avoiding emotionally painful and shameful incidents that would overwhelm a fragmented or underdeveloped ego. Dissociative disorders include psychogenic amnesia, derealization and depersonalization (e.g., feeling unreal or estranged from one's body), identity confusion, rapid mood changes, and multiple personality development.

Steinberg (1989) developed the Structured Clinical Interview for DSM-III-R Dissociative Disorders (SCID-D), in order to differentiate dissociative disorders and states from the Schneiderian first-rank symptoms of thought disorder (e.g., schizophrenia). The SCID-D involves initial and retest or reliability interviews in which the subject is questioned in great detail about the unusual features of dissociation. During the structured clinical interview, the examiner rates the subject's responses and records the ratings in the SCID-D booklet.

Rated responses to structured interview questions facilitate differential diagnosis. If an offender suffers from a dissociative disorder, there may be mitigating circumstances, which should be taken into consideration in adjudication or sentencing. Should an offender have a chronic thought disorder, such that he or she does not realize the nature and wrongfulness of one's actions, the offender may be incompetent to stand trial or could be found not guilty by reason of insanity (Wrightsman, Nietzel & Fortune, 1994). Differential diagnosis is profoundly important in forensic psychiatry due to implications of the findings.

An offender who presents poor memory, lack of empathy, rapid mood change, identity confusion, and other symptoms linked to dissociative disorders or thought disorders may be simply malingering or attempting to avoid criminal consequences by appearing mentally disturbed. Fortunately, there are clinical interview checklists for assessing the unusual behavior and underlying motives of criminals (e.g., Rogers, Dolmetsch & Cavanaugh, 1981). In addition, there are structured clinical interview formats for investigating the extent of criminality.

Hare et al. (1990) devised an Interview Schedule for the Psychopathy Checklist: Clinical Version (PCL:CV). This protocol facilitates specification of psychopathic traits, differentiating them from psychotic, organic, and mood disorders. The schedule guides the examiner through questions concerning 10 features of psychopathy: superficial, grandiose, manipulative, lacks remorse, lacks empathy, doesn't accept responsibility, impulsive, poor behavior controls, lacks goals, and irresponsible. The PCL:CV, similar to the SCID-D, secures data from face-to-face interviewing of the offender, reviewing medical chart and extant documentation, and contacting collateral sources.

There are other methods available to psychiatrists and allied health professionals for differential diagnosis of conditions related to offender behavior.

Recent technological advances, such as magnetic resonance imaging (MRI) techniques, and electroencephalographic (EEG) mapping methods, permit the clinician to systematically evaluate irregularities in brain activity associated with hyperactivity, addiction, and subclinical seizure disorder. These conditions have been linked to delinquency and criminality (Blackburn, 1993; Eyesenck & Gudjonsson, 1989). In addition, there are specialized blood tests, typically measuring enzymes and byproducts of metabolic processes, which can be helpful in diagnosing mental disorders. In addition, neuroendocrine testing, in which patient responses to pharmacological demands are measured, can also be used to diagnose depression.

Specialized medical testing contributes not only to refinement of diagnostic impressions, but also to identification of treatment options. In particular, psychiatric examination, with and without specialized testing, frequently leads to pharmacotherapy. Medication trials (e.g., administering an antidepressant drug such as the serotonin reuptake inhibitor called Prozac to a depressed patient) are used by physicians to treat symptoms and refine diagnoses.

The psychiatric examination is an important, underutilized component of correctional case management. Beginning with the history and physical, the physician secures valuable information about the etiology or cause of conditions relevant to the assessment and classification of offender behavior. The Mental Status Examination (MSE), the cornerstone of comprehensive psychiatric examination, continues the systematic process of describing constellations of symptoms and identifying recurrent patterns of behavior. Responses to questioning in the initial interview and the MSE raise important diagnostic issues. Frequently, the psychiatrist uses structured clinical interviews or specialized medical testing to refine the emergent diagnostic impressions. In this manner, the clinician gains greater certainty before rendering a forensic opinion, starting a medication trial, or committing an individual to a psychiatric hospital setting. The psychiatric examiner is concerned with the traditional elements of the medical model of helping (see Brickman et al., 1982) in which etiology, diagnosis, and prognosis of disease processes are determined by medical experts.

Psychological Evaluation

The psychological evaluation shares many methods and procedures with the psychiatric examination. In each type of assessment, the professional in charge of the process is a highly trained expert, who brings specialized knowledge and skill to bear upon the assessment question. Similarly, the psychiatrist and psychologist share interviewing as a primary modality. While the mental status examination and structured clinical interview are central components of psychiatric differential diagnosis, interviewing is only one part of the psychological evaluation. A complete psychological evaluation involves interviewing (including facets of the MSE), behavioral observation, and testing.

The distinguishing characteristic of the psychological evaluation is the emphasis placed upon testing. Measurement of intelligence, academic and vocational abilities, personality, and other attributes has been a major concern of psychology (Anastasi, 1988). Psychological testing developed rapidly in the twentieth century because of advances in public schooling and the necessity of classifying large numbers of soldiers during and after World Wars I and II. Demand for correctional services also increased in the period after World War II; however, psychological evaluation is not always used in correctional classification systems. While the goal of psychiatric examination is to diagnose mental disorders when they exist, psychological evaluation is less concerned with diagnosis and more concerned with describing the various traits and factors involved in human adjustment.

Psychiatric diagnoses are based on global clinical portraits of the individual. With the advent of structured clinical interview formats and decision-trees, psychiatric examination became somewhat more standardized. Psychological evaluation, since its inception, attempted to measure as objectively as possible, specific attributes of human nature. Psychological testing, in particular, used large standardization samples of identified populations to investigate variance in a trait of interest. Standardization in psychological testing contributed to the development of norms, based on descriptive statistics. Comparing an individual's score to norms in a known group enabled an objective estimate of how rare or typical, abnormal or normal, the individual appeared. Elevated scores on psychological test scales, constructed to measure particular variables, could be interpreted as statistically and clinically significant. Thus, the movement toward standardization and psychometric validation of psychological tests increased the reliability, validity, and utility of the measures.

The comprehensive psychological test battery includes a limited number of highly reliable and valid instruments or procedures that together predict near future behavior. Psychiatric examination involves the condensation of large amounts of information into a confident diagnosis. Psychological evaluation through testing focuses upon linear additions to explain variance in a hypothetical population of scores. That is to say, psychological testing involves adding only those tests to the battery that will improve the accuracy of behavioral predictions. A comprehensive psychological test battery includes several classes of tests needed to measure variables relevant to the assessment question.

There are several categories of tests and measurement procedures that constitute a psychological test battery. First, there is a division of possible measurement devices into three classes: objective, projective and performance tests. Objective tests measure a psychological variable or dimension in a relatively direct manner by comparing individual scores to norms or standard scores. Projective testing involves indirect measurement of aspects of human adjustment by means of individual responses to unstructured tasks. The verbal, written, or graphic responses to projective test protocols reveal underlying psychodynamics and psychic contents relevant to the study of personality, as well as perceptual processes.

Objective tests tend to be paper-and-pencil instruments in which individuals complete a test item by marking one of two or more responses on an answer sheet. Questions or items are contained in a test booklet. The format for responding to questions may be forced choice (e.g., a "True" or "False" response on an answer sheet or a choice between two opposite traits) or multiple choice, involving a range of responses which vary according to some dimension or along a continuum. Objective tests may be brief, such as the 21-item Beck Depression Inventory (Beck, 1978), requiring only minutes to complete. However, most objective tests measure several psychological traits and factors in one instrument, producing separate scale scores and requiring an hour or more for test-taking.

The longer objective tests, such as the Minnesota Multiphasic Personality Inventory (Graham, 1987), are composed of several smaller scales, which measure in a reliable and valid manner, a particular or homogeneous dimension. Individual responses are scored by counting answers to items grouped in a particular scale, summing these "hits" into a scale score, then comparing the person's obtained score to norms or standard scores. The scoring process is facilitated by use of templates, which can be placed on top of the answer sheet in order to highlight answers related to one scale at a time. In addition, answer sheets can be scored by computer software programs. Computer scoring involves entering all responses by means of a keyboard or telephone, or scanning the answer sheet directly into the computer.

Projective test materials are obtained from the commercial suppliers. Distribution of objective and projective tests and supporting materials is limited to purchasers who have training and experience in the appropriate uses of psychological tests. Test suppliers may require purchasers to complete qualification forms in order to obtain most projective tests and many objective tests. Projective testing demands the most training and experience because subject responses are open and unique to the individual. The psychologist must interpret the subject's responses to an ambiguous task that mobilizes unconscious processes. The interpretations may be guided by explicit criteria, sometimes resulting in scores similar to objective test scale scores. However, the individual completing the projective test is not limited to any specified or predetermined responses.

Performance tests are similar to projective tests in that the subject responds to an item by performing a task. Unlike projective testing, performance tests use specific tasks that have one or a few desired responses. Performance is scored with respect to accuracy, time required to complete the task, and level of difficulty involved in the task. Performance tests compare what a person is able to do with known standards for performing particular tasks, similar to the assessment process in objective testing. The standards may be associated with chronological age or mental age in intelligence and academic testing. Standards may be derived from studying the performance of individuals in known groups and determining which criteria are associated with mastery of the task at what level of efficiency. Vocational aptitude tests and work samples compare subject responses to those of known groups. Performance testing differs from objective and projective testing because the emphasis is placed upon actual task performance, involving sensation, motor coordination, and particular activity.

While objective, projective, and performance testing methods are concerned primarily with the selection of instruments for a comprehensive psychological test battery, behavioral observations and physiological assessment techniques are also included in psychological evaluation. Behavioral observation refers to a systematic approach for describing the subject's demeanor, response style, and particular dimensions of adjustment. Behavioral observation may be brief and general or highly specific to a variable associated with the assessment question.

In most psychological reports, there are general observations regarding whether or not the subject appeared anxious, angry, depressed, or detached. In addition, observations about the apparent motivation and activity level are recorded in the written report. Such observations may reflect considerable clinical inference or may be limited to empirical evidence obtained during the MSE or another specific protocol. The general behavioral observations in a psychological report indicate the subject's involvement in the assessment process, as well as some preliminary features of his or her adjustment.

Specific behavioral observations are obtained usually to measure, according to some predetermined criteria, selected problem areas related to the assessment question. Behavioral observation methods arose from the evolution of behavioral assessment, a branch of cognitive-behavior therapy (Bellack & Hersen, 1988). There are behavioral techniques for objectively measuring anxiety and fear, depression, health-related disorders (e.g., risk of coronary heart disease), marital dysfunction, sexual disturbance, addictive and appetitive disorders, and child behavior problems. The assessment of social skills is especially relevant to the behavioral observation of offenders.

Juvenile and adult offenders often present very low levels of social skill. Situational social anxieties and difficulties, as well as global social incompetence, interfere with the rehabilitation of offenders in institutional and community corrections. Assessment of social skills includes real-life observation, role-play, self-rating, and self-monitoring (Becker & Heimberg, 1988). Social skills assessment methods tend to focus on particular behaviors in specified situations. Objective rating and scoring systems enable determination of whether a subject is shy or avoidant, anxious or even socially phobic, angry or aggressive, or assertive and comfortable. Social skills training may be indicated for identified problems with initiating a conversation, making a request for change, resisting peer influence, taking time out from escalating conflict, concluding a telephone call, and engaging in other behavioral domains.

Specific assessment of particular offender behaviors and global observation of indicators of adjustment are important in the psychological evaluation of offenders. Behavioral observation methods and procedures strengthen the predictive value of a psychological test battery composed of objective, projective, and performance measures. Behavioral observation enables a more intensive investigation of aspects of the criminal lifestyle, such as social skills deficits. Physiological assessment methods are essentially very discrete means of observing behavior relevant to an assessment question.

Physiological assessment involves close measurement of human reactions to environmental stimuli. Typically, physiological assessment requires some biofeedback technology and instrumentation for detecting and quantifying a psychophysiological response of interest (Sturgis & Gramling, 1988). For example, electromyography (EMG), involving placement of surface electrodes over a musculoskeletal group such as the forearm, measures electrical depolarization of muscle fibers during emotion, stress, or generalized arousal. There are sensors or measuring devices for most psychophysiological functions. Lie detection or polygraphy involves measurement of several responses, such as breathing and perspiration, in response to potentially anxiety-provoking questions by the examiner. Psychophysiological responses to questions are integrated by a chart recorder and evaluated by the examiner. While the responses are objective, the reliability, validity, and utility of the polygraph examination is based on the examiner's knowledge and skill. Therefore, polygraph results can be admitted as evidence in trials only as a data base for expert opinion through the stipulation of prosecution and defense (Wrightsman, Nietzel & Fortune, 1994). Nevertheless, psychophysiological assessment of selected functions can be very helpful in refining the diagnosis or classification of the offender.

Sex offenders constitute one criminal group that usually participates in some physiological assessment of genital arousal (Sturgis & Gramling, 1988). An offender consents to participate in laboratory-based assessment of the sexual arousal pattern. It is possible through penile plethysmography to specify the response topography of the individual. However, the procedure in itself cannot "prove" or rule out pedophilia or other sexual deviance. The protocol involves measurement of slight changes in penile tumescence by means of the Barlow strain gauge attached by the subject to the mid-shaft of the penis. Each subject's responses to potentially sexual stimulus slides are compared to responses to neutral slides (i.e., the baseline). Deviant arousal is usually present in sex offenders and other sexually deviant individuals because they have conditioned interest in the inappropriate object (e.g., the child's immature body) or criminal act (e.g., rape or sexual aggression) through actual contact or masturbation to fantasy over time. With child molesting, there is usually a history of viewing the child, fantasizing about contact, grooming or developing the victim, and engaging in other preparatory behaviors before the onset of actual offending.

Physiological assessment and behavioral observation are useful adjuncts to the standard psychological test battery, which includes objective, projective, and performance tests specifically selected to improve the near-future prediction of a particular offender's behavior. While behavioral observation would be included to some extent in any psychological evaluation and the resulting report, specialized physiological and behavioral data would be most relevant to certain classes of criminal conduct including sex offending, undersocialized aggressive behavior, hyperactive delinquency, and juvenile arson. As criminologists learn more about the behavioral topography of particular offenses, specialized assessment techniques will become increasingly relevant. For the present, the comprehensive psychological test battery tends to include certain well-established, standardized tests.

Conclusions

The assessment phase of correctional case management represents a major component in matching the needs of a new client to the resources of the correctional system. Assessment methods from several professional disciplines answer questions raised during intake, resulting in meaningful data that can be applied toward a biopsychosocial diagnosis of the offender.

Descriptive and analytical approaches to assessment attempt to improve the understanding of the typical characteristics, motivations, and needs of the client who requires a correctional intervention. There are basic data gathering methods, used by the case manager and other members of the treatment team, including review of extant documentation, interviewing, home visitation, and collateral contact. Throughout the process of data gathering, the interviewer continues to build a relationship with the correctional client, protecting his or her rights to confidentiality and reducing the obstacles imposed by coercive power in corrections. A diagnosis of an offender is comprised of data derived from the assessment phase integrated with information from the psychosocial history, the psychiatric examination, and the psychological evaluation. The diagnosis thus obtained is differential in nature and is biopsychosocial in span.

The psychosocial history is routinely used in most mental health agencies. History taking, which is conducted typically by social workers, addresses the relevancy of critical life events in the evolution of offender behavior. Some theories (e.g., the psychoanalytic model) emphasize the remote causes of delinquent conduct and adult criminality. Assessment methods based on such theories would focus on life history issues. Other theories, such as the cognitive-behavioral perspective that is dominant in contemporary corrections, are much less concerned with historical factors and are much more interested in current living conditions and recent patterns of behavior. Whatever may be the personal practice theory of the professional, the psychosocial history provides a wealth of information about the past and present, thereby making possible some predictions of near-future interpersonal behaviors, lifestyle options, and risk factors for relapse or recidivism, thus contributing to the differential diagnosis of the offender.

The psychiatric evaluation is a standard feature in mental health settings. In correctional settings, an in-depth assessment of the characteristics and predispositions of the offender would ideally include contributions from other members of the treatment team. Although a comprehensive psychiatric examination is rare in most correctional settings, recent interest in the biological bases of abnormal behavior and the inheritance of criminal temperament increase the relevancy of completing a medical history and physical examination, the mental status examination, and a structured clinical interview. The mental status examination and clinical interview contribute to differential diagnosis.

The psychological evaluation shares many features with the psychiatric examination. Both methods are based on the medical model of helping in which a highly skilled expert conducts an assessment in order to specify diagnosis, prognosis, and treatment recommendations. A comprehensive psychological test battery includes object, projective, and performance measures selected specifically to describe and predict individual differences in behavior. Results from psychological testing, behavioral observation, and specialized assessment techniques are combined by the psychologist in a report, which addresses the original assessment questions and indicates direction for follow-up efforts. The psychological evaluation helps to refine the clinical portrait of the individual and therefore adds a measure of additional confidence in the emergent differential diagnosis.

References

American Psychiatric Association (1987). *Diagnostic and Statistical Manual of Mental Disorders* (Revised Edition). Washington, DC: Author.

American Psychiatric Association (1994). *Diagnostic and Statistical Manual of Mental Disorders* (Fourth Edition). Washington, DC: Author.

Anastasi, A. (1988). *Psychological Testing* (Sixth Edition). New York, NY: Macmillan.

Beck, A.T. (1978). *Beck Depression Inventory*. New York, NY: The Psychological Corporation.

Becker, R.E. & R.G. Heimberg (1988). "Assessment of Social Skills." In A.S. Bellack & M. Hersen (eds.) *Behavioral Assessment: A Practical Handbook* (Third Edition) (pp. 365-395). New York, NY: Pergamon.

Bellack, A.S. & M. Hersen (eds.) (1988). *Behavioral Assessment: A Practical Handbook* (Third Edition). New York, NY: Pergamon.

Blackburn, R. (1993). *The Psychology of Criminal Conduct: Theory, Research and Practice*. Chichester, England: John Wiley & Sons.

Bowlby, J. (1969). *Attachment and Loss* (Vol. 1). New York, NY: Basic Books.

Chess, S. & A. Thomas (1984). *Origins and Evolution of Behavior Disorders: From Infancy to Early Adult Life*. New York, NY: Brunner/Mazel.

Ellis, L. (1988). "Criminal Behaviour and r/K Selection: An Extension of Gene-Based Evolutionary Theory." *Personality and Individual Differences*, 9:697-708.

Eysenck, H.J. & G.H. Gudjonsson (1989). *The Causes and Cures of Criminality*. New York, NY: Plenum.

Graham, J.R. (1987). *The MMPI: A Practical Guide* (Second Edition). New York, NY: Oxford University Press.

Hare, R.D., T.J. Harpur, A.R. Hakstian, A.E. Forth, S.D. Hart & J.P. Newman (1990). "The Revised Psychopathy Checklist: Reliability and Factor Structure." *Psychological Assessment*, 2:338-341.

Herrnstein, R.J. & C. Murray (1994). *The Bell Curve: Intelligence and Class Structure in American Life*. New York, NY: The Free Press.

Mednick, S.A. & K.O. Christiansen (eds.) (1977). *Biosocial Bases of Criminal Behavior*. New York, NY: Gardiner Press.

Mednick, S.A., W.F. Gabrielli & B. Hutchings (1984). "Genetic Influences in Criminal Convictions: Evidence from an Adoption Cohort." *Science*, 234:891-894.

Merluzzi, T.V. & M.D. Boltwood (1989). "Cognitive Assessment." In A. Freeman, K.M. Simon, L.E. Beutler & H. Arkowitz (eds.) *Comprehensive Handbook of Cognitive Therapy* (pp. 249-266). New York, NY: Plenum.

Millon, T. (1981). *Disorders of Personality*. New York, NY: John Wiley.

Mirin, S.M., R.D. Weiss & S.F. Greenfield (1991). "Psychoactive Substance Use Disorders. In A.J. Gelenberg, E.L. Bassuk & S.C. Schoonover (eds.) *The Practitioner's Guide to Psychoactive Drugs* (Third Edition) (pp. 243-316). New York, NY: Plenum.

Peters, R.D., R.J. McMahon & V.L. Quinsey (eds.) (1992). *Aggression and Violence Throughout the Life Span*. Newbury Park, CA: Sage Publications.

Rogers, R., R. Dolmetsch & J.L. Cavanaugh (1981). "An Empirical Approach to Insanity Evaluations." *Journal of Clinical Psychology*, 37:683-687.

Ross, C.A. (1989). *Multiple Personality Disorder: Diagnosis, Clinical Features and Treatment*. New York, NY: John Wiley.

Southern, S.C. & M.F. Schwartz (eds.) *Freedom to Love: Overcoming the Oppression of Compulsive Sexual Behavior*. St. Louis, MO: Masters & Johnson Institute.

Steinberg, M. (1989). *Structured Clinical Interview for DSM-III-R Dissociative Disorders*. New Haven, CT: Yale University Medical School.

Sturgis, E.T. & S. Gramling (1988). "Psychophysiological Assessment." In A.S. Bellack & M. Hersen (eds.) *Behavioral Assessment: A Practical Handbook* (Third Edition) (pp. 213-251). New York, NY: Pergamon.

Wechsler, D. (1981). *Wechsler Adult Intelligence Scale-Revised*. New York, NY: The Psychological Corporation.

Wilson, J.Q. & R.J. Herrnstein (1985). *Crime and Human Nature*. New York, NY: Simon & Schuster.

Wrightsman, L.S., M.T. Nietzel & W.H. Fortune (1994). *Psychology and the Legal System* (Third Edition). Pacific Grove, CA: Brooks/Cole.

Chapter 5

Classification, Treatment Planning, and Referral

Introduction

Data gathered during the assessment phase of correctional case management converge on a tentative diagnosis, which addresses individual needs and concerns of the individual, as well as a preliminary classification, which enables matching of offender characteristics with available program resources. Classification refers to matching the major characteristics of offenders with potentially effective interventions (Gottfredson & Tonry, 1987). Interventions include treatment program and modality, case disposition, security level, and unit assignment. Another function of classification is prediction, which is relevant in sentencing and correctional decisionmaking. Prediction involves assessing future risk for reoffense, elopement, or another aspect of recidivism. Classification and prediction are essential to correctional case management in institutional settings. However, classification decisions are also important in treatment planning and referral in community corrections.

Assessment produces the data base for classification decisions. Diagnosis represents a special case of assessment that fits easily with classification. In fact, one of the oldest classification systems in mental health is directly linked to diagnosis, the *Diagnostic and Statistical Manual of Mental Disorders* (DSM) of the American Psychiatric Association (1987, 1994).

Major Classification Systems

In this part of the chapter, the authors will describe and discuss some major offender classification systems. Those that have been selected have importance and significance for correctional case managers.

DSM-IV Classification

The most recent edition of the manual, the *DSM-IV* (APA, 1994), involves multiaxial assessment to arrive at classification and diagnostic decisions. Multi-

axial assessment reviews descriptive data on five axes to facilitate clinical decisionmaking. Each person is evaluated on the axes:

1. Axis I Clinical Syndromes and V Codes.

2. Axis II Development Disorders and Personality Disorders.

3. Axis III Physical Disorders and Conditions.

4. Axis IV Severity of Psychosocial Stressors.

5. Axis V Global Assessment of Functioning.

On Axis I, clinical syndromes include the major mental disorders commonly
associated with psychiatric illness, such as depression, schizophrenia, and delu-
sional disorder (i.e., paranoia). These mental disorders are quite relevant to correctional classification. Mentally disturbed offenders are typically held in protective custody or a forensic hospital, rather than placed in the general population
of a jail or prison. The V codes on Axis I refer to conditions not attributable to a
mental disorder that are nevertheless a focus of treatment. The V codes, like the
clinical syndromes, are categorized by four or five-digit codes, which are associated with particular conditions in the *DSM-IV*. For example, 296.34 refers to
recurrent severe major depressive disorder with psychotic features.

Axis II of the *DSM-IV* addresses developmental disorders and delays of
childhood, as well as personality traits and disorders in adulthood. For example, attention deficit/hyperactivity disorder (ADHD) would be coded 314.01 on
Axis II. While ADHD figures prominently in much juvenile delinquency, conduct disorder is stereotypically associated with predisposition for juvenile
crime. Conduct disorder has the following features in the *DSM-IV*:

1. Aggression toward people and animals.

2. Inclinations toward destruction of property.

3. Stealing and deceitfulness.

4. Propensity to violate rules and norms, e.g., running away; truancy.

The diagnosis of conduct disorder requires the presence of three or more of the
aforementioned features within the past twelve months, with at least one criterion manifested within the past six months.

Antisocial personality disorder (301.7, *DSM-IV*) is a major diagnostic category in correctional case management. While offenders presenting antisocial
personality are in the minority, even in correctional settings, this diagnostic
group includes most of the severe, recidivist criminals (Wilson & Herrnstein,
1985). An offender would be classified as having an antisocial personality disorder using the *DSM-IV* if he or she presents three or more of the following
characteristics since age 15:

1. Fails to conform to social norms or engages in unlawful activities.

2. Uses deceitfulness or lying in order to obtain pleasure or profit.

3. Is impulsive and lacks self-control.

4. Starts fights and becomes involved in physical assaults.

5. Places the safety of self and others in jeopardy.

6. Is irresponsible and disregards liability for actions; also does not work.

The *DSM-IV* criteria for adult personality disorders require that the patient be at least 18 years old.

Axis III affords the clinician an opportunity to record any physical problem relevant to the management of the case. Offenders present the full range of acute and chronic physical disorders, such as cancer and heart disease, as well as less common problems posing serious health risks in correctional settings, including HIV and tuberculosis (Durham, 1994). Axis IV presents a scale to report the overall severity of psychosocial stressors within the past year. The psychosocial stressors are rated from none to catastrophic in severity, arising predominantly from acute events or enduring circumstances. Psychosocial stressors include marital, family, financial, occupational, and legal problems that impact on the person's emotional adjustment.

Axis V of the *DSM-IV* contains a global assessment of functioning (GAF) scale. This scale facilitates classification of the individual according to overall psychological, social, and occupational functioning. The scale ranges from 10 (Persistent danger of severely hurting self or others) to 100 (Superior functioning in a wide range of activities). Many juvenile and adult offenders score in the 40 to 70 range of the GAF.

The five axes of the *DSM-IV* classification system provide a uniform means for organizing substantial data about the mental functional and behavioral adjustment of correctional clients. Although the system is best suited to psychiatric diagnosis, it can be used accurately by other allied health and correctional professionals. Resulting diagnostic impressions are used to make treatment recommendations and assign individuals to programs and therapeutic environments. Most of the data needed for

DSM-IV classification can be gathered during the mental status examination or comprehensive psychiatric evaluation. Psychological testing may secure additional relevant information.

MMPI Classification

The Minnesota Multiphasic Personality Inventory (MMPI) was the first objective personality test to be widely used in the prediction of mental disorders and personality traits. The MMPI was developed in 1943 and distributed in a variety of individual and group formats. While the MMPI can be hand scored and profiles can be charted on standard forms, the 566-567 item test is usually scored by one of the major testing services (e.g., The Psychological Corporation or National Computer Systems). The MMPI was restandardized by the University of Minnesota panel responsible for its ongoing development, producing the MMPI-2 (cf. Graham, 1987). However, the original MMPI, in spite of some dated language, remains in common use, due to the extensive research base that has accrued over time.

The MMPI produces profiles, narrative interpretations from computer software or an atlas (e.g., Graham, 1987), and hundreds of research-based subscale scores and clusters. All of these features contribute to considerable refinement in differential diagnosis, personality portrayal, and classification. Also, the MMPI contains validity scales to detect carelessness, random responding, lying, faking good or bad, atypical or deviant response sets, and psychological defensiveness or denial.

There are 10 major clinical scales on the MMPI.

1. Hypochondriasis.
2. Depression.
3. Hysteria.
4. Psychopathic Deviate.
5. Masculinity-Femininity.
6. Paranoia.
7. Psychasthenia.
8. Schizophrenia.
9. Hypomania.
10. Social Inversion.

Significant elevations on the scale scores (e.g., the standard or t-score is greater than 70 on the MMPI or 65 on the MMPI-2) indicate that the subject has endorsed more of the features or characteristics associated with the clinical syndrome attached to the scale.

Scale 4 (Psychopathic Deviate), is of particular usefulness for correctional case managers. An elevation on Scale 4 is virtually stereotypical of the career or recidivist criminal.

Scale 4 was developed to identify psychopathic or antisocial personality. While major criminal types were excluded from the original criterion group used to norm the MMPI, individuals were included who regularly engaged in lying, stealing, sexual promiscuity, fighting, and problem drinking. A wide range of amoral and antisocial behaviors were included in the development of the scale. Since the test can be used with adolescents, delinquent conduct was included as well. High scorers on Scale 4 are typically outgoing, immature, energetic, adventurous, impulsive, and hostile. Very high scores (t=80 and above) are associated with predisposition to engage in physical violence. The antisocial features of high Scale 4 are mitigated or reduced in importance when the subject is an adolescent or college student since rebelliousness and risk-taking curiosity are considered normative in these groups. Clinical significance of Scale 4 elevations are reduced also by higher scores on Scale 5, indicating greater feminine orientation in males. The Scale 5 elevation softens the otherwise negative interpretation of Scale 4.

Particular scale score elevations and combinations of scores can be meaningfully interpreted within the extensive MMPI literature (Graham, 1987). In interpreting the MMPI, the examiner first considers the validity indices in order to determine whether the profile of scores is representative of the individual. Next, the entire profile is reviewed, noting pattern of elevations and even below-average scores on some scales. For example, a very low score on Scale 2 (Depression) and an elevation on Scale 9 (Hypomania) could indicate the presence of bipolar affective disorder or manic-depressive illness.

After reviewing the overall profile, particular elevations are considered, especially to gain insights about everyday behavior and personality functioning. Finally, combinations of scores are examined to define types. Two- and three-digit codes (e.g., elevations on Scales 4 and 8 resulting in the 4-8 code) can be used to determine extensive clinical information, including likely diagnosis and prognosis. An atlas or interpretation manual (e.g., Duckworth, 1985; Graham, 1987) is typically used to discern central clinical features.

Emergent interpretations can be checked against elevations on subscale or supplementary scale scores, which are produced typically by computer-scoring software. Some of the subscale and supplementary scale scores are very useful. For example, elevations on the MacAndrew Alcoholism scale (MAC) are excellent subtle predictors for problems with chemical dependency and other addictive behaviors. However, research has shown that there are too many false positives (i.e., diagnosing a problem when none exists) when using the MAC with African-American males. Many of the other subscales are useful in determining the severity and subtypes of mental disorders identified in the clinical scales and subsequent configural analyses.

Megargee and Bohn (1979) developed a system for classifying criminal offenders based on the MMPI profile. They identified 10 criminal types in their classification system: "Item," "Easy," "Baker," "Able," "George," "Delta," "Jupiter," "Foxtrot," "Charlie," and "How."

The MMPI criminal taxonomy has been used with good results in federal and state correctional systems. The system has also been used to match individuals and treatment resources in community settings.

Group Item offenders, lacking significant psychopathology and criminal careers, were the best adjusted in the standardization studies (Megargee & Bohn, 1979). Therefore, Item offenders did not require intensive psychological or correctional treatment. While they benefited from the structure and overall program in the Federal Correctional Institute at Tallahassee, it appears that they could progress in other settings with alcohol education and chemical dependency treatment.

Group Easy offenders, the best adjusted and controlled of the 10 types, with the greatest intellectual potential, were nevertheless underachievers and generally undependable. The authors recommended academic programs, community-based treatment, and insight-oriented psychotherapy for Easy offenders. When they are incarcerated, their sentences should be brief, since they need to work on their self-sabotaging behavior patterns in the real world.

Group Baker offenders, unlike Item and Easy, clearly have intrapsychic and interpersonal problems. However, their problems are less severe than the remaining groups. Baker offenders appear shame-based, passive-aggressive, and alcoholic. They tend to have recurrent legal problems due to their alcoholic lifestyles. Depressed and defensive Baker types benefit from supportive counseling and group approaches. They benefit from structure and guidance in the environment. Alcoholics Anonymous is clearly indicated and provides some of the best outcomes with this population.

Group Able is a classification that includes socialized delinquents and sensation-seeking extroverts. They are sociable, active, and manipulative. Ables are usually white, middle-class individuals who have fallen prey to a hedonistic lifestyle. They do well in prisons and other institutional settings, but tend to relapse by committing drug-related and property crimes when they are loosely supervised in the community. Therefore, aftercare, involving residential treatment and halfway housing, is a paramount concern. Able offenders benefit the most from group therapy, involving some confrontation from peers. Frequently, they require chemical dependency treatment, as well.

Group George offenders are similar to Group Able inmates, but they are more depressed and generally less well adjusted. They are much more solitary and isolative, preferring to "do their own time," rather than becoming involved in the lives of peers. Some of them may be career criminals or participants in organized crime activities. They tend to take advantage of educational and vocational programs in the prison setting. A member of this classification group would be unlikely to participate in psychotherapy. However, they can form loyal and stable relationships. Therefore, programs emphasizing group task achievement or teamwork could be beneficial.

Beginning with Group Delta, there is a transition from minimal-moderate impairment to serious psychological and criminal deviancy. Megargee and Bohn (1979) described this group as hedonistic, amoral, and impulsive persons with entrenched hostility and alienation. This group experienced the worst family histories and most chaotic lifestyles. The Delta offender is most psychopathic of the types, and therefore, they present the worst recidivism rates. Since they do not adjust well in institutional or community settings, correctional decisionmaking is probably most concerned with reducing risk of reoffense through incapacitation by incarceration. Since they are predatory and aggressive, they are usually isolated from first offenders and tend to reside with similar peers. Over time, as Deltas mature, they tend to grow out of some of their high-incidence criminality. Thus, incarceration may function to remove them from society until they have acquired chronologically some self-control. Their present-oriented life perspective may make them candidates for reality-based therapies or cognitive-behavioral interventions. Yet, their prognosis in therapy is generally poor.

Group Jupiter is composed primarily of African-American males who present deprivation and poor social history. They could be described as multi-problem offenders. However, they tend to do better than expected when placed in adequate housing and when provided occupational opportunities. When stress is high, Jupiter offenders can be hostile and assaultive. Social welfare interventions are helpful with this group.

Group Foxtrot experiences difficulty in nearly every sphere of life. Although they present extensive criminal histories, their offender behavior is symptomatic of pervasive psychopathology. They are impulsive, disorganized, and antisocial. Since they present psychological, interpersonal, educational, and vocational deficiencies, Foxtrot offenders could benefit from virtually any program. Due to their cognitive distortion and poor adjustment, this classification of offenders responds best to behavior modification interventions. They also benefit from social skills training. They require a high degree of structure in any correctional setting.

The Charlie Group of offenders, who are hostile loners, show poor adjustment in most settings. Many of their problems can be traced to severe family problems and life trauma. They are antisocial, paranoid, and aggressive. Their life histories and resulting alienation contribute to lack of empathy and sociability. They tend to have disciplinary problems when forced to interact with others. Therefore, solitary and lower stimulation settings are best. Charlie offenders were most likely to be incarcerated for parole violations, rather than new offenses. Given their street-wise paranoia, they do well in dangerous, crime-ridden environments. However, they have serious difficulty relating to the "straight" world. This group has a poor prognosis, but they could benefit from cognitive-behavioral interventions provided the confrontation level is not too high.

The How Group is the last of the 10 MMPI classification groups. Due to their instability, anxiety, disorganization, and poor reality testing, offenders in this classification generally require psychiatric treatment. They do poorly in correctional settings and can present a danger to themselves or others. Therefore, How offenders are encountered in state hospitals and forensic settings. They will probably need medication in order to function at all in the community. Some of these individuals have become "street people," by virtue of the trend toward deinstitutionalization in mental health services. In corrections, this group is treated as mentally disordered or disturbed offenders.

The 10 groups in the MMPI classification system (Megargee & Bohn, 1979) represent important categories of correctional inmates. The system was used originally in secure, prison settings. However, it has been used over the years since its inception for community correctional decisionmaking. The classification system has been enlisted in making assignments to halfway houses and transitional living arrangements, special treatment programs, and specialized probation/parole caseloads (Motiuk, Motiuk & Bonta, 1992). Building on the utility of this system, other researchers and practitioners have identified particular typologies within particular criminal groups, affording finer grain analysis of their characteristics, problems, and needs.

Behavioral Classification

Behavioral classification involves observation and rating of offender characteristics. The observations and ratings are condensed into a meaningful typology by which similar offenders are grouped for some correctional purpose. One of the major systems uses behavioral classification: the Behavioral Classification System for Adult Offenders (Quay, 1983), also called the Adult Internal Management System (AIMS) (Quay, 1984). This system does not rely upon direct input from the offender. Instead, staff members complete two rating instruments, the Checklist for the Analysis of Life Histories, used in organizing information from the psychosocial history, and the Correctional Adjustment Checklist, based on staff member observations of the offender's behavior in a correctional setting.

The AIMS is used primarily in institutional corrections to assign inmates to housing units. However, the classification system can be used in any correctional setting, including jails and halfway houses, to make treatment and security decisions. The AIMS approach to classification has many applications in correctional management. The system has not only reduced disciplinary problems in prisons, but also separated vulnerable and predatory inmates (Quay, 1984).

The AIMS classification groups inmates into one of five personality types: (1) Aggressive Psychopath, (2) Manipulative, (3) Situational, (4) Inadequate Dependent, and (5) Neurotic Anxious (Quay & Parsons, 1971). Later, the personality types were described according to Roman numeral indicators (I through V) to reduce reliance upon negative stereotypes (Quay, 1984).

Group I inmates present the highest rate of disciplinary infractions. They are the "heavies" in correctional institutions, having little empathy for others and using aggression and other antisocial behaviors to confront, control, or intimidate. These aggressive-psychopathic offenders are troublesome and do not respond well to authority or treatment.

Offenders from Group II are highly manipulative individuals who are indirect in expressing their hostility and resentment. They fit the classic stereotype of the "con artist" who uses verbal persuasion and deception to victimize others. Group II inmates are unreliable and untrustworthy, requiring close supervision like the Group I offenders. In institutional settings, they operate behind the scenes organizing inmate gangs and illicit activities. Therefore, they are reluctant to abandon a criminal lifestyle, even in a secure setting.

Group III offenders are the best adjusted in the AIMS system. They do not intentionally victimize others, instead having some empathy and concern for peers. They make good group members and contribute to the therapeutic milieu in some settings. Situational offenders can be reliable and industrious. Therefore, they may enjoy success in trustee roles and vocational, academic, and rehabilitation programs. Group III inmates present the fewest disciplinary problems.

Offenders classified in Group IV have low to moderate rates of disciplinary infractions. They are passive individuals who are dependent upon the structure and support in their environments. Group IV offenders are vulnerable to victimization by stronger, aggressive, and manipulative predators. They may participate in selected correctional programs. However, they also tend to complain or "whine," making them difficult to supervise.

Group V inmates are the most likely to be victimized in correctional settings. They are anxious, distressed, and neurotic individuals who can be overwhelmed by the psychosocial stressors in correctional settings. They need careful supervision, as well as mental health attention. Like Group IV inmates, they may have few friends or supporters. Thus, they do not become involved in the institutional community or culture. They tend to require medication or individual psychotherapy, rather than benefiting from group training and rehabilitation efforts.

Quay (1984) argued that the AIMS addresses not only institutional, but also offender needs. It does focus attention on the issues of security and housing. However, underlying these concerns are characteristics of offenders and their needs. For example, Groups I and II require high structure and surveillance in custody in order to reduce the expression of criminality. Groups IV and V require moderate structure to reduce their distress, yet they need enough flexibility to pursue treatment, especially in chemical dependency and psychiatric programs.

Levinson (1988) described education, work, and counseling treatments for Heavy (I & II), Moderate (III), and Light (IV & V) groups. Groups I and II offenders benefit most from individualized, behavioral approaches, including programmed learning. They require clear, short-term goals and tasks in vocational and academic programs. Group III inmates can be afforded a high level of responsibility. They thrive on projects requiring personal initiative and creativity. In addition, they do well in classrooms and groups. Light (Groups IV and V) offenders need supportive interventions in educational, work, and counseling programs. Some may benefit from group endeavors, but most of them require careful individual attention, whatever the focus of the correctional program.

The behavioral classification system has been applied to adults and juveniles. The classification system for juveniles identified four basic types: (1) Undersocialized Aggressive, (2) Socialized Aggressive, (3) Attention Deficit, and (4) Anxiety, Withdrawal, and Dysphoria (Quay & Parsons, 1971). While these types are similar to Quay's adult classification scheme, juvenile typologies tend to emphasize underlying needs and problems of young offenders. In addition, juvenile classification systems emphasize the developmental level or maturity of the offender.

I-Level Classification

The Interpersonal Maturity Level Classification System, known as the I-level Classification System, was derived from theories of personality development (Sullivan, Grant & Grant, 1957; Warren, 1966). For these theorists, personality development was related to increasing cognitive complexity, personal integration, and interpersonal maturity. These theories predicted that individuals could be classified according to their current level of development, from the disorganization of the infant to the complexity of the adult presenting the highest levels of social and moral reasoning. I-level Classification developed from the application of the personality development theory in the Community Treatment Project of the California Youth Authority (Harris, 1988; Warren, 1966, 1983). The Community Treatment Project (CTP) was initiated to increase the effectiveness of treatment and supervision in the community by means of differential intervention, matching of offenders to treatment approaches and matching of offenders to treatment providers according to the I-level typology. I-level classification has been used with juveniles and adults in a variety of residential and community settings throughout the United States and several foreign countries.

Two methods are used to classify offenders according to developmental level: the CTP I-level interview (Palmer, 1974; Warren, 1966) and the Jesness Inventory (Jesness, 1983, 1988; Jesness & Wedge, 1985). The interview method requires considerable training and clinical skill, while the inventory procedure relies upon individual responses to 155 items. According to Harris (1988), each method has its strengths and weaknesses, resulting in some overall concerns about the reliability of I-level classification decisions.

Classification by I-level involves determination of developmental level and subtype. There are seven levels (encompassing various behaviors) in this classification system.

1. Infantile.

2. Asocial Passive or Asocial Aggressive.

3. Immature Conformist, Cultural Conformist, or Manipulator.

4. Neurotic Acting-Out, Neurotic Anxious, Cultural Identifier, or Situational-Emotional Reactor.

5. Differentiation of Self and Others.

6. Cognitive Complexity.

7. Flexibility and Tolerance.

I-level 1 is not included in the classification system because this disorganized, infantile state is seldom encountered among juvenile delinquents. Persons functioning in this developmental stage present profound mental and interpersonal disorders. I-levels 5-7 are omitted because rarely does any delinquent score in the 5 range, which indicates good differentiation of self and others. Levels 6 and 7 are infrequent among adults. I-level 6 indicates a high level of cognitive complexity or personality integration. I-level 7 is associated with high interpersonal flexibility and tolerance. The highest stages of personality development are associated with greater intelligence, creativity, and morality (Jennings, Kilkenney & Kohlberg, 1983; Loevinger, 1976; Reitsma-Street & Leschied, 1988).

According to the theory of I-level personality development, delinquent behavior has different meanings or functions at each stage or level. Therefore, different treatments or interventions are needed based on the current maturity of the offender. In general, highly structured interventions such as residential treatment and behavior modification best fit the needs of juveniles classified in the lower levels. Most of the remaining delinquents functioned well in group counseling (sometimes using Transactional Analysis); however, those classified in the higher levels were viewed as ready for individual counseling, as well. Some anxious and situational offenders benefit from family counseling or intervention with the parents. Homogeneous groupings in and out of the classroom, ideally with matched teachers, resulted in some therapeutic gains as well (Harris, 1988).

The matching model has been applied to several classification schemes in treatment and rehabilitation programs. The Conceptual Level Matching Model (CLMM), described by Reitsma-Street and Leschied (1988), is theoretically similar to I-level personality classification. The CLMM attempts to match the conceptual level of offenders with environments that either afford the greatest communication potential and optimal structure or strain and challenge, or are accessible and tolerable given the current level of conceptual functioning. This approach to understanding personality development is based on the conceptual systems theory of Harvey, Hunt, and Schroder (1961), but the underlying constructs are similar to those advanced by Piaget, Erikson, Loevinger, and other developmental theorists.

Conceptual Level (CL) is an estimate of cognitive maturity within the social or interpersonal domain. In the CLMM, persons are classified according to their current CL, then matched with an environment that produces stability and enhanced communication or an environment that strains the existing CL, creating opportunities for personal growth. Lower CL requires high structure, in terms of guidance, control, and rules. Higher CL is associated with greater tolerance of ambiguity, empathy, and curiosity. In correctional settings, the CLMM is especially helpful in organizing educational programs. However, the CLMM has been used in custodial management, determining the optimal degree of limit-setting based on the current CL of the resident. In general, the higher CL offenders fare better in community settings, self-motivated tasks, and therapy.

The CLMM and I-level classification systems afford novel perspectives of structure and supervision in correctional settings. Each of these classification methods reframe structure in terms of optimal levels of control, rule-setting, and guidance. This perspective advances corrections beyond concerns for safety, as manifested in locked doors and ongoing surveillance. Classification based on interpersonal maturity addresses the goal of facilitating growth by modifying the correctional environment to fit the developmental needs of the offender.

While this developmental perspective may be most applicable in the treatment of juvenile delinquency, the matching model or differential intervention perspective is useful in planning transitions for adult offenders as well. Information about the current conceptual functioning and interpersonal maturity of the offender should be helpful in determining whether institutional or community placement is indicated.

Level of Supervision Classification

An obvious concern in any correctional classification system is the level of supervision needed for an individual client or an identified group of offenders. Concerns about supervision affect decisionmaking in granting bail, probation, work release, parole, and community versus institutional treatment. Level of supervision frequently reflects extent of risk for elopement, violation of probation/parole agreement, and reoffense. Risk also reflects concerns about near-future dangerousness or likelihood of harming oneself or others in less structured environments.

There are a number of salient predictors in the decision to release an offender from custody into community treatment or supervision. Harris' (1988) "Predictors for Community Treatment" (Probation and Parole), is a very useful model for correctional case managers (Table 5.1).

Table 5.1
Predictors for Community Treatment (Probation and Parole)

1. Seriousness of offense
2. Attributions of offender
3. History of criminal activity
4. History of drug and alcohol use
5. History of violence
6. Past behavior in institutions
7. Age of offender
8. History of employment
9. Status of marriage and family life
10. Status of mental functioning
11. Contact with criminal associates
12. Length of sentence

The first salient predictor, seriousness of the offense, refers to the extent of injury or harm to victims or society in general. For example, rape assaults in which a weapon is used may produce greater physical and emotional harm than other forms of sexual coercion. In addition, crimes that result in large financial losses for victims or the community are considered more serious. Similarly, an offense occurring in the context of other criminal behavior, especially as part of patterned offender behavior, can be considered serious, rather than situational. In some states, victim impact statements are introduced when considering sentencing options.

Another predictor for risk is the attributions of the offender. Whenever an offender persists in denying charges (even after being found guilty or pleading no contest), prognosis in negatively affected. In addition, the offender's blaming others for the crime increases risk. The individual's history of criminal activity (including data about delinquent conduct when available), violence or aggression, and chemical dependency are important considerations in criminal justice decisionmaking, as well.

Decisions regarding level of supervision are influenced by the offender's past institutional behavior. Frequencies of infraction and disciplinary responses should be considered in assigning inmates to living units and programs. The age of the offender is another predictor of risk. In general, the young offender has greater likelihood of engaging in crime. Most delinquents "mature out" of criminal conduct. However, when an offender first engages in serious patterned delinquency at a young age, there is substantial risk of chronic recidivism.

Stability in employment and marital status reflect investment in conventional behavior, as well as a stake in conformity. Therefore, these predictors reduce estimates of risk. Having criminal associates and struggling with emotional problems or mental disorders increase risk of disruptive and rule-breaking behavior. Even the length of an offender's sentence should be taken into consideration in making correctional decisions. Individuals enjoying shorter sentences may not be motivated sufficiently to participate in treatment programs. Individuals experiencing longer sentences may lack motivation as well. Inmates serving long sentences may present more infractions and disruptive institutional behavior. They could have difficulty in making transitions back to community settings.

While level of supervision decisions usually take into consideration salient risk predictors from the individual's past, other factors contribute to correctional problem-solving and rehabilitation. Model case management systems in Ohio and Wisconsin (Crooks, 1994; McShane & Krause, 1993; Van Voorhis, 1992) emphasized client needs assessment in classification. By linking risk and needs assessment, a comprehensive system for management and rehabilitation is created.

In 1973, the Wisconsin Bureau of Community Corrections secured state and federal funds to develop a workload system for new probation officers. By 1975, they initiated the Case Classification/Staff Deployment Project, in which characteristics of offenders contributed to the assignment of staff to specialized caseloads. The Wisconsin classification system was adopted in 1981 by the National Institute of Corrections (NIC) as a model for community supervision. Ultimately, the system consisted of four elements: (1) an offender risk assessment scale, (2) an offender needs assessment scale, (3) a workload budgeting and deployment system, and (4) a management information system.

In the Wisconsin/NIC model the risk and needs assessment scales are scored based on the weight of each item in a regression equation used to predict recidivism. Then, the probationer or parolee is assigned to one of three levels of supervision. At six-month intervals during community supervision, the scales are readministered and the offender is reclassified as needed. Workload decisionmaking and budgeting decisionmaking were based on time studies of the activities required to meet the targeted supervision standards. A management information system (MIS) was devised to match offender caseload supervision requirements to the resources of the bureau. Risk and needs assessments determine the intensity or quantity of supervision, while the resulting case management classification (CMC) determines the quality and nature of services.

The CMC process identified four types of offender caseloads: selective intervention, casework control, environmental structuring, and limit setting. Selective intervention requires the least agency resources. Situational offenders enjoy adequate family and social support, as well as educational and vocational skills. Since their adjustment is good, this classification of offenders have fewer needs than other groups, requiring less supervision and correctional intervention.

Individuals on casework control need significant supervision and agency services. Successful rehabilitation of these offenders typically involves careful attention to underlying chemical dependency and adjustment problems.

Environmental structuring is used with offenders who have low intelligence and poor social skills. They require many community resources in order to avoid relapse.

The limit setting classification is reserved for offenders who have dedicated themselves to a criminal lifestyle. They are a manipulative, antisocial group that generally does not benefit from rehabilitation. When correctional resources are limited, they receive the least social services. However, their classification dictates a high level of surveillance and strict, no-nonsense limit setting in order to protect the community.

The NIC Model Probation Management System matches client risk/needs classification to correctional resources available in a given jurisdiction. Case management classification (CMC) is usually reserved for cases scoring highest on the risk and needs assessment. Therefore, probationers in the maximum supervision category are assigned to one of the four types of offender caseloads. Cases classified as regular or minimum in the risk/needs assessment are assigned to limited supervision. Probationers on limited supervision can be tracked in the case management system by attending to the payment of fees, attendance at community counseling sessions, completion of community service (volunteer labor), or fulfillment of other court directives. Since these activities can be tracked by computer, little face-to-face contact with the probation officer is needed.

Computers are used in the NIC model probation system to develop workload standards for correctional case management. The MIS in a particular jurisdiction could establish that it takes an average of 12 hours to complete a presentence investigation (PSI). Therefore, an intake caseworker who completes PSIs and has 120 hours available each month for this function can complete routinely 10 investigations per month. Maximum supervision cases may require an average of eight hours per month. Thus, the intensive supervision case manager may be able to provide this level of service to only 15 clients according to the MIS workload standards. Due to the extraordinary demand for services and the equivocal outcomes from investing such resources in maximum cases, many correctional systems are reconsidering the value of intensive supervision. Some studies (Durham, 1994) established that probationers and parolees receiving intensive supervision actually do worse than regular clients in terms of recidivism.

Although some correctional professionals in the field mistrust standardized level of supervision procedures and instruments as being out of touch with the real world or infringing upon their discretion, there is a trend toward use of objective scales in correctional decisionmaking. The Level of Supervision Inventory (LSI) (Andrews, 1982) has been used extensively in Canada and throughout North America to make correctional decisions.

The LSI is a psychometric tool, which follows the logic of the NIC model and other recent advances in classification. Risk and offender needs can be scored by correctional professionals or determined by client self-report (Motiuk, Motiuk & Bonta, 1992). The LSI has been used to predict staff evaluation of offender progress, recidivism while on probation, adjustment to halfway house placement, frequency of misconduct in community supervision, and severity of reoffense. The LSI evidenced better predictive validity than the Megargee-MMPI classification system in one study (Motiuk, Bonta & Andrews, 1986).

Overall, the level of supervision approach to classification has some advantages to more psychologically oriented systems. Correctional professionals readily understand classification based on risk factors for reoffense and client needs for services. This descriptive approach is very close to the real-life data in the daily correctional environment. Some of the other classification systems emphasize personality and psychological dimensions that are not readily observable. In addition, several of the sophisticated typologies, especially those based on interview methods, may be difficult to evaluate or apply. While one trend in classification, represented by the NIC model, is to construct a computer-based management information system to accomplish the goals of differential intervention, the level of supervision methods can be augmented by psychologically oriented approaches. In effect, corrections may be in a sense "rediscovering psychology."

An Omnibus Model for Classification

Each of the classification systems has its merits and liabilities. Some systems apply primarily to adults (e.g., Megargee's MMPI typology) while other approaches are tailored to adolescents (e.g., I-Level classification). Certain methods address concerns in prisons and other secure settings, while a few approaches focus on the level of supervision in community corrections. In order to address increasing demands for accurate classification with the growing offender population, it is desirable to offer a comprehensive or omnibus classification system, combining promising aspects from several models.

Van Voorhis (1988) explored the construct and predictive validity of five offender typologies. In the course of her research, she identified some commonalities among the systems, which can be used to construct an omnibus model of classification. Some additional categories have been added based on the authors' clinical experience (Table 5.2).

Table 5.2
An Omnibus Classification System

1. Low Conceptual Level
2. Mentally Disordered
3. Neurotic
4. Immature Dependent
5. Situational
6. Subcultural
7. Character Disordered
8. Power Oriented
9. Manipulative
10. Neurologically Impaired
11. Chemically Dependent
12. Violent
13. Sadistic

The category of Low Conceptual Level includes individuals who function at a very marginal, overly concrete level. They have not acquired adequate moral reasoning skills and tend to not learn contingencies (i.e., If I do this [then] this will happen) from their experiences. They require high structure in their environment in order to avoid rule-breaking and being victimized by others.

Mentally Disordered offenders present major clinical syndromes of psychosis, such as paranoia, which can be readily diagnosed by a psychiatrist or mental health professional. Occasionally, they commit criminal acts for which they cannot be held responsible or they are incompetent to stand trial. When they are encountered in correctional systems, high structure in the forms of surveillance and orderly routine are needed. Most receive psychotropic medication to manage symptoms of their conditions. Major depression and bipolar affective disorder may be encountered frequently in adult offender populations.

The category of Neurotic offender incorporates numerous conditions, which are related in terms of the presence of anxiety. Neurotic offenders may be compulsive, passive-aggressive, histrionic, avoidant, and borderline. All can be considered essentially self-sabotaging. They became involved in criminal activities to "act out" or externalize inner conflicts, frequently with authority figures. Neurotic offenders act out in order to reduce tension or anxiety within oneself or the family system. Many delinquents are essentially neurotic, as the I-level classification system indicates.

Immature Dependent offenders are somewhat less disturbed than the aforementioned classifications. However, they experience debilitating social anxiety at times. Lacking social skills, they do not know how to behave in a productive, rule-abiding manner. Typically, they fall under the influence of older, stronger criminals who manipulate or coerce them into criminal activity.

The Situational offender is the best adjusted type in several classification systems. Due to extraordinary psychosocial stress or extreme anomie, or normlessness, in particular contexts, Situational offenders experience lapse in judgment or self-control. They do not perceive themselves as deviant and do not seek criminal associates.

Like the Situational offender, the Subcultural type has difficulty recognizing criminal cognition and behaviors. They are influenced by prevailing norms in the home and neighborhood environment. Yet, they possess a "stake in conformity" or the normal desire to fit into some reference group. They may become involved in gang-related activities.

Character Disordered offenders reflect the classic stereotype of the antisocial individual. Emerging as conduct disorder of childhood, such individuals are impulsive, self-centered, and aggressive. They are easily frustrated and fail to learn altruism, empathy, and prosocial behavior. Therefore, only surveillance or incarceration influences their choices to commit crime.

Power Oriented offenders are a special subgrouping of antisocial individuals. However, they are distinct enough in motive and conduct to have their own category. Power Oriented individuals violate the boundaries of others (e.g., committing rape, stealing property, or otherwise inflicting injury) in order to feel in control or self-assured. They relate to most situations as zero-sum games (i.e., there is a winner and others lose). As a result, these types of offenders are extremely sensitive to opportunities to coerce and dominate others.

Manipulative offenders represent a subgroup of antisocial individuals as well. They present adequate to above-average communication and social skills, since they tend to be extroverted. Manipulative offenders derive meaning in life from "conning" and managing the impressions of others. In this manner, they hide their true nature and avoid criticism, judgment, and responsibility. These offenders become involved in street scams and white-collar crimes. They are able to make rational choices and plan their crimes.

Neurologically Impaired criminals engage in criminal incidents and chronic offender behavior by virtue of lack of control. They present neurological deficits that make it difficult to control or regulate impulses. The largest group in this category are the juveniles experiencing Attention Deficit/Hyperactivity Disorder (APA, 1994). Their impulsivity, hyperkinetic behavior, and difficulty in concentrating or learning increase the risk that they will become adult offenders. Some of these individuals are sensation-seeking or risk-taking, while others cannot seem to manage the ordinary stresses of daily life without engaging in deviant or violent behavior.

Chemical dependency is related to most offender behavior (Durham, 1994). Some acts are criminal specifically because they violate state or federal laws related to drug possession or distribution. Many Chemically Dependent offenders engage in petty or property crimes in order to maintain a chemically dependent lifestyle. Some substance abusers commit serious and violent crimes when they are under the influence of a mood-altering chemical.

The category of Violent offenders reflects a common-sense approach to classification. Many of the other types of offenders may engage periodically in violent behavior. The Violent offender commits offenses which are primarily violent in nature. If there is some choice between demand or violence, this type of offender will use force or a weapon. Some offenders perpetrate a violent act due to situational or subcultural concerns, and therefore, they should be included in categories other than Violent.

Sadistic offenders use violence for personal and sexual gratification. Unlike Violent offenders, who may be predisposed to instrumental violence in order to accomplish criminal goals, the Sadistic individual's chief motive is to inflict harm and suffering on the victim. Some seemingly benign offenses, such as exhibitionism, express essentially sadistic motives, for example, deriving sexual gratification from the fear response on the victim's face. The most horrific crimes, such as serial murder, fit into the Sadistic category.

The omnibus model of classification emphasizes both the descriptive characteristics and the underlying psychosocial motives of the offender. Both level of supervision and differential intervention can be applied to increase the depth and utility of the classification system. Supervision and rehabilitation decisions can be based upon careful consideration of criminogenic needs.

The analysis of criminogenic needs evolved from recent advances in the psychology of criminal conduct (Andrews, Bonta & Hoge, 1990). A psychological understanding of criminal behavior is essential in modifying risk for recidivism within corrections. In other words, risk for relapse or recidivism is inexorably linked to needs of individuals and known groups of offenders. Criminogenic needs are dynamic attributes of offenders and their circumstances that can be changed over time by correctional interventions in order to reduce risk of recidivism.

In a review of predictive validity of incremental changes in criminogenic needs (Andrews, Bonta & Hoge, 1990), six indices were associated with risk modification, while three other familiar criteria demonstrated nonsignificant

CLASSIFICATION, TREATMENT PLANNING, AND REFERRAL

association with risk. The two most important indices of criminogenic needs were antisocial attitudes, including thinking errors and cognitive distortions, and antisocial associates, or ongoing attachments with known offenders. Having an antisocial personality was also a predictor for recidivism due to the constellation of needs linked to psychopathy (e.g., risk-taking and rule-breaking). Trouble at school or home was a predictor of relapse, as well. Finally, history of drug abuse and alienation produced patterns of needs associated with criminality.

Three factors frequently associated with reduced risk for criminality were nonsignificant in the statistical analysis (Andrews, Bonta & Hoge, 1990). Conventional success orientation, empathy, and personal distress (a combination of high anxiety and low self-esteem) nevertheless have potential for explaining some of the variance in criminal recidivism. Criminogenic needs should be addressed in effective correctional counseling and case management programs. Effectiveness in corrections is based upon achieving reductions in recidivism for different classes of offenders by means of modifying needs, which then become intermediate goals for treatment.

Level of supervision (i.e., management) and differential intervention decisions take into account the classification of the offender and his or her needs. Management and rehabilitation levels can be addressed simultaneously through attention to the structure afforded by the correctional environment.

In general, high structure is reserved for high-risk offenders, who present pervasive, well-established criminogenic needs, satisfied by ongoing offender behavior. Low structure is typically associated with community treatment and pre-release programs for offenders having reasonable potential for rehabilitation and adequate self-control. However, there is a trend to move from high, through moderate, to low structure over time in a given correctional system. This trend fits with a modern correctional case management model in which management is shifted from the correctional professional to client self-regulation, as criminogenic needs and risk factors are reduced.

Treatment Planning and Referral

Effective treatment planning and referral begins with careful assessment, diagnosis, and classification. The omnibus model of classification presents some treatment options based on characteristics of known groups of offenders, including their amenability or responsivity to treatment and their particular criminogenic needs, which must be addressed in corrections. The degree of structure in the correctional setting is one of the first variables in correctional decisionmaking. Each of the categories in the omnibus classification system is matched with the optimal structure in the initial stage of differential intervention. This is depicted in Table 5.3.

Table 5.3
Differential Intervention Level of Structure by Classification

High Structure	Moderate Structure	Low Structure
Low Conceptual Level	Neurotic	Situational
Mentally Disordered	Immature Dependent	Subcultural
Character Disordered	Neurologically Impaired	
Power Oriented	Chemically Dependent	
Manipulative		
Violent		
Sadistic		

The organization of classes from high to low structure suggests the difficulty in case management with some groups of offenders. In addition, classification by degree of structure bridges the gap from basic treatment amenability issues to genuine matching of offender needs with available treatment resources. Some offenders (e.g., Sadistic) primarily require surveillance to incapacitate or reduce their criminal activities. Other offenders (e.g., Situational) benefit from the least restrictive environment required to modify needs associated with risk for future offender behavior. Certain treatment components address not only risk of reoffense, but also risk for technical violations of probation/parole agreements. Fundamentally, decisions regarding structure should be made to help offenders stay out of prisons and other secure settings, which are increasingly costly to government and society.

The next step in treatment planning is matching interventions to the needs of individual offenders according to known characteristics of the offender's classification and the optimal degree of structure. **Classification** by structural requirements may be depicted in this manner:

1. Offenders with high needs for structure include those who are classified as: (a) having low conceptual levels; (b) are mentally disordered (psychotic or schizophrenic); (c) are character disordered; (d) are power oriented; (e) are manipulative; (f) are violent; and, (g) are sadistic.

2. Offenders requiring moderate structure include those who are classified as: (a) neurotic; (b) immature and/or dependent; (c) the neurologically impaired; and, (d) those who are chemically dependent.

3. Offenders who require low structure include those who are clas-
    sified as: (a) having situational problems; and (b) are subcultur-
    ally different.

Differential interventions, taking into account classification and structure,
can be described in this manner:

1. Low conceptual levels: Behavior modification
2. Mentally disordered: Psychotropic medications
3. Character disordered: Cognitive therapy
4. Power oriented: Group therapy
5. Manipulative: Vocational education
6. Violent: Restricted environment
7. Sadistic: Surveillance
8. Neurotic: Individual psychotherapy
9. Immature/dependent: Social skills training
10. Neurologically impaired: Psychoeducational programs
11. Chemically dependent: Therapeutic community
12. Situational problems: Community resources
13. Subcultural difference: Recreational therapy

Some interventions may be used among various types of various classes of
offenders. If structure is reduced over time in the correctional program, then
selected interventions may apply early in the treatment of some classes of
offenders and toward the end of treatment for other offender types. Interventions such as behavior modification fit certain correctional settings (e.g., a
point/token economy in a residential treatment center for juvenile offenders),
but also apply generally across a range of classifications and environments.

Differential intervention involves the best fit between a particular offender's
characteristics and needs and the program resources available in a given correctional setting. Differential intervention ultimately addresses the particular, even
unique, needs of an individual. The goal of matching treatment options to specific needs is aimed at reducing the risk of relapse. Therefore, an individual treatment plan should be constructed for each offender. The plan may incorporate
some general recommendations or terms, which have been established as effective for most offenders. Yet, the core of differential intervention involves selecting from a menu of possible interventions the most promising, efficient array of
resources. In this manner, the strength of the matching model is brought to bear
upon the individual, who is, of course, the focus of case management.

An individual treatment plan conforms to the guidelines or format required
by the correctional agency. However, each treatment plan is an expression of
the professional's formulation of the case. This formulation is based on assessment results, diagnostic impressions, and classification characteristics. In mental health practice, the case formulation contains information related to the eti-

ology and prognosis. The clinical understanding expressed in the formulation leads naturally to diagnostic impressions and treatment recommendations, which are separate headings in the individual treatment plan.

We recommend that professionals in corrections follow the method of mental health practitioners in formulating their cases and making corresponding treatment decisions. The formulation includes a summary of the psychosocial history, including information relevant to understanding the remote causes and current symptoms of criminal conduct and any relevant clinical syndromes. The results of the psychiatric examination, if one were completed, would be included. Findings of the psychological evaluation are recorded in the formulation as well. Typically, observations about etiology and prognosis are recorded in the first paragraph, while information about current status, including residence, are included in a second paragraph. The second paragraph also incorporates the reasons for referral to community caregivers (e.g., evaluation and treatment) and the mandate or rationale for correctional treatment. The written formulation, which is contained in the chart or case folder, converges on diagnosis and classification.

The diagnostic impressions constitute the next section of the proposed treatment plan. The impressions may take the form of a brief descriptive narrative, resulting in a particular classification. In many settings, especially if correctional counseling is available, *DSM-IV* multiaxial diagnoses may be useful. Regardless of the diagnostic or classification system used in the correctional agency, the impressions should clearly indicate risk factors and criminogenic needs. The diagnostic impressions should be related to correctional resources in the agency, contributing to correctional decisionmaking regarding level of supervision and differential intervention.

Treatment recommendations are offered in the final section of the individual treatment plan. Depending upon the resources and limitations of the correctional setting, the plan may include recommendations for structure, supervision, and counseling. Ideally, the matching model guides the process of selecting interventions for a given offender. The recommendations section of the individual treatment plan will include terms of probation or parole in community corrections. In addition, recommendations take the form of referrals to particular programs, resources, and caregivers.

In institutional and community corrections, referrals may be verbal or written, informal or formal. Since treatment team members need to communicate efficiently even in small agencies or institutions, written referrals are usually indicated. Written referrals provide information about the offender and the reason a particular resource or program is recommended. The formal referral is recorded in the case record to document implementation of the ongoing treatment plan. In community corrections, the case manager will receive regular or periodic reports from community caregivers, which may then be filed to document compliance, progress, or completion. In institutional programs, counselors, officers, and other correctional professionals may meet on a regular basis to "staff" or discuss particular cases. The results of staffings or case conferences are documented in the case record.

The individual treatment plan is modified as more data are obtained and treatment components are completed. Team members make recommendations for new interventions that promise to reduce additionally the offender's risk for relapse. Frequently, the treatment team decisions and community referrals address needs, which can be considered intermediate treatment goals. The referrals and recommendations in the treatment plan are included in the case record to document progress. The written record is used to conduct case audits in which there is attention to quality assurance and policy adherence. The individual treatment plan facilitates communication among professionals and forms an objective base for organizing correctional interventions. If there are problems with compliance with mandated terms of intervention, then the case record affords data for decision-making in such matters as revocation or custody.

Conclusions

The classification phase of correctional case management forms the web among assessment, diagnosis, and treatment. Classification refers to assigning individuals who share significant characteristics to potentially effective interventions. In recent years, there have been major advances in the prediction of offender risk of recidivism and the estimation of client needs. Various classification systems were created to organize data derived from risk and needs assessments.

One of the oldest classification systems, the *DSM-IV* multiaxial assessment, emphasized differential diagnosis of clinical syndromes, such as paranoia or psychosis. The *DSM-IV* is especially relevant in cases involving mentally disordered offenders. This psychiatric model provides the most accepted criteria for diagnosing conduct disorder of childhood and antisocial personality disorder.

Megargee's MMPI classification system is also psychological in nature. The MMPI includes 10 clinical scales and numerous subscales and supplementary scales. Client responses to the MMPI produce a profile that can be meaningfully interpreted. Megargee identified 10 criminal types based on configural analyses of MMPI profiles.

Some classification systems are less concerned with underlying psychological characteristics and more focused on social and behavioral features. Quay's Adult Internal Management System (AIMS) identified five criminal personality types, each having particular needs. Two classification systems emphasized developmental and cognitive factors. I-level classification is well-suited to classifying juvenile offenders according to their interpersonal maturity. The Conceptual Level Matching Model has been used with offenders to fit environmental structure to present conceptual complexity.

Concerns about structure are directly related to level-of-supervision decisions. Salient predictors are used to release offenders from custody or assign them to community supervision. Level-of-supervision classification emphasizes the following factors: seriousness of offense, attributions of offenders, past institutional behavior, stability in employment, and marital status. The Level of

Supervision Inventory (LSI) was developed to classify offenders according to basic characteristics, risk factors, and emergent needs. The LSI has been as effective as Megargee's MMPI system in matching offenders to available resources in institutional, transitional, and community settings.

The level-of-supervision approach was used by Wisconsin, and later the National Institute of Corrections, to construct a model community supervision program. The NIC model identified four types of offender caseloads, requiring special case management approaches: selective intervention, casework control, environmental structuring, and limit setting.

Based upon a review of recent literature, we developed an omnibus model for classification. This comprehensive model includes 13 criminal types: low conceptual level, mentally disordered, neurotic, immature dependent, situational, subcultural, character disordered, power-oriented, manipulative, neurologically impaired, chemically dependent, violent, and sadistic. Each class of offenders has characteristic needs for degree of structure (high, moderate, or low) and particular types of interventions. Level of supervision (i.e., management) and differential intervention decisions take into account the characteristics of the offender and his or her needs. Criminogenic needs include antisocial attributions, antisocial associates, trouble at school and home, history of drug abuse, and alienation. These needs establish intermediate goals for treatment, which is ultimately intended to reduce risk of relapse.

An individual treatment plan should be completed in order to reduce offender risk of relapse or recidivism. Treatment planning involves communicating with all members of the treatment plan, developing a formulation of the case, forming diagnostic impressions, and making treatment recommendations. Referrals arise from staffings, case conferences, and treatment team meetings. Referrals are used to implement the individual's treatment plan. There is follow-up to determine and document compliance, progress, and program completion.

Classification is a critical case management function in contemporary corrections. There is increasing awareness that effective supervision and rehabilitation require some attempts to match offenders with potentially therapeutic correctional environments. By systematically varying the degree of structure and implementing particular interventions, corrections can move from institutional to community settings. Offenders must be encouraged to develop behavioral, cognitive, and moral maturity through comprehensive approaches to differential intervention.

References

American Psychiatric Association (1987). *Diagnostic and Statistical Manual of Mental Disorders* (Third Edition-Revised). Washington, DC: Author.

American Psychiatric Association (1994). *Diagnostic and Statistical Manual of Mental Disorders* (Fourth Edition). Washington, DC: Author.

Andrews, D.A. (1982). *The Level of Supervision Inventory (LSI)*. Toronto, CN: Ontario Ministry of Correctional Services.

Andrews, D.A., J. Bonta & R.D. Hoge (1990). "Classification for Effective Rehabilitation: Rediscovering Psychology." *Criminal Justice and Behavior*, 17:19-52.

Crooks, C.W. (1994). "The Case Management System Experience in Ohio." In P.C. Kratcoski (ed.) *Correctional Counseling and Treatment* (Third Edition) (pp. 114-132). Prospect Heights, IL: Waveland Press.

Duckworth, J. (1985). *MMPI Interpretation Manual for Counselors and Clinicians* (Second Edition). Muncie, IN: Accelerated Development.

Durham, A.M. (1994). *Crisis and Reform: Current Issues in American Punishment*. Boston, MA: Little, Brown and Company.

Gottfredson, D.M. & M. Tonry (eds.) (1987). *Prediction and Classification: Criminal Justice Decisionmaking*. Chicago, IL: University of Chicago Press.

Graham, J.R. (1987). *The MMPI: A Practical Guide* (Second Edition). New York, NY: Oxford University Press.

Harris, P.W. (1988). "The Interpersonal Maturity Level Classification System." *Criminal Justice and Behavior*, 15:58-77.

Harvey, O.J., D.E. Hunt & H.M. Schroeder (1961). *Conceptual Systems and Personality Organization*. New York, NY: John Wiley.

Jennings, W., R. Kilkenney & L. Kohlberg (1983). "Moral Development Theory and Practice for Youthful and Adult Offenders." In W. Lauffer & J. Day (eds.) *Personality Theory, Moral Development and Criminal Behavior* (pp. 281-355). Lexington, MA: D.C. Heath.

Jesness, C.F. (1983). *The Jesness Inventory* (Revised Edition). Palo Alto, CA: Consulting Psychologists Press.

Jesness, C.F. (1988). "The Jesness Inventory Classification System." *Criminal Justice and Behavior*, 15:78-91.

Jesness, C.F. & R.F. Wedge (1985). *Jesness Inventory Classification System: Supplementary Manual*. Palo Alto, CA: Consulting Psychologists Press.

Levinson, R.B. (1988). "Developments in the Classification Process: Quay's AIMS Approach." *Criminal Justice and Behavior*, 15:24-38.

Loevinger, J. (1976). *Ego Development*. San Francisco, CA: Jossey-Bass.

McShane, M.D. & W. Krause (1993). *Community Corrections*. New York, NY: McMillan.

Megaree, E.I. & M.J. Bohn, Jr. (1979). *Classifying Criminal Offenders: A New System Based on the MMPI*. Beverly Hills, CA: Sage Publications.

Montiuk, L.L., J. Bonta & D.A. Andrews (1986). "Classification in Correctional Halfway Houses: The Relative and Incremental Predictive Criterion Validities of the Megaree-MMPI and LSI Systems." *Criminal Justice and Behavior*, 13:33-46.

Montiuk, M.S., L.L. Montiuk & J. Bonta (1992). "A Comparison Between Self-Report and Interview-Based Inventories in Offender Classification. *Criminal Justice and Behavior*, 19:143-159.

Palmer, T. (1974). "The Youth Authority's Community Treatment Project." *Federal Probation*, 38:3-14.

Quay, H.C. (1983). *Technical Manual for the Behavioral Classification System for Adult Offenders*. Washington, DC: Department of Justice.

Quay, H.C. (1984). *Managing Adult Inmates: Classification for Housing and Program Assignments*. College Park, MD: American Correctional Association.

Quay, H.C. & L.B. Parsons (1971). *The Differential Behavioral Classification of the Juvenile Offender*. Washington, DC: US Bureau of Prisons.

Reitsma-Street, M. & A.W. Leschied (1988). "The Conceptual-Level Matching Model in Corrections." *Criminal Justice and Behavior*, 15:92-108.

Sullivan, C.M., M.Q. Grant & J.D. Grant (1957). "The Development of Interpersonal Maturity: Applications to Delinquency." *Psychiatry*, 20:373-385.

Van Voorhis, P. (1988). "A Cross Classification of Five Offender Typologies: Issues of Construct and Predictive Validity. *Criminal Justice and Behavior*, 15:109-124.

Van Voorhis, P. (1992). "An Overview of Offender Correctional Systems." In D. Lester, M. Braswell & P. Van Voorhis (eds.) *Correctional Counseling* (Second Edition) (pp. 73-92). Cincinnati, OH: Anderson Publishing Co.

Warren, M.Q. (1966). *Interpersonal Maturity Level Classification: Diagnosis, and Treatment of Low, Middle, and High Maturity Delinquents*. Sacramento, CA: California Youth Authority.

Warren, M.Q. (1983). "Applications of Interpersonal Maturity Theory to Offender Populations." In W. Lauffer & J. Day (eds.) *Personality Theory, Moral Development and Criminal Behavior* (pp. 23-50). Lexington, MA: D.C. Heath.

Wilson, J.Q. & R.J. Herrnstein (1985). *Crime and Human Nature*. New York, NY: Simon & Schuster.

Chapter 6

Foundations for Problem-Solving and Case Management Intervention

Introduction

Historically, the term corrections has generally been taken to mean rehabilitation of the offender. The notion of rehabilitation is associated with three central values that comprise the ideology of most correctional counselors. The first value is expressed in the belief that most offenders have, at least minimally, the potential for change in behavior with respect to distorted or dysfunctional values, attitudes, and behaviors. The second value is incorporated in the belief that intrapersonal and interpersonal changes can take place via the therapeutic encounter of the offender with the correctional counselor during individual counseling, or by way of the therapeutic encounter of the offender involved in family or group counseling approaches. The third value lies in the belief that the criminal justice system or, more precisely, structures within that system, such as institutions for incarceration or imprisonment, as well as community correctional settings, can become therapeutic milieux; that they can become more humanized.

The issue of punishment versus corrections should be clear with respect to correctional counseling: correctional counseling has to do with the rehabilitation of offenders; punishment has to do with removing and incapacitating offenders via imprisonment or incarceration so that they cannot act out or aggress against individuals or groups in society. Punishment also has to do with creating and implementing laws and legal statutes that may make potential offenders think or believe that they will face certain punishment (the notion of individual or personal deterrence from crime). It may include the use of stigmatization of offenders by the dramatic implementation of punishment, for example, capital punishment accompanied by wide media attention, so as to provide a more universal deterrence from criminal behavior for other, like-minded criminals.

Case management, within the last decade or so, has increasingly become the counseling method of choice of clinical practitioners who work with clients that have a multiplicity of social, psychological, or behavioral problems. Case management has become a widespread treatment approach across a variety of public and private, profit and non-profit, state and local, health and mental health agencies. In these kinds of settings, the use of case management has been found to be particularly appropriate for counseling chronically mentally disturbed persons; particularly for those who have been placed into community-based, deinstitutionalized settings.

Criminal offenders mirror chronically mentally disabled clients in that they often also have a multiplicity of severe and persistent social and psychological disorders and, in some cases, severe psychological pathologies. These problems make it extremely difficult for them to function in an appropriate, responsible, competent, and meaningful manner with respect to their individual, family, group, and community relationships.

Correctional case management is a counseling process that can be used with many types of offenders, including offenders who are imprisoned or institutionalized, but it is particularly relevant and appropriate for offenders who have been placed in community correctional settings. Commonly, these types of offenders may be on probation, which can be defined as the legal status of a suspended criminal sentence, contingent upon the continuance of good behavior; or on parole, meaning that the offender has been adjudicated, but has been conditionally released to serve an indeterminate or unexpired sentence, again contingent upon good behavior. Community corrections refer to correctional settings that exist as alternatives to incarceration or imprisonment. By definition, these are deinstitutionalized settings.

More precisely, correctional case management, as discussed in Chapter 1, is a systematic process by which the identified strengths and needs of offenders are matched, in a stepwise and logical process, with appropriate treatment resources, programs, and services. Furthermore, with respect to offenders, correctional case management is a treatment approach that can be used to bridge the gap and narrow the range of differences among programs, services, and resources that are likely to exist between community and institutionalized care structures because of the politically and economically driven mandate for community-based care manifested by the phenomenon of deinstitutionalization of services and programs in all areas of social services. Many of these new care structures are likely to represent the privatization of correctional services.

The goals of correctional case management counseling, for all types of offenders in deinstitutionalized settings, whether one is discussing mentally disordered persons in an aftercare program, a substance abuser in a halfway house, or the parolee or probationer "doing time" at home on electronic monitoring, are the same: rehabilitation of the offender (change, modification, or accommodation of personal behavior); and, reintegration into the family or community in particular, and into the larger society in general (assumption and demonstration of normative, i.e, appropriate social roles and responsibilities).

The purpose of this chapter, and the next one, is to develop a foundation from which a framework for correctional case management counseling intervention with offenders can be developed. This is accomplished in the chapter as the authors:

1. Present a theoretical base that can support correctional case management.

2. Describe the steps in the correctional case management prob-
    lem-solving process.

3. Describe correctional case management generalist techniques.

Theoretical Base

A number of therapeutic approaches exist that contain viable methods for
correctional counseling with offenders. In the opinion of the authors, the degree
and extent of social and psychological syndromes and disorders that one is likely to encounter in a cohort group of parolees and probationers are likely to be
widespread. Therefore, virtually any approach, ranging from supporting and
sustaining strategies (relationship strategies) thorough psychotherapies (insight-
oriented strategies) of various sorts may be applicable. There may be, however,
some specific treatment methods of choice with offenders. The authors believe
that this is accurate with respect to what has been variously described in the
counseling and psychological literature as the "cognitive" or "cognitive-behavioral" or "social learning" perspectives.

The argument may be developed as follows. Community-based correctional counseling is a type of mental health counseling that is directed at criminal
offenders. These type of clients are generally non-voluntary. The primary counseling goal with these types of clients is to prevent them from offending or re-
offending (recidivism). Commission of an offense may result in the revocation
of probation or parole, and this often leads to imprisonment. Correctional counseling, by definition, must operate to externally manage, direct, compel, and
reward pro-social and appropriate behaviors by parolees and probationers.
Therefore, correctional counseling may be viewed as a particular type of
behavioral treatment approach. The externalization aspects of behavioral methods implicit in this approach can be naturally combined in clinical practice
with cognitive methods. This results in a hybrid approach that the authors will,
from here on, refer to as the "cognitive-behavioral" method. Beck, with various
colleagues, was largely responsible for the development of this approach (Beck
& Weishaar, 1989). Recent examples of this synthesis may be seen in the work
of Freeman, Pretzer, Fleming, and Simon (1990).

The two methods have a natural counseling complimentarity because, in
combination, they are directed toward the internal and external dimensions of
the client and of his or her problems. The approach is, sui generis, psychosocial.
Although more additional systematic research is needed, there is some research
evidence to suggest that such combined approaches may be effective with
clients in criminal justice settings, and, particularly, with delinquents (Kennedy,
1984; Hains & Hains, 1988).

To further understand this approach, one needs to explore its theoretical
roots, and consider some of its contemporary definitions. The writers believe
that the general theoretical formulations for the cognitive-behavioral approach

originated with Adler as a consequence of certain disagreements that he had with Freud about the process of psychological development. In expressing his concept of "individual psychology," Adler attached greater importance to the influence of the environment, life-style, and distorted attitudes and behaviors of patients as factors in personality development rather than, for example, certain other personality factors such as the libido and the unconscious (Weiss, 1973).

Since Adler, and essentially in a revisionistic fashion, the original theoretical formulations in this approach have served to sprout a constellation of related theoretical notions; each, in many cases, identified by its originator. Numerous examples can be cited. The "rational psychotherapy" (later to be called "rational emotive therapy") approach of Ellis (1962), with its emphasis upon the client's ability to cognitively distinguish between and act upon rational versus irrational belief systems, has direct applications for correctional counseling with offenders. Glasser's (1965) "reality therapy" is probably the best known of the cognitive therapies. In differentiating between reality therapy and conventional psychotherapy, Glasser makes a key point about his approach which is instructive for correctional counselors: "We emphasize the morality of behavior. We face the issue of right and wrong which we believe solidifies the involvement" (1965:44). Other important examples of cognitive approaches that have usefulness for correctional counseling are extant in the clinical literature. The reader is directed to Greenwald (1973) and his research about direct decision theory; or, the applications of reality therapy to correctional clients by Raubolt and Bratter (1976); and, the very important work by Yochelson and Samenow (1976) which describes the dysfunctional cognitive processes of offenders, and presents a series of correctional counseling techniques to address their errors in thinking. In addition, there are some more recent approaches with offenders, which can be used on a group or individual basis, that show promise. Chief among these, in the opinion of the writers, are the works of Prendergast (1991), in treating sex offenders in correctional settings and in outpatient clinics; and, Englander-Golden and Satir's (1990) "say it straight training program," which is a research-based, multiple risk factor prevention program directed at juvenile delinquents and substance abusers.

Kendall and Braswell (1993) are correct in noting that the cognitive-behavioral approach developed from two major social-psychological mainstreams: the emergence of a behaviorist position with respect to understanding the internal mechanisms of individual self-control; and, the development of cognitive-learning theories of psychotherapy. More specifically, the cognitive-behavioral approach is a theoretical model that purports to explain the phenomena of offender behavior by conceptualizing the behavior as a product of illogical and irrational thinking manifested by behaviors that are antisocial, dysfunctional, and destructive toward the self, other persons, and the community and society in general. Werner (1986) captures it this way: "A cognitive approach holds that the principle determinant of emotions, motives, and behavior is an individual's thinking which is a conscious process" (1986:91). More definitely, for Lazarus (1976), the approach derives from learning principles, and, particularly, from social learning, cognitive processes, and behavioral principles that appear to be experimentally related to how and why individuals learn and unlearn adaptive and maladaptive behaviors. In short, the cognitive-behavioral method contains a number of concepts concerning the nature of the therapeutic relationship, the nature of personality development, and the nature of personality change, which supply the elements for an effective strategy that can be used by case management correctional counselors in order to work effectively with a variety of offenders in community-based correctional settings.

The Steps in the Correctional Case Management Problem-Solving Process

In this section of the chapter, we shall describe nine steps in the correctional case management problem-solving process. These steps represent the flow or process of doing correctional case management. In a sense, they represent an overview of what needs to be done and a structure or model for doing it. These steps are depicted in Figure 6.1.

Figure 6.1
Nine Steps in the Correctional Case Management Problem-Solving Process

1. Identification of the problems to be solved.

2. Placing the offender's problems in an historic and current context.

3. Hypothesizing about the offender's problems.

4. Deciding what data are needed in order to accept or reject the tentative assessment.

5. Obtaining the data to confirm or reject the tentative assessment.

6. Confirming the tentative assessment.

7. Designing a strategy for correctional case management counseling intervention.

8. Putting the intervention plan into action.

9. Evaluating the planned change interventions.

The process of doing correctional case management is dependent upon a thorough understanding of assessment and diagnosis (described in Chapter 4), along with a thorough understanding of classification, treatment planning and referral (described in Chapter 5). The material in these two chapters forms the basis from which an identification of the problems in social and psychological functioning derive, and suggests avenues for treatment or intervention in order to move parolees and probationers toward personal rehabilitation and societal reintegration goals. As we proceed to describe the nine steps that are involved in this process, two points need to be emphasized. First, in real life, such a process is dynamic and ongoing since data regarding the probationers and parolees change or are added and, consequently, assessments and treatment approaches are often changed or modified. Second, each step in the process is built upon the previous step; therefore, the progression is assumed to be linear. Instead, more often than not, the dynamic interaction between the offender and the case manager is uneven and characterized by periods of both acceleration and regression, and more commonly resembles a matrix.

The **first step** is the identification of the problem or problems to be solved. The problems that clients in the criminal justice system present are usually multiple in nature. These problems usually center on criminal behaviors or acts by offenders that bring them into contact with the criminal justice system. The presentation of the problem or problems in social functioning begins as the correctional case manager, via the therapeutic relationship with the client, allows the client to present his or her view of the problem, and of his or her role in its formation. In the case of multiple problems, the case manager may wish to prioritize these problems and focus on the most pressing ones. In the prioritization process, problems that can be readily addressed with the provision of concrete services, for example, economic assistance, medical services, educational services, employment services, or problems that can be managed by information and referral services, should be immediately acted upon at this stage.

The essential goal that has to occur at this step is the development of a therapeutic relationship with the client. Without such a relationship the client may not feel comfortable about entering into a planned change process. At this point it is also important that the client be emotionally or psychologically able to acknowledge that he or she has problems in social functioning which brings the client into contact with the criminal justice system. That is to say, the client has to "own the problem." The client must also be experiencing a certain amount of social and emotional stress in regard to these problems, and be motivated to the point of being willing to engage in a planned change process with the case manager. The caveat for the case manager here is to clearly understand that in order to bring about some resolution of the problems, the parolee or probationer must be willing, in a genuine and authentic way, to admit his or her role in the formation of the problems, and be motivated to use the help of the case manager. If this condition does not hold then the case manager's activities toward rehabilitation and reintegration of the client may just end up as "rescue fantasies."

Some signs that point to client modifiability include: feelings of depression, anxiety states, various manifestations of psychological and physiological stress, withdrawal, and feelings and expressions of guilt. Offenders who may not be able to profit from case management activities need to be eliminated at this point in the process. This category would include, for example, overtly psychotic or schizophrenic clients (a category of offenders not likely to be placed on probation or parole anyway), and persons with certain kinds of developmental disabilities, or with certain kinds of organic mental syndromes or brain dysfunctions which foreclose on their ability to become involved in logical discussion, appropriate communication, and conceptualization.

It is problematic as to whether or not antisocial personality disorders ought to be included. The authors believe that they ought to be included if two key points can be established: that they are able to admit their role in the problem, even if such as admission is only a surface response; and, if they show some sign of remorse or guilt about their behavior (contrary to popular belief, antisocial personalities have a conscience [superego]; albeit, an infantile or deficient or defective one). In short, clients who do not have the emotional or psychological capacity and ability to understand and act upon the real world of the "here and now" usually cannot be helped by cognitive-behavioral methods because these are reality-level therapies.

The question becomes, then, what types of offenders are suitable planned change targets for case managers? The types of problematic behaviors presented below are a suggested, but not exhaustive, list:

1. Persons with certain kinds of disorders of infancy, childhood, or adolescence, for example: conduct disorders, or using a legal term: juvenile delinquents.

2. Persons with psychoactive substance-induced or substance-use organic mental disorders, for example: alcohol, amphetamine, cannabis, cocaine, hallucinogen, inhalant, opiod, and phencyclidine types.

3. Persons with certain kinds of sexual disorders (paraphilias), principally: exhibitionism, pedophilia, and voyeurism.

4. Persons with impulse control disorders, for example, kleptomania, and pyromania.

5. Individuals with certain kinds of personality disorders; and, especially: the antisocial personality disorder.

6. Persons with problems in personal relationships, including interpersonal relationship problems in parental, marriage, and family functioning; and, problems in relationship to other siblings, parents, relatives, friends, co-workers, and employers. Symptoms include difficulties in role relationships, communication problems, sexual dysfunctions, problems in parenting skills, child abuse and neglect, spouse battering, and anxiety often expressed via hostility, anger, aggression, irritability, withdrawal, depression, suicidal ideations, and self-mutilation and self-destructive behaviors.

The **second step** has to do with placing the client's problems in both an historic and present context. The major activity that the case manager becomes involved in at this point is that of data gathering in terms of the broad sociopsycho-environmental context of the client. The case manager at this juncture is "looking over the terrain" of the probationer or parolee with respect to the most pressing social problems that were presented in the previous step, while simultaneously gathering data that will result in a better understanding of the client. The point is to develop an ecological perspective about the parolee or probationer. Sources for these data include family members and relatives, friends, co-workers, employers, and all sorts of collaterals that are or have been important in the client's psychological and sociological life space. These sources should also include other agencies and services that the probationer or parolee may have used in the past. From all of these sources the case manager begins to get an idea of the nature and scope of the probationer or parolee's social problems, and some inkling about how to intervene in terms of problem resolution.

During the **third step**, the case manager hypothesizes about the client's problems in social functioning. This is done as he or she synthesizes the data presented by the client in step one with the data about the client's social and psychological environment obtained during step two. What the case manager should do here is to speculate about the cause-effect relationships among these data. This step results in a tentative diagnosis or assessment of the problem or problems in social functioning.

At **step four** the case manager must go about confirming the tentative assessment that had been developed in step three. At this point the case manager begins to focus his or her thinking about what kinds of additional data are needed, and how one would go about obtaining these data in order to accept or reject the tentative assessment.

Step five involves the operationalization of step number four. Here, the case manager begins an active process of obtaining data with respect to the specific confirmation or denial of the tentative assessment. In contrast to step number two, the focus here is very narrow. This is the point at which the case manager may examine various reports and documents concerning the client. Now, various types of tests and measurements may be used, such as: health and medical examinations, psychometric tests, educational measurements, work and vocational evaluations, and so forth. This is also the point at which one may wish to consult with other human service experts such as psychiatrists, clinical psychologists, clinical social workers, physicians, nurses, and counselors/therapists of various sorts. It may also become necessary to refer the offender for additional testing or evaluation if needed. At this step in the process the case manager is trying to obtain highly focused data concerning the problems of the offender in order that he or she can have some degree of confidence concerning the assessment. A kind of "sorting out" concerning the validity of problems in social functioning has to occur here.

At **step six**, the case manager should have arrived at a point where the data that he or she has obtained strongly suggests that the tentative assessment of the offender's problems in social functioning appears to be accurate. At this point, the tentative assessment may also seem to suggest or support a plan of treatment or planned intervention with respect to the modification or remediation of the social problems in order to facilitate the rehabilitation of the offender and to promote his or her reintegration into society. If this seems to be the case, the case manager should feel confident about formulating his or her plan of action for planned change intervention. If this comfort level has not been achieved, then the case manager needs to continue to gather and evaluate the data base. Particular scrutiny should be directed at the client's view of the problems and at data from collateral sources; especially, data derived from persons that are socioculturally and emotionally close to the client, that is to say "significant others." A reiteration of steps one to four may be in order.

In **step seven**, the case manager draws-up a design or strategy for intervention. Such a plan always includes a set of short-term and long-term (more than one year) planned intervention goals, along with a set of actions or techniques, expressed in behavioral terms, to accomplish these goals. These goals and sets of actions are tailored to each of the parolee or probationer's social and psychological problems. The plan must always involve the case manager and the client in the change process. Intervention plans must recognize the principle that case managers intervene with and on behalf of the client. There has to be mutuality, agreement, and therapeutic work by both parties. Sometimes it is important to reduce both sets of activities to a written contract or case management grid (see Enos & Hisanaga, 1978). This type of procedure helps to strengthen the client's acknowledgment of the problems and foster responsibility for working toward their resolution.

Step eight is the actual "doing" of the intervention. It is the putting into action of the planned change strategy. Implementation of the treatment plan with respect to the use of correctional case management generalist intervention techniques will be described in the next section of this chapter. The use of correctional case management counseling intervention techniques will be discussed in Chapter 7.

The last step, **step nine**, refers to evaluating the planned change efforts. It should be understood that evaluation occurs on an ongoing basis as the work continues with the client, even when the goals are not yet completed. Evaluation also occurs at termination; whether the goals have been achieved or not, or are incomplete. In the instance of incomplete goals, the case manager must constantly monitor the client's progress toward attaining the goals and the effects of the interventions. If progress toward the goals is not being effectuated, or if the goals have not been achieved within the timeframe for the intervention effort, the case manager must begin a review of the steps in the intervention process. He or she must closely examine the data bases in steps one and two of the process to determine if the data are reliable. Consideration must also be directed at the assessment to determine if the assessment was accurate.

At termination, a final evaluation also must occur with respect to the goals that have not been achieved. Again, the case manager must look at the data bases in steps one and two as well as his or her assessment of the problems in social function. With respect to goal attainment, examining the data bases and the assessment serves as a kind of feedback loop. In areas where the interventions are not or have not been successful, an examination of the data bases serves as a corrective. In the examination new data may become apparent or the data may be viewed in alternate ways. This, in turn, will affect the assessment, and ultimately may cause the case manager to venture into different intervention avenues.

There are a number of quasi-experimental types of clinical outcome models available for the evaluation of individual or group case management goals. The nine steps in the psychosocial assessment process can fit nicely into these types of single-subject, group or multi-group designs (Jayaratne & Levy, 1979; Posavac & Carey, 1980; Kazdin & Tuma, 1982). The authors recommend their use when case managers desire a more quantitative and less impressionistic evaluation of the degree of attainment of the case management goals.

The Correctional Case Manager Generalist

We shall now proceed to describe the role behaviors of the correctional case manager as a generalist practitioner. In doing this, we will focus upon some techniques that he or she can use in order to bring about change with respect to the behavior of an offender. These techniques include: case finding, networking, advocacy, enabling, setting limits on behavior, professional intervention, and support (see Figure 6.2).

Figure 6.2
Correctional Case Management Generalist

A generalist practitioners who directs his or her counseling efforts toward the external (social/environmental) world of the offender.

Techniques

Case Finding
Networking
Advocacy
Enabling
Setting Limits on Behavior
Professional Intervention
Support

The correctional case manager, as a generalist, directs his or her counseling energies toward the external world of the offender. This can be thought of as a kind of meso- or macro-level intervention approach, and is characterized by the correctional case manager acting on behalf of the client in relation to a variety of social systems and social institutions of various types and sizes. In this role, the case manager is principally interested in linking the offender with a wide array of social welfare and social services from which he or she may obtain appropriate resources which can then be used to assist in personal rehabilitation and reintegration into society. More specifically, the correctional case manager as a generalist, is interested in linking the offender with concrete services, such as: social welfare income maintenance programs; food, clothing, and housing assistance programs; physical, rehabilitative, vocational, and educational training programs; and, health promotion, medical treatment, and health maintenance programs. In addition, the correctional case manager as a generalist also strives to link the offender with appropriate community based mental health programs. Such programs may include: public and private (nonprofit) individual, family, and group mental health, psychotherapy, and counseling services; support groups; and, various peer-counseling and self-recovery programs which are of particular value to the addicted parolee and probationer and his/her family such as Alcoholics Anonymous (AA), Moderation Management (MM), and Narcotics Anonymous (NA). These kinds of activities generally involve the case manager generalist in a broad range of networking or professional liaison activities with other professional helping persons and with community agencies. Thus, the case manager as generalist must have a good awareness of the number and types of social service and social welfare service agencies in his or her community. He or she must also understand the structure, function, and services available via the programs in these agencies.

The case manager generalist must also have a diagnostic understanding of the particular rehabilitative and reintegration needs of his/her clients, their motivation for rehabilitation and reintegration, and the quality and levels of their physical, intellectual, educational, and emotional capacities in relation to how these might be brought to bear on the efforts toward rehabilitation and reintegration. This is a necessary condition in order to make a good therapeutic match between the offender and the specific agency program or service, or perhaps the specific individual or type of service personnel that the offender may need via referral. In the experience of the writers, it is most important to make a good match between the idiosyncratic needs of an offender and a particular service provider.

Case Finding

In this role, the case manager generalist functions as a social epidemiologist. In this sense it is an outreach role that encompasses early identification of problems in the social and physical environment that may pose current or future risks for the client. Having identified some of these risk factors, the case manager generalist must then try to prevent them from impinging upon or altering the course of successful rehabilitation and reintegration by the offender. It is a primary case management technique that consists of detection and prevention.

There are numerous minefields in the parolee or probationer's social and physical environment. The primary area of analysis for the case manager in the case finding role is the family. The case manager needs to view the family as an organically inter-connected system consisting of at least three subsystems: its structure, its level of interaction, and its developmental history.

In terms of an analysis of the structure of the family, several areas need to be evaluated. This sort of analysis begins with an examination of the composition of the family, including primary family members as well as extended family members, and persons who are not related but who interact with the family. Within the infrastructure of the family, the case manager must evaluate the nature and quality of the interrelationships between and among the family members. This includes an evaluation of the relationships among several subsystems including the marital pair, the marital pair as parents, the siblings, and relationships with other subsystems outside the kinship boundaries of the family. The key issue here is the extent to which the family is cohesive or nonintact. One way to evaluate the structure of a family has to do with the issue of socialization. Socialization refers to the process by which individuals acquire the social values and norms of the family or the community, or of society in general. Disorganized and dysfunctional families often consist of parents who are abusive or neglectful, or who present faulty models of socialization and learning for their children. Minuchin's seminal work (1967) concerning structural family therapy, presents some important elements that characterize the kinds of organized and disorganized families under discussion here.

Networking

This role is sometimes described in the literature about generic or generalist or case work practice as the "broker" or "linkage" role. In this role, the case manager may apply several networking techniques on behalf of the offender in order to facilitate a successful counseling experience. Networking cannot be successful unless the case manager understands the structural and functional aspects of the community in which he or she works. The case manager also has to have a good deal of technical expertise about various programs and services for which his or her client may be eligible. It is also predicated upon the case manager having a profile in the community's criminal justice and social services arenas. The case manager, therefore, will need to establish a network of professional and collateral contacts that could be utilized in order to secure needed services for the client.

Sometimes networking can be conducted at arms-length via a process of information and referral. In addition, many communities now have computerized information and referral services networks. Networking, however, often must transcend the technological and informational levels. It works best when it becomes personalized. This means that to be successful, a case manager must know the service delivery system not only in terms of its programs and services but also in terms of its personnel. Networking means utilizing the human, personal touch in order to help an offender access the social and rehabilitation services systems. Often, it is built upon a reciprocal or quid-pro-quo basis. The key element, however, is the quality and efficiency of the interpersonal-interprofessional network that the case manager as generalist builds and cultivates.

Advocate

Sometimes the case manager has to act more assertively or aggressively on behalf of offenders in order to help them achieve their reintegration or rehabilitation goals. This occurs when the opportunity structure of social services is blocked, fragmented, incomplete, or simply does not exist. When these kinds of situations occur in a community the case manager often must advocate on behalf of his or her client.

The advocacy role can be played-out in a number of ways. The case manager may lobby on behalf of his or her client by virtue of presenting technical or factual data in the client's favor for admission to a program or service. The argument may also be fashioned in a rational-logical mode via a consideration of the advantages and disadvantages of developing a particular program in the community or a special service in an existing agency. Sometimes, the effort may center on a humanistic consideration of the client and his or her family circumstances when advocating for the admission of the offender into a program or for extending the eligibility of certain services to the offender. Or, an appeal can be directed at various agency directors for coordination of various programs and services, or to individual agency directors concerning the issue of closing gaps in fragmented service areas. Sometimes the argument can be formulated in terms of a crisis. Here, the case manager can argue the need for a program with respect to the danger posed to a community if it does not have such a program. Many programs for the control of drug dealing in neighborhoods, for example, have come about through the use of this technique.

The advocate, of course, has to lobby or argue persuasively or, perhaps, confront various audiences. The range of such audiences, in both the public and private sectors, might range across individual program or service providers or executives; community criminal justice advisory groups; social services councils; various city, municipality, county, or state human services councils, commissions or boards; or, certain political, financial, religious, or educational elites. Obtaining memberships in, or serving on some of these boards or councils, may facilitate the advocacy role. In this case, the membership, per se, serves as a secondary gain for the case manager. Ultimately, the case manager generalist as a successful advocate wants to achieve two things: first, the development of needed service opportunities for his or her clients; and, in a more ideologically derived sense, the humanizing of social and human service bureaucracies on behalf of their clients.

Enabler

In utilizing the enabler technique, the case manager helps the offender make maximal use of appropriate programs and services in the community. Many types of enabling activities are apparent. For example, a basic stance is one of describing and discussing information about various programs or services and the array of associated options, contingencies, and opportunity costs associated with each program or service with the offender. This is followed by encouraging the offender to act upon the information. A discussion of options, contingencies, or opportunity costs is often effective with offenders who are resistant to act upon service options. Explaining the risk (contingency) of the possibility of a revocation of probation if the offender fails to act on a service opportunity, for example enroll in a drug treatment program, can be highly persuasive with these kinds of offenders.

Another stance might involve the expression of a professional opinion concerning the importance or the need for the client to use certain programs or services. This kind of enabling is important for offenders who may have certain psychological, organic, or developmental deficiencies that make it difficult for them to make responsible or rational choices. Sometimes they need to float upon the ego of the case manager who makes the choices for them. Many offenders who are neurotic (characterized by high levels of fear and anxiety) or mentally retarded, for example, fit into this category. Sometimes the case manager may have to take these kinds of clients in hand in order to enable them to use the service opportunities.

There are some important considerations in the enabling process that need to be considered. The enabling process must first be tempered with an understanding by the case manager that the program or service that he or she is promoting is appropriate for the offender, and that the offender should have a reasonable chance of success in the program. Second, the case manager cannot enable clients to act on a goal unless they are willing or motivated to take action. The case manager cannot create motivation. He or she can, however, promote offenders toward motivation by support, reassurance, encouragement, and, when appropriate, by persuasion. Concerning persuasion, sometimes the process of logical discussion, when directed at the client and his or her problematic life situation, may stimulate a measure of anxiety, or perhaps create a crisis state that may cause them to become motivated to make use of a service. Case managers must not use force or coercion. Similarly, they cannot want or wish for their clients to accomplish something out of their (case managers') own needs for self-reassurance, ego-gratification, or self-aggrandizement. Conversely, the case manager generalist must respect the offender's right to self-determination in terms of acting on service options, even if that self-determination is ultimately exercised in a self-defeating way. Sometimes counseling success derives from failure because failure may create a sense of crisis and urgency in offenders, which could serve to mobilize and motivate them to take action. But, self-determination with clients in the criminal justice system is always predicated upon legal constraints and prohibitions. One cannot allow self-determination to be acted-upon in a way that is destructive to self or society.

Setting Limits on Behavior

This technique refers to an activity on the part of the correctional case manager by which the boundaries that will circumscribe the behavior of an offender are identified and enforced. These boundaries began with the limits on behavior and the standards for normative behavior that were prescribed by the judicial order with respect to his or her placement in a community-based correctional setting.

Behavioral expectations and limits on behavior were also established during steps seven and eight of the problem-solving process as the long-term and short-term counseling goals were developed, the actions and techniques to accomplish these goals were determined, and the roles of the case manager and the offender in terms of achieving the goals were delineated. Limits have to be specific and clearly and unambiguously communicated. Limits also have to be realistic in the sense that they have to be manageable by the offender. The offender must also clearly understand the consequences that are attached to violations of the limits. For example, if a counseling session is missed, a clearly defined consequence must follow. It is especially important that limit setting be enforced whenever there is any demonstration of behavior that is or may be potentially dangerous to the offender or to other persons. Failure to follow through on violations of limits, or ignoring violations, tends to re-enforce psychologically pathological and socially deviant behaviors.

An additional point about setting limits must be noted. There are limits to the nature of the counseling relationship. For example, the correctional counselor does not interact socially with offenders, see them outside of counseling sessions, loan them money, co-sign a note, or share or disclose parts of the counselor's personal history that are not appropriate to share. There are other areas of interpersonal interaction, as well, that each counselor needs to identify and isolate from the counseling relationship.

Professional Intervention

Professional intervention refers to techniques used by the correctional case manager that are principally directed at changing the social environment of the offender. Often, offenders lack the assertiveness, maturity, or confidence to act on their own behalf to change problematic environmental situations. In some cases, they do not have the educational, intellectual, or social skills to enable them to effectively deal with many of the problems that they face in the community. In such cases, it may be necessary for the case manager to act for them. The case manager may act on behalf of the client, with the client, or together with significant others who are closely tied to the client.

A number of examples can illustrate the use of this technique. For example, the case manager may accompany an offender to a job interview, help an offender enroll in an educational or vocational training program, enroll the offender in a health program, or take them to an outpatient mental health clinic program. In some situations, the correctional case manager may act more unilaterally. For example, they may intervene on behalf of the offender with the manager of a housing complex, find the offender a new place to live, or meet with a potential employer in order to help secure a job for the client. Numerous other examples are readily apparent.

Professional intervention is not just "doing" for the client. The use of this technique is primarily designed to facilitate several processes within the offender. First, it allows the offender to temporarily rely upon the personality and ego strength of the counselor in order to help complete a task that the offender, at that particular time, was unable to accomplish. In the second instance, it may result in the solution of some short-term problems. As a secondary gain, the solution of short-term problems may serve to free up the emotional energies of the offender and to relieve stress. When freed up in this way, the offender may then be able to focus his or her energies upon solving other, more significant and pressing problems. It should be remembered that it is probably difficult for an offender to gain much from a counseling encounter if he or she is hungry, worried about being out of a job, or has been evicted from an apartment. The third value of the use of this technique is more subliminal and psychoeducational in nature. As the case manager intervenes professionally on behalf of the offender, a demonstration of behavior concerning socially acceptable ways of dealing with problems is being communicated to the offender. Sometimes, offenders will internalize these kinds of pro-social behaviors by unconscious imitation. This phenomena will be discussed in more detail in Chapter 7.

The professional intervention technique consists of a number of activities that are generally designed to deal with short run and crisis oriented problems. The technique is directed at the vagaries of an offender's social environment. Albeit, sometimes we may only be dealing with the symptoms of the problems. To be more effective, the correctional counselor needs to show the offender how to manage these kinds of problems by himself or herself. The case manager cannot continue to solve environmental problems for the client. Continuing on that path will result in increasing dependency. This may lead to an inability of the offender to take charge of his or her life circumstances.

Support

Support is the last of the generalist intervention techniques. Support refers to the process of giving the offender encouragement and reassurance. There are at least three situations when support can be used effectively. In the first instance, support is used to give an offender a sense of hope, and to try to persuade and convince the offender that he or she has chosen a right course of action by entering into the counseling relationship. It is a type of activity that tries to convey to the offender the idea that someone cares, that perhaps something can be done, and that we can work together to overcome the problems. It is a form of reassurance that is used to help sustain the offender/case manager relationship. Support is demonstrated to the offender by the nature of the counseling relationship. It occurs when the relationship is constructed by the counselor in such as way as to inspire confidence in the capabilities of the counselor, and in the belief in the innate abilities of the client to overcome his or her problems. It is a kind of existential moment during which the offender comes to see that he or she can take responsibility for personal contingencies and responsibilities, and that he or she has the power to balance out freedom with authority. It starts with the attitude of: "I'm glad that you have come; now let's work together to solve your problems."

In the second instance, it can be used when the offender seems to have the ability and capacity to act effectively but is hesitant about his or her ability to be successful. If it appears that the action that the offender wants to take, or the behavior that he or she wants to change, can be realistically accomplished; then, the case manager should communicate support for this activity or change. It is intended to communicate to the offender a "can-do attitude." It is an activity that provides a kind of psychological push for a reluctant person who may have a poor self-concept. It is a type of "hurdle help."

In the third instance, support can be used to reinforce positive actions and behaviors. This step follows from the previous one. It gives recognition for positive accomplishments. Every step toward positive change, even little hesitant ones, should be rewarded verbally and nonverbally by communicating support and approval. It is a reinforcement of the attitude, attributed to Mao Tse Tung, that a journey of a thousand miles beings with a single step. We need to reward even little positive "baby steps" taken toward rehabilitation. In many cases, the approval is often communicated in an exaggerated way, not for hyperbole, but for emphasis. Approval of positive behavior needs to be communicated emphatically.

In using the technique of support, the case manager generalist begins to shift the focus in working with the offender from social and environmental concerns toward the attitudes, values, and behavior of the offender. As such, support is a technique that bridges generalist intervention techniques with correctional counseling techniques. These techniques will be discussed in detail in the following chapter.

Conclusions

The chapter began with the writers expressing the point of view that in order to be an effective correctional counselor one should align with a central value held by professional counselors of all types: the need for and the importance of the rehabilitation of the offender. This point is clearly oppositional to the idea of punishment and retribution. This difference may be explained by understanding that institutionalization of offenders, via imprisonment, stresses management and control of behavior. By contrast, correctional counseling primarily takes place in community-based, deinstitutionalized settings. By definition, the point of deinstitutionalization was to offer an alternative to institutionalization in the hope that the proximity of the family, neighborhood, and community would have a therapeutic milieux effect (Jones, 1953; Cumming & Cumming, 1968). As the writers view it, the key to change in behavior by the offender comes about through the interpersonal encounter between the counselor and the client, or as a consequence of a therapeutic encounter among various persons in a group counseling setting. In addition to a commitment to the ideal of rehabilitation, this point represents a second value stance that is very important for correctional counselors to incorporate. One cannot become an effective correctional counselor if one has difficulties in understanding and empathizing with clients and with their personal, family, or community problems. Correctional counselors, in their own neurotic way, seem to believe that they can make a difference by professional involvement in problem-solving activities with offenders and with their families and communities. People who are uncomfortable in this type of role are perhaps personally better suited to the law enforcement or administration of justice aspects of criminal justice. The profession is expansive enough to incorporate many types of personalities and viewpoints.

In addition, the writers presented a theoretical base that could effectively underpin correctional case management counseling: cognitive-behavioral theory. This theory essentially represents a blending of behavioral notions that have to do with understanding the inner, psychological world of an individual, along with an emphasis, beginning with Adler, toward developing psychotherapies that focus on the cognitive and learning aspects of individual personalities. The cognitive-behavioral approach has a great deal of relevance for case management correctional counseling because it forces the offender to examine his or her thinking errors, and also because it requires an acknowledgment of deviant behaviors by the offender. It is these aspects of reality therapy that make it useful for correctional counselors in their everyday work with offenders.

In this chapter the writers also described nine steps that encompass the process of doing case management correctional counseling. The nine steps provide an overview of what needs to be done with and for the offender, as well as a model or structure for doing it. The steps included:

1. Identifying the problems.

2. Placing the problems in an historic and present context.

3. Hypothesizing about the problems and developing a tentative diagnosis or assessment.

4. Examining the need for additional data to support the tentative assessment.

5. Confirming or rejecting the tentative assessment.

6. Accepting the tentative assessment.

7. Drawing up a design or strategy of planned change interventions.

8. Implementing the interventions.

9. Evaluating the planned change efforts.

Finally, correctional case management, from the standpoint of generalist practice, was described. It was viewed as a systematic process by which identified strengths and weaknesses of the offender were matched with appropriate treatment programs and services in the community. More precise specifications of the case manager generalist techniques were also presented, including the:

1. Case finder technique.

2. Networker technique.

3. Advocate technique.

4. Enabler technique.

5. Setting limits on behavior technique.

6. Professional intervention technique.

7. Support technique.

Correctional case management generalist techniques can be thought of as a series of actions or strategies that the case manager engages in with and on behalf of offenders in order to affect their social and physical environments. The intention is to impact and change or modify these environments in some sort of concrete or direct way. The areas for change, modification, or adjustment in the offender's life derive from the assessment, diagnostic, classification, and treatment planning and referral process. The case manager generalist functions as a sociotherapist rather than as a psychotherapist, in order to help the parolee or probationer achieve his or her treatment goals of rehabilitation and reintegration into society.

References

Beck, A.T. & M. Weishaar (1989). "Cognitive Therapy." In A. Freeman, K.M. Simon, L.E. Beutler & H. Arkowitz (eds.) (1989). *Comprehensive Handbook of Cognitive Therapy*. New York, NY: Plenum Press.

Cumming, J. & E. Cumming (1968). *Ego and Milieu*. New York, NY: Atherton Press.

Ellis, A. (1962). *Reason and Emotion in Psychotherapy*. New York, NY: Lyle Stuart.

Englander-Golden, P. & V. Satir (1990). *Say it Straight*. Palo Alto, CA: Science and Behavior Books.

Enos, R. & M. Hisanaga (1978). "Goal Setting with Pregnant Teenagers." *Child Welfare*, 58:541-552.

Freeman, A., J. Pretzer, B. Fleming & K.M. Simon (1990). *Clinical Applications of Cognitive Therapy*. New York, NY: Plenum Press.

Glasser, W. (1965). *Reality Therapy*. New York, NY: Harper and Row.

Greenwald, H. (1973). *Direct Decision Theory*. San Diego, CA: Edits.

Hains, A.A. & A.H. Hains (1988). "Cognitive-Behavioral Training of Problem-Solving and Impulse Control with Delinquent Adolescents." *Journal of Offender Services and Rehabilitation*, 12:95-113.

Jayaratne, S. & R.L. Levy (1979). *Empirical Clinical Practice*. New York, NY: Columbia University Press.

Jones, M. (1953). *The Therapeutic Community*. New York, NY: Basic Books.

Kazdin, A.E. & A.H. Tuma (eds.). (1982). *Single-Case Research Designs*. San Francisco, CA: Jossey-Bass.

Kendall, P.C. & L. Braswell (1993). *Cognitive-Behavioral Therapy for Impulsive Children* (Second Edition). New York, NY: The Guilford Press.

Kennedy, R.E. (1984). "Cognitive Behavior Interventions with Delinquents." In A. Meyers & W.E. Craighead (eds.) *Cognitive Behavior Therapy with Children* (pp. 351-376). New York, NY: Plenum Press.

Lazarus, A.A. (1976). "Introduction and Overview." In A.A. Lazarus (ed.) *Multimodal Behavior Therapy*. New York, NY: Springer Publishing Co.

Minuchin, S. (1974). *Families and Family Therapy*. Cambridge, MA: Harvard University Press.

Posavac, E. & R. Carey (1980). *Program Evaluation*. Englewood Cliffs, NJ: Prentice-Hall.

Prendergast, W. (1991). *Treating Sex Offenders in Correctional Institutions and Outpatient Clinics*. New York, NY: Springer Publishing Co.

Raubolt, R.R. & T.E. Bratter (1976). "Treating the Methadone Addict." In A. Bassin, T.E. Bratter & R.R. Rachin (eds.) *The Reality Therapy Reader* (pp. 326-344). New York, NY: Harper and Row.

Weiss, D. (1973). *Psychoanalytic Schools from the Beginning to the Present Day*. New York, NY: Jason Aronson.

Werner, H.D. (1986). "Cognitive Theory." In F.J. Turner (ed.) *Social Work Treatment: Interlocking Theoretical Approaches* (Third Edition) (pp. 91-130). New York, NY: Free Press.

Yochelson, S. & S.E. Samenow (1976). *The Criminal Personality: Volume II, the Change Process*. New York, NY: Jason Aronson.

Chapter 7

Counseling Intervention Techniques

Introduction

The purpose of this chapter is to address, in some detail, the process and method of correctional case management intervention through the use of counseling techniques. More specifically, we will describe, apply, and present examples of counseling techniques which the case manager can use with offenders. Three techniques will be examined: confronting problematic behaviors; engaging the personality dynamics of the offender; and, exploring the developmental history of the offender. These techniques are depicted in Figure 7.1.

Figure 7.1
Correctional Case Management Intervention Counseling Techniques

Purpose

These three techniques are used selectively and differentially in order to help offenders obtain insight and change in behavior.

Techniques

1. Confronting problematic behaviors.
2. Engaging the personality dynamics of the offender.
3. Exploring the developmental history of the offender.

The counseling techniques compliment the generalist techniques that were discussed in the previous chapter. Like the generalist techniques, the counseling techniques are based upon an understanding of the material from Chapter 4 concerning the assessment and diagnostic process. The information concerning classification, treatment planning, and referral described in Chapter 5 is also very relevant. In addition, the problem-solving process, described in Chapter 6, provides a model or structure for implementing these techniques.

In contrast to the correctional case manager as a generalist, the case manager as a counselor directs his or her professional energies toward the internal or personal, emotional, and psychological world of the offender. It is a world inhabited by the feelings of the offender, and by his or her interpretations of those feelings. Therefore, the focus of the counseling effort is upon the intrinsic aspects of the persona. It is an approach that uses a series of techniques that are directed at the cognitive, affective, and behavioral domains of the offender. The goals of rehabilitation and reintegration of offenders into society can, ultimately, only be accomplished in a full sense if offenders, through the vehicle of the counseling process, obtain insight and understanding concerning their: cognitive or thinking distortions; dysfunctional affective moods, feelings, and emotions; and, pathological and socially deviant behaviors. Furthermore, they stand only a slim chance of rehabilitation unless the correctional counseling process challenges them to change or modify the problematic aspects of these areas of functioning.

The case manager as a generalist, and the case manager as a counselor, should not be viewed as dichotomies or as distinctive and separate areas for correctional case management activities. In many cases, the kinds of problems that offenders bring to the case management professional can usually be dealt with by the use of generalist intervention techniques. However, offenders, like other persons with problems in social and psychological functioning inhabit, at the same time, both an external social world and an internal psychological world. Because of this, case management correctional activities must include the use of parallel, and often simultaneous generalist and counseling techniques in order to achieve real change.

Understanding the Use of the Counseling Intervention Techniques

In Chapter 6 we presented the rationale for the use of the cognitive-behavioral approach with offenders. To reiterate, the cognitive-behavioral approach developed from a synthesis of certain behavioral positions that sought to explain the inner psychological mechanisms of individual self-control, with the emergence of psychotherapies that tended to view behavior as a product of conscious and learning processes. The areas of cognitive and behavioral dysfunctions that this method is principally directed at have been largely identified by Freeman, Pretzer, Fleming, and Simon (1990). They have described a number of methods for challenging, controlling, and eliminating various kinds of "dysfunctional automatic thoughts and cognitive distortions [and] maladaptive beliefs and assumptions." (1990:49). In the correctional counseling literature, Yochelson and Samenow (1976) were pioneers concerning the identification of the thinking errors of offenders. They also provided key information about how to deal with these kinds of thinking errors. From our standpoint, the correctional case manager as a counselor must direct his or her counseling interventions toward correcting the dysfunctional and distorted thinking patterns of the offender. In addition, counseling energy must also be directed at nonproductive and maladaptive belief systems and incorrect assumptions about self, others, and society that many offenders carry. The counseling techniques presented in this chapter will give the correctional case manager some tools to help in accomplishing that mission.

In order to more precisely understand how to use these techniques, we must first understand the phenomena and the significance of the blending of the behaviorist individual self-control position with psychotherapeutic cognitive-behavioral methods. The key to understanding this blending has to do with the concept of insight.

Almost without exception, psychotherapeutic approaches (especially psychoanalytic, i.e., Freudian and neo-Freudian approaches) are insight-oriented change strategies. Insight-oriented therapies are directed toward giving the client insight or understanding about the genesis of his or her problematic behaviors or actions. Most differences of opinion about this point center on the role and importance of developmental history and the role of suppressed and repressed psychological material (the unconscious).

For Freud, insight meant that we could understand our striving (drives or wishes) and perhaps control or redirect them in the sense that we did not have to become prisoners of our developmental history but could, instead, act upon various choices. Acting upon choices was voluntary. Adler was more emphatic about this issue. For Adler, an individual could change the reality of his or her sense of "inferiority" by conscious actions and should be persuaded to act upon various choices by the therapist. Jung, by contrast, equated insight with a kind of universal religious order through which a person could become "saved" (Rieff, 1963).

The three variations on the theme of insight are presented by way of background so that the correctional case manager as a counselor may understand that insight is a very problematic concept. In actuality, insight may be better understood as a construct. That is, we cannot observe, empirically, by our senses, that an offender has gained insight, but we can infer, by a process of mental assembly, that such an action has occurred via a demonstration of a change in behavior or attitude. For example, an offender may have gained insight about the effect of his behavior upon someone else as he or she expresses feelings of guilt about the behavior. From the expression of guilt, we infer the attainment of insight.

In terms of the counseling activities of the correctional case manager, the writers believe that three things need to occur via the counseling interaction: the counselor must confront the offender about his or her problems in psychosocial functioning; the counselor needs to engage the offender in a process of discussing and reflecting upon the dysfunctional aspects of his or her personality dynamics or characteristics; and, the counselor needs to explore those aspects of the offenders' developmental history that may have contributed to the present problems that the he or she has in psychosocial functioning. The ultimate outcome of the use of these three techniques should be the acquisition of insight about his or her behavior by the offender. Insight development is what all three techniques have in common.

However, insight is not enough. The case manager should influence and persuade the offender to change problematic behaviors and attitudes. Offenders must be directed to act upon that insight. We believe that the case management counseling techniques that we will proceed to discuss can be used to systematically and effectively move offenders in a planned change direction.

Correctional Case Management Counseling Techniques

The counseling techniques that we will now describe are designed to:

1.   help the offender make an authentic acknowledgement of the problem. This makes the offender own the problem. This activity also helps to disabuse the offender about notions of victimization.

2.   correct errors as expressed or verbalized by illogical thinking and cognitive distortions. This kind of activity provides a means of helping offenders to refocus, reframe, and restructure their thinking processes in order to eliminate errors and distortions so as to be in conformity with normative societal values and goals.

3.   bring the offender to the point of insight or conscious awareness. This helps the offender make connections between his or her personality dynamics and behavior. It is also used to bring into consciousness the negative aspects of his or her developmental history and socialization, and the relationship of these elements to current problems in psychosocial functioning. This helps the offender locate the historical source of the problem.

Confronting Problematic Behaviors

Through the use of this technique, the case manager engages the offender in a process of logical discussion during which the offender is forced to confront and consider the following issues:

1.   His or her role in the formation of the problem.

2.   The consequences and effects of his or her behaviors and actions, both in the individual sense, as well as the impact of the behaviors or actions upon significant others and larger personal and social systems with which the offender interacts.

3.   Alternative or more socially acceptable ways of responding to problems and situations, as well as a consideration of contingencies and opportunity costs associated with various ways of responding and behaving.

This technique is used when we are sure that the offender has the ability to use and tolerate confrontation. Through confrontation about these issues, the correctional counselor brings into awareness for the offender those areas of his or her individual construction of psychological or social reality that are adverse, or in opposition to the aggregate of socially acceptable behaviors or actions. The process involves a verbal consideration of issues and options for the purposes of developing self-awareness and challenging the offender to change. Appropriate areas of problematic behavior by offenders that lend themselves to confrontation by the case manager include:

1. deceitfulness.

2. failure to control impulsive urges.

3. failure to control aggressive behavior.

4. indifference to the feelings of others.

5. irresponsible behavior.

6. inappropriate sexual urges or fantasies.

In the beginning phase of confrontation work with the offender, the case manager discusses with the offender the logical sequence of behaviors, alternatives, and consequences. Much of this kind of work is accomplished by the use of questioning. Questioning is used to identify the deviant behaviors, confirm the data that substantiates and corroborates the behavior, clarify what the behavior means to the offender, and challenge and dispute the offender's distorted view of the behavior.

In the second phase, the case manager counselor argues in favor of the positive alternatives and against the less positive choices that the client may be considering. In this part of the encounter, greater use is made of questions that are posed in a conditional tense (i.e., implying a supposition or conjecture on the part of the offender). These kinds of questions are not phrased as absolutes but, instead, require the offender to reflect upon, contemplate, or consider his or her behavior. The questions are commonly posed as "shoulds" or "coulds," for example, "What should you have done?" or "What could you have done?" The question may imply that the counselor has read the mind of the offender: "Could it be that you really wanted to...?" The question may also be constructed to make the offender label a negative behavior: "What you did really caused a lot of problems, didn't it?" Or, the question may be asked in order to personalize or make the offender acknowledge the behavior: "You really screwed up there, didn't you?" The creative case manager can devise numerous other examples.

In the third phase, it may have become necessary for the case manager to debate the offender concerning the array of alternatives, and the consequences and contingencies and opportunity costs attached to each one. The correctional counselor may have to forcefully dispute the offender's reasoning and arguments, while reiterating the importance of the socially responsible choices. It is during this last phase that many of the thinking errors and cognitive distortions of offenders are addressed, confronted, and disputed. At this point in the confrontation process, the correctional counselor is dealing with absolutes. The absolutes are expressed not as questions, but as professional opinions. The communication to the client always contains a message concerning the consequence of failure to act or change. For example, a direct interpretation by the counselor of the meaning of the behavior of the offender may be made: "I think that you really want to mess up so that you can go back to the pen." Often, the counselor may express an opinion concerning the motivation of the offender to change: "I don't think that you are really interested in participating in the A.A. meetings." Often, the counselor needs to point out "con" games: "I think that you are only saying that because you think that that's what I want to hear." The counselor can be very direct: "If you continue to act that way, your parole will be revoked." And, sometimes, paradoxical statements can be very effective: "It's ok if you come late to our counseling sessions; there are many other clients who need more time to see me." An innovative counselor can develop many variations of directive communications. The writings of Berne (1964); Watzlawick, Beavin, and Jackson (1967); and Englander-Golden and Satir (1990), are good sources of information about therapeutic communications that can be used in correctional counseling and psychotherapy.

In summary, the use of this technique is designed to confront the offender concerning his or her behavior in order to help the offender gain insight about how these behaviors may contribute to or exacerbate problems in psychosocial functioning. For example, an asocial client might be directed to consider the nature of his aggressive behavioral reactions to other people and how these kinds of actions might provoke retaliation. This can evolve via a consideration of a parolee's statement that "people are just no good and you have to get them before they get you." Here, via logical discussion, the client would be directed to reflect upon the usefulness of aggressive behavior, re-consider using more appropriate behaviors, and forced to explore the maladaptive behavioral response: the rationalization that the aggression is "ok" because people are going to "get you." With respect to the last point, the offender would be forced to consider that the rationalization might be serving to help him or her avoid stress, or self blame, or as a justification for avoiding an unpleasant task.

Engaging the Personality Dynamics of the Offender

The technique of engaging the personality dynamics of the offender is directed at making offenders consider the role their personality characteristics play in the formation, persistence and exacerbation of their problems. Hollis (1972) describes this technique as an important means in the process of dynamic understanding by the client since it causes the client to bring "reason and judgement to bear upon the characteristics of his personality and his functioning that has been brought to his attention" (1972:131). This is an important point because we know, at least intuitively, but also from some research, that offenders, as personality types, tend to deny their role in their problems. They also tend to project blame onto others. In short, as Jennings, Kilkenny, and Kohlberg (1983) found, they have problems in moral reasoning. The use of this technique also involves having the offender examine and reflect upon the means that they characteristically used to deal with feelings of guilt and anxiety about behavior. Many offenders, in the opinion of the writers, comprise personality types who commonly use certain ego defense mechanisms in stereotypical and routinized ways to deal with guilt and anxiety. These defenses routinely include: denial, rationalization, projection, and compartmentalization. In keeping with cognitive-behavioral theory, we view the use of these defenses as examples of irrational and illogical thinking that are consciously used by offenders in order to help them avoid guilt, concern, or responsibility for behaviors that are antisocial, dysfunctional, and destructive toward themselves, toward other persons, and toward the community and society in general. We thus favor Adler's position that distorted attitudes and behaviors are consciously determined and are among the key factors in personality development, rather than Freud's psychodynamic approach which emphasized the interplay among various unconscious mental processes (the id, ego, superego, libido, etc.) as the key determinants in human feelings, thoughts, ideas, and actions. By contrast, for an excellent description of the psychodynamic view concerning this issue, the reader is directed to Liebert and Spiegler (1987).

In the experience of the authors, denial is the most common form of cognitive distortion used by offenders. Denial means that offenders simply put out of consciousness responsibility for or acknowledgment of behavior. It is the most primitive and child-like of responses. Rationalization is another common example of faulty thinking used by offenders. It refers to the process of how people make connections between their behavior and the consequences that flow from the behavior. It is used by offenders to explain away deviant behavior by attributing it to other sources and, usually, to other persons. For example, an offender who has sexually molested a child might attribute that behavior to the fact that he was "high on cocaine" at the time of the molestation. Another form of faulty thinking used by offenders is projection. It refers to a process that offenders use to project or attribute their socially unacceptable and deviant wishes and desires onto others, thus creating a rationale for why they acted out. For example, offenders often state that they stole something because if they had not stolen it, someone else would have. Or, they sometimes state that they acted out because someone else disliked them. More psychologically manipulative offenders, such as anti-personality disordered offenders, have the attitude that people are "marks" to be taken advantage of. Compartmentalization is also among the principal forms of faulty and illogical thinking manifested by offenders. Compartmentalization refers to a process whereby the offender divides his personality into two parts: the expressive part and the instrumental part. For Nettler (1976), the problem in doing this is confusion between what people really want to do versus what they want to achieve. In the case of offenders, they consciously separate their feelings about the criminal act from the healthy parts of their personality. An example of this kind of behavior as a normative and vital survival skill may be may be understood by considering the phenomena of war. Soldiers in battle must consciously separate out killing the enemy from killing per se. The offender, however, uses compartmentalization in a distorted way. A mafiosi member, for example, often has a normal family life. He consciously separates his family life style from his life as a "wise guy" who maintains another life style with a mistress. In the case of sexual offenders, they sometimes compartmentalize their personalities as victims of sexual abuse as child, while at the same time, replaying that developmental script by sexually victimizing children. There are, of course, other types of ego defense mechanisms that are characteristic of offenders. We have limited our discussion to those that we believe have singular importance with respect to the personality construct of offenders.

There are two principal activities that the case manager as counselor can use in order to engage the personality dynamics of the offender in counseling. These activities are: comparing and contrasting, and substitution and sublimation. The work of Tate (1967) is informative about these activities.

In using the comparing and contrasting approach, the offender is first obliged to consider how problematic aspects of his or her personality compare and contrast with other people. The areas of disagreement, or dissonance, between the offender and normative society are uncovered, and the offender is directed toward changing aspects of his or her personality. Minimally, the case manager should direct energy toward narrowing the range of disagreements. What should occur with comparing and contrasting is a kind of values refocusing. Enos and Black (1982) have described how this can be done:

First, the distorted values and attitudes that form the persona of the offender are identified and presented to the offender by the case manager. Here, the professional responsibility of the case manager is to function as a kind of "reality test" in order to objectify and appraise the distorted values and attitudes for the offender.

Second, the case manager describes the distorted and illogical thinking processes that the offender has used to define other persons, objects, and situations. The purpose here is to help the individual understand his or her cognitive distortions. During this step, the case manager becomes the correctional representative of "every man or woman" in society for the offender. Simply put, the personality dynamics of the counselor become the personal yardstick against which the offender is evaluated.

Third, the case manager interprets the purpose that these distorted values and attitudes serve for the offender. With offenders in general, the purposes that these kinds of values and attitudes serve are to isolate and defend their personalities from feelings of guilt for deviant behavior, or to absolve them from taking responsibility for their behavior. Offenders who are antisocial personalities, or con artists, spend a great deal of emotional energy trying to distance their personalities from feelings of guilt. This is why these types of persons are sometimes referred to as "psychopaths." Neurotic offenders, such as those we characterize as having high levels of fear and anxiety, spend much of their psychic energy dealing with overwhelming and punishing guilt about their behavior. This is characteristic, for example, of some kinds of sexual offenders.

Fourth, the case manager defines the offender's behavior as dysfunctional. The case manager then incorporates the areas of change in values and attitudes by the offender as planned change goals in the treatment plan. Change in behavior with respect to the attainment of these goals is regularly monitored and evaluated. Progress toward the attainment of these goals may determine the continuance or discontinuance of the offender in a community-based correctional setting.

An example at this point might further clarify the process of implementing the use of the technique of engaging the personality dynamics of the offender:

A female offender who lives in a psychologically retreatist subculture of drug addiction and prostitution, and whose chronic responses to life's demands are denial and repression, might be forced to consider the usefulness of these kinds of maladaptive responses. This could occur as the case manager forces this offender to clarify her expressed feelings that "no one likes or loves her and that others always take advantage of her." In this way, the client might come to understand that her personality is characterized by a weak self-concept that reinforces the belief that she is unable to take control of her life. This poses difficulties for her in life because this imagery of herself sets her up to expect that people will mistreat her. In effect, this imagery of herself moves her, like an invisible hand, toward chronic addiction and prostitution.

Through the use of comparing and contrasting, the case manager focuses upon the value and moral dimensions of the client's personality system. In the counseling and clinical literature one can find several models of treatment directed at these dimensions. Some of them appear to be effective both as tools for the diagnosis and classification of offenders, as well as for treatment. Historically, this approach evolved from the work of Aichorn (1965) with delinquent youth. Aichorn emphasized the role of education in preventing the development of anti-social attitudes, behaviors, and personalities. Later, Redl and Wineman's (1962) descriptive research about ego-defective, aggressive youth, and methods for their treatment, played a major role in helping us understand the dimensions of moral and re-educative approaches to treatment. More recently, the research of Kohlberg and his associates, which was derived in part from Piaget's (1965) research concerning moral reasoning and cognitive development in children, has been very instrumental in giving us insight about moral stages of personality development vis-à-vis the personality of the offender (Kagan & Lamb, 1985; Kohlberg, 1987). Van Kaam (1986) has also contributed some important information about moral education and correctional counseling. Van Kaam believes that correctional counseling is a form of moral education, and that it also is a means for helping offenders to become "freed up" from their morally ineffective ways of behaving. But, most importantly in the opinion of these authors, Van Kaam states that, through correctional counseling, offenders might learn to extinguish their morally ineffective reactions "after insight into their inhibitory power is gained during the counseling sessions. They may be replaced through the conditioning of morally more effective responses generated by their new openness to moral values" (1986:49).

In discussing group therapy programs that have been derived from moral development theories, Lester and Van Voorhis (1992) captured the essence of the therapeutic intention in these treatment approaches in stating that these programs attempt to "provide experiences where individuals can formulate thoughts about moral issues, discuss them with others, and be challenged in the course of these discussions" (1992:189). The following case example of a white-collar offender describes the type of personality that is an almost ideal type for personality-centered interventions directed at the offenders' value and morality makeup (Example 7.1).

Example 7.1
The Case of Gary Edward

Gary Edward, the former owner of a construction firm, was sentenced to two years of probation after he admitted that he had made a false statement while testifying during his bankruptcy trial. In addition to being placed on probation, he was fined $5,000 by the judge.

Gary Edward had agreed to sign court documents that indicated that he had hidden a stock brokerage account from his bankruptcy referee. In return for admitting his guilt in this matter, federal government prosecutors agreed to drop additional perjury and fraud changes against him. These other charges included allegations that he had hidden ownership of a luxury automobile, valuable paintings, jewelry, a coin collection, and cash from the trustee. In addition, it was alleged that he concealed his membership on a corporation board, and vastly over-reported his expenses, including rent, alimony, child care payments, and educational expenses for his children. Gary Edward was heard to say to his ex-wife after the probation hearing that "the problem with this country is there are just too damn many rules and regulations for a businessman to keep up with."

The second activity with respect to the technique of engaging the personality dynamics of the offender has been variously called substitution or sublimation. Substitution and sublimation refer to the incorporation of new and positive attitudes, values, and behaviors by the offender. The net effect is a changed personality. Incorporation occurs through an involuntary and unconscious process. Think of it in the sense of an authentic religious conversion. Although many prisoners claim to have found God in prison, some of these conversions appear to be authentic. One can note the conversion of heavyweight boxing champion Mike Tyson to the Muslim faith while recently imprisoned.

Substitution or sublimation may occur as the case manager, through inter-actions with the offender, projects or models normative, that is to say, socially and psychologically acceptable attitudes, values, and behaviors. Pullias and Young (1969) describe this process as an intrinsic part of the teaching role. In their view, a role for the teacher is to describe for students the kinds of life problems and experiences that the teacher had encountered and had dealt with successfully. Rogers (1957) made the same point when he discussed the impor-tance of the therapist to be genuine in his relationship with the client. For Rogers, genuineness meant that the therapist must be aware of himself even in ways that may be regarded as being unorthodox for therapy, such as sharing feelings with the client through self-disclosure.

If the process has been successful, the offender will have incorporated some of the attitudes, values, and behaviors of the counselor, and will play them out in his or her lifestyle. It is not really possible to measure, in any objective way, how the process of incorporation takes place. The correctional case manager may not be aware that a positive identification has taken place. However, the process may be inferred because there are often physical or verbal clues. For example, the offender might say: "I want to go to college too so that I can become a correc-tional officer (like you)." Or, the case manager might notice that, over time, the parolee may have adapted her style of dress, or the use of cosmetics, in the same manner as the case manager. Modeling behavior is a very powerful therapeutic device. Some social service agencies in the youth field are designed around this approach, for example Big Brothers and Big Sisters, Inc.

Exploring the Developmental History of the Offender

Exploring the developmental history of the offender refers to the use of a technique whereby the dynamic of developmental history (especially the impact of experiences of abuse and neglect as a child, or of faulty parental role model-ing upon the child) is explored. The correctional counselor is interested in both understanding how these negative experiences impact upon current problems in social or psychological functioning by the offender, and in communicating that association to the offender in order to help the offender gain insight.

Most of the work in applying this technique is accomplished by two activi-ties: ventilation and interpretation. For example, consider a parolee who contin-ually makes unwise romantic and relationship choices of men in her life and, as a consequence, gets caught-up in their criminal activities as a passive partici-pant. The criminal activity may be a form of compensation that helps her deal with her negative developmental experiences. This point was made by Van Kaam (1969), as he described the process by which Adler, through his observa-tion of patients, developed the construct of the "inferiority complex." Van Kaam commented that those patients who felt less important, less worthwhile, and less perfect than others used compensations of various sorts to counteract and guard against these kinds of feelings of inferiority.

With respect to the example in the previous paragraph, the case manager should help her ventilate or express emotions and feelings about her past and current relationships with all of the significant people in her life: her parents, husband, siblings, friends, and significant others. Ventilation is designed to elicit the offender's phenomenological and experiential view of his or her relationships with other people. An avenue for interpretation could occur as the offender shares with the case manager her recollections of physical abuse by her father as a child, and his statement to her that she would never be any good. Insight to help move her toward behavioral change could occur as the case manager interprets her behavior in the here and now as a kind of self-fulfilling prophecy that is being played-out through her unconscious choice of men who abuse her. Interpretation might take the form of having the offender reflect upon the counselor's supposition that her choice of men who abuse her might spring from a suppressed feeling that she has little self-worth as a consequence of the physical and emotional abuse she experienced as a child.

For some offenders, it may be more appropriate to use nonverbal means to achieve ventilation. Art, music, and poetry, for example, can be used as expressive avenues for offenders (Black & Enos, 1981). For other offenders, just getting out the bottled-up feelings brings about a powerful emotional catharsis so that they can move on to a constructive life path. Sometimes, however, ventilation is not enough. Ventilation may need to followed by interpretation so that a conscious link to behavior can be established.

A case manager must not use interpretation in order to blame someone who has been victimized, nor to stigmatize them. The purpose of interpretation is to promote understanding and insight about behavior. The recently concluded murder trial in South Carolina of Susan Smith, who had pleaded guilty to the charge of murdering her two young children and was subsequently convicted, is a case in point. Most Americans wondered why or how a mother could drown her own children. As the trial progressed, a great deal of information about Susan Smith's developmental history was revealed. One of the facts that was revealed was her history of long-standing sexual abuse by her stepfather (to which he admitted during his testimony at the trial). This dynamic helps us understand the genesis of her behavior, while not necessarily excusing, justifying, or mitigating the behavior.

Case Study

A case study will now be presented in order to further illustrate how the three correctional counseling techniques can be used with an offender. Imagine that you are the correctional counselor.

The Case of Susan Ellen

Susan Ellen is a Caucasian, 41-year-old, single mother. She has a 12-year-old son. She completed the tenth grade and has only marginal work skills. Susan Ellen has spent most of her employment life in menial positions, principally as a domestic worker. A previous boyfriend, Richard, "turned her on" to cocaine about 10 years ago. Since then, she has been addicted to it. She supports her addiction by petty theft, shoplifting, and prostitution. She was recently arrested for drug dealing. After a short term in state prison, she was released on parole. While she was in prison, her son, Craig, was placed in family foster care by the state child protective services division in her city. Craig has a congenital heart problem and requires daily medication. When Susan Ellen gained parole, her son was returned to her. However, he was recently removed from her care by the child protective services department because of chronic neglect and lack of medical supervision. Craig has been placed with another foster family. Susan Ellen is very anxious about her situation. She is also very depressed about the fate of her child. She has been assigned to your intensive supervision caseload.

You, as her correctional case manager, have referred her to the local mental health clinic. She had previously been evaluated at the clinic. Her primary diagnosis was chronic substance use and substance dependency. She is taking medication for depression. Susan Ellen is currently enrolled in a substance abuser support group at the clinic, although her attendance is irregular. She works part-time in a local convenience store. This income is augmented by a Supplemental Security Income (SSI) grant. Susan Ellen seems to be eligible for vocational rehabilitation services, and for a training or educational grant from the state labor and employment board as well. You plan to look into these possibilities with her soon. You previously helped her enroll in the general education development program at the local high school in order to help her obtain her high school equivalency diploma. She seems to be very interested in learning how to use computers.

You have been concerned for some time now about the fact that the community has no drug therapy program. There is only a support group, run by the clients, at the local mental health clinic. As a member of the city's human services resource advisory commission, you have been trying to influence the other members of the commission to support the application of the local mental health clinic for a "seed" grant from the city in order to develop a comprehensive drug abuse treatment program. The commission recently voted to recommend approval of the grant application to the mayor and city council.

Case Management Counselor Techniques with Susan Ellen

As the reader may have observed, all of the appropriate case management generalist intervention techniques have been applied to Susan Ellen's situation. However, the case manager is concerned about Susan Ellen's depression, about the possibility that she may violate her parole, and about her situation regarding the removal of her son. The case manager has a good working relationship with this offender and, in her professional opinion, believes that Susan Ellen is motivated for change, has the mental, physical, and emotional capacity to change, and can benefit from the therapeutic opportunity provided by the counseling interventions.

Confronting Problematic Behaviors

- You provide Susan Ellen with information from the child welfare protective services agency about the conditions that pertain to visiting her son at the home of his foster parents. You inform her that if she violates these conditions, she may not be able to see her son, and she may destroy her future chances of getting him back.

- You have her describe for you her life as a cocaine addict. As she draws this picture, you point out the consequences of her behavior in terms of her arrest and the removal of her son.

- You engage in some futurism exercises with her by verbally painting two scenarios: in one scenario, she continues to use cocaine and eventually becomes so addicted that she has to be institutionalized, or she overdoses and dies. Then you paint a different scenario in which she enters a treatment center and successfully completes the program and joins Narcotics Anonymous. Following this, she obtains her high school diploma, enrolls in the local community college, becomes employed part-time as a computer operator, and is reunited with her son. Ask her to describe for you what values, attitudes, and behaviors she would have to demonstrate in order to play-out the positive life script.

Engaging the Personality Dynamics of the Offender

- You discuss some of the difficulties you experienced in trying to complete your college degree in criminal justice while having to work 20 hours a week at a fast-food restaurant. Discuss how you were able to balance out your work, school, and social life. Draw a verbal analogy between how you were able to accomplish this and Susan Ellen's need to obtain a high school diploma so that she can progress beyond menial jobs.

- Ask Susan Ellen to describe for you what kind of a person she thinks that she is. In the course of the discussion, she tells you that she feels that she is not very pretty, that she is "dumb," and that no one could ever really love her for herself. She tells you that she has always felt this way about herself, even as a child. In the course of the discussion you begin to reflect or bounce these feelings that she has about herself upon her. You do this by forcing her to consider if there is a link between her poor self-concept and why she commits burglaries and petty crimes and has become a drug addict. A reflective question to her might be. "Could it be possible that because you feel so poorly about yourself you take cocaine in order to escape from yourself and from your problems?" The task here for the case manager is to allow the client to reflect upon her social and psychological construction of her personality and to help her make the link between this definition of herself and her problems in social functioning.

The point of this exercise is to not allow Susan Ellen to feast upon her negative perceptions of herself. Ellis (1962) is instructive about this point in discussing the importance of developing rational beliefs that allow a client to understand that people in their life space may often reject them but that they (clients) do not have to reject themselves by internalizing (accepting or validating) that rejection.

Ask Susan Ellen to describe for you why the child welfare department removed her son from her care and placed him with a foster family. As she recounts the situation, you ask her to elaborate upon various circumstances. It develops that she believes that her need for drugs means that she has to have a "fix" regularly, and that while she is "high" she can't always supervise her son. Also, as she describes it, even with a regular job, much of her income had to go to support her drug habit, therefore, she cannot always buy enough food or clothing for her son. These things, she explains, plus the lack of support from the father of the child, and her rejection by her family, force her to steal in order to exist. At this point the case manager helps Susan Ellen reflect upon her behavior by asking her to consider that her description of the situation involving the reasons for the removal of her child was constructed by her upon a base of rationalizations for behavior: "I'm an addict, therefore, I have to do drugs;" denial of her role in the problem formation by taking upon herself the role of the victim; and, projecting the blame upon others, such as her family and the father of her child.

Although there may be a realistic base to support some of Susan Ellen's arguments, again, she cannot be allowed to feast upon these arguments. In using cognitive-behavioral approaches, offenders are not allowed to rationalize away maladaptive behaviors. Instead, Susan Ellen must be helped by the correctional counselor to see and understand the linkage between her distorted ideations and how these serve to construct an inappropriate social and psychological reality: a reality at odds with conventional society. From this process insight may develop, and, hopefully, with encouragement of the case manager, Susan Ellen will act upon that insight.

Exploring the Developmental World of the Offender

The case manager asks Susan Ellen to recount her family history. In that discussion, she reveals some information that she had not presented before. She says that when she was six, she and her younger brother witnessed their father murdering their mother. She and her brother were placed in foster family care after her father was sent to the penitentiary. At age eight, Susan Ellen and her brother went to live with an aunt and uncle. After one year, the aunt and uncle adopted both children. Susan Ellen tells you that her aunt and uncle physically abused her, and they neglected her in favor of her brother. Her brother could do no wrong in their eyes. When Susan Ellen was 12, her adoptive mother was deserted by her adoptive father and the family became destitute. She stated that they had to "go on welfare" (i.e., Aid to Families with Dependent Children). One night while her adoptive mother was visiting her boyfriend, Susan Ellen's brother accidentally set the mattress in the apartment on fire. Fire destroyed part of the apartment. Shortly thereafter, child protective services caseworkers investigated. Both children were then temporarily placed in an emergency shelter home and then in a foster family home. Eventually, they were returned to the custody of the adoptive mother.

There are many problematic areas in Susan Ellen's developmental history that the case manager could focus on: the trauma of witnessing the murder of her natural mother, her physical abuse and neglect by her adoptive parents, the emotional abuse she felt because her adoptive parents favored her brother, the desertion of the family by the adoptive father, and the series of abandonments through placement and replacement in family foster family care.

As Susan Ellen tells her story, or at some appropriate point after she has told it, the case manager may ask her if she sees any parallels between her past life script and the current way that she is functioning with respect to her son. The parallels are not precisely the same but they are very similar. The case manager tells Susan Ellen that sometimes when we have been traumatized as children, as adults we tend to play-back the same script with our children. The intention here is to make Susan Ellen's unconscious awareness connect with a conscious awareness of her behavior in the here and now. The case manager promotes this connection by causing her to consider and to reflect upon the issue of her physical abuse and emotional neglect by her adoptive parents. When Susan Ellen demonstrates an understanding of the link between her family history and her current problems in social functioning, insight is formed. The next point, as always, is to help Susan Ellen exercise the option of constructing a more socially and psychologically acceptable social reality by acting upon the insight that has been generated.

We reiterate that the problem-solving process with offenders (Chapter 6) occurs, in real-life situations, as an ongoing process. It is certainly not static and it may not always be linear. We need to continually examine the impact of our generalist or counselor interventions in relation to an offender's progress toward the achievement of the case management treatment goals. At any point in our work with the client, new data may emerge. These data can act as feedback to inform the progress and process of our work. The net result may be to change or modify any of the nine steps in the problem-solving process. The case manager must remember not to become locked in to previous diagnoses, classifications, or impressions, or wedded to only certain sets of data.

Conclusions

In this chapter we focused upon the role of the correctional case manager as a counselor. The interventions of the case manager as a counselor are very different from those of the case manager as a generalist. Basically, the generalist practitioner intervenes, unilaterally or with the offender, with respect to changing or modifying problem areas in the offender's social and physical environment. The counselor, by contrast, is primarily interested in changing or modifying an offender's values, attitudes, and behaviors. An offender's values, attitudes, and behaviors constitute his or her persona or intrinsic characteristics. The counseling techniques are used to help an offender gain insight about problematic aspects of his or her behavior, personality, or the influence of the developmental history upon the present problems in psychosocial functioning.

In the chapter we also presented three counseling intervention techniques that could be used in order to help offenders attain insight. These techniques were: confronting the problematic behaviors of the offender, engaging the personality dynamics of the offender, and exploring the developmental history of the offender. Case examples and a case study were presented that described how these techniques could be applied by the counselor with various types of clients.

In the aggregate, these techniques comprise a reality level psychotherapy derived from the cognitive-behavioral approach. In the experience of the authors, most correctional case managers can accomplish a great deal of therapeutic progress in the life of offenders by utilizing one or more of the generalist intervention techniques described in Chapter 6. Other correctional case managers, particularly those working in various community settings that afford intensive supervision of offenders, who have sufficient clinical training, experiences, and appropriate supervision, along with recourse to competent clinical consultation, may be competent to use these counseling techniques. Education beyond the bachelor's degree in a relevant academic discipline, such as counseling, psychology, or social work, is usually indicated and should be encouraged for correctional case managers who wish to function as counselors in the manner in which we have described the roles and activities in this chapter. However, quite often, a case manager may be able to properly apply these techniques by virtue of having attained a good working knowledge through increasingly responsible and intensive probation or parole supervision work, by in-service training, or by participation in technical workshops, conferences, and seminars.

In any case, in reality, the world of correctional counseling is replete with offenders who have various types of serious social and psychological problems. For example, numerous substance abusers, white-collar criminals, sexual offenders, and con artists of various sorts, come to community correctional settings with a large amount of long-standing pathological baggage. As discussed in Chapter 1, much of this phenomena can be traced to concentrated efforts over the last two decades toward deinstitutionalization. For instance, Cole (1995) notes that in 1980 there were 1.4 million Americans under community supervision and, that by 1990, this figure had increased to 3.2 million, which is an increase of almost 130 percent. This increase can also be traced to concerns about jail and prison overcrowding. These developments have contributed to the expansion of community-based supervision and treatment settings, as well as to a variety of innovative alternatives to sentencing and incarceration. The outcome is that these developments are here and we must work with them.

References

Aichorn, A. (1965). *Wayward Youth*. New York, NY: The Viking Press.

Berne, E. (1964). *Games People Play*. New York, NY: Grove Press.

Black, C. & R. Enos (1981). "Using Phenomenology in Clinical Social Work: A Poetic Pilgrimage. *Clinical Social Work Journal*, 9:34-43.

Cole, G.F. (1995). *The American System of Criminal Justice* (Seventh Edition). Belmont, CA: Wadsworth Publishing Co.

Ellis, A. (1962).*Reason and Emotion in Psychotherapy*. New York, NY: Stuart.

Englander-Golden, P. & V. Satir (1990). *Say it Straight*. Palo Alto, CA: Science and Behavior Books.

Enos, R. & C.M. Black (1982). "A Social Construction of Reality Model for Clinical Social Work Practice." *The Journal of Applied Social Sciences*, 58:83-97.

Freeman, A., J. Pretzer, B. Fleming & K.M. Simon (1990). *Clinical Applications of Cognitive Therapy*. New York, NY: Plenum Press.

Hollis, F. (1972). *Casework: A Psychosocial Therapy* (Second Edition). New York, NY: Random House.

Kagan, J. & S. Lamb (eds.) (1985). *The Emergence of Morality in Young Children*. Chicago, IL: The University of Chicago Press.

Kohlberg, L. (1987). *Child Psychology and Childhood Education: A Cognitive-Developmental View*. New York, NY: Longman.

Lester, D. & P. Van Voorhis (1992). "Group and Milieu Therapy." In D. Lester, M. Braswell & P. Van Voorhis (eds.) *Correctional Counseling* (Second Edition) (pp. 175-210). Cincinnati, OH: Anderson Publishing Co.

Liebert, R.M. & M.D. Spiegler (1987). *Personality: Strategies and Issues*. Chicago, IL: The Dorsey Press.

Nettler, G. (1976). *Social Concerns*. New York, NY: McGraw-Hill.

Piaget, J. (1965). *The Moral Judgment of the Child.* New York, NY: The Free Press.

Pullias, E.V. & J.D. Young (1969). *A Teacher is Many Things.* Bloomington, IN: Indiana University Press.

Redl, F. & D. Wineman (1962). *Children Who Hate: The Disorganization and Breakdown of Behavior Controls.* New York, NY: Collier Books.

Rieff, P. (1963). "Introduction." In P. Rieff (ed.) *Freud: The History of the Psychoanalytic Movement* (pp. 16-23). New York, NY: Collier Books.

Rogers, C.R. (1957). "The Necessary and Sufficient Conditions of Therapeutic Personality Change. *The Journal of Consulting Psychology*, 21:95-103.

Tate, G. (1967). *Strategy of Therapy.* New York, NY: Springer Publishing Co.

Van Kaam, A. (1969). *Existential Foundations of Psychology.* Garden City, NY: Image Books.

Van Kaam, A. (1986). Correctional Counseling and Moral Education. *Journal of Correctional Education*, 37:48-53.

Watzlawick, P., J.H. Beavin & D.D Jackson (1967). *Pragmatics of Human Communication: A Study of Interactional Patterns, Pathologies, and Paradoxes.* New York, NY: W.W. Norton.

Yochelson, S. & S.E. Samenow (1976). *The Criminal Personality: Volume II, The Change Process.* New York, NY: Jason Aronson.

Chapter 8

An Overview of Group
and Family Approaches

Introduction

Whenever the correctional case manager is working with an offender, there are group and family issues. Every client is potentially a member of some known offender group or classification. In addition, organizational efficiency may require group delivery of services, such as offering group counseling for sex offenders in intensive supervision. There are concerns about helping the client fit with groups of friends, co-workers, and other community members, as well.

Every aspect of the criminal justice system affects not only the offender, but also his or her family. Single offenders have parents, siblings, and extended family members who may be concerned about such issues as arrest, bond, adjudication, sentencing, and incarceration or community supervision. Entry of the offender into the criminal justice system typically triggers a crisis in the nuclear family. The offender's spouse and children share feelings of shame, loss of control, and fear of the future.

The correctional case manager needs to understand group and family dynamics in order to have an adequate understanding of the client. Family members frequently serve as collateral contacts during the assessment phase of the correctional case management process. The case manager can facilitate productive family relations in response to perceived crises, ongoing demands, and losses. The correctional professional must possess competency in understanding group dynamics and leading groups in order to fulfill numerous roles and functions.

Group Dynamics and Group Leadership

Group dynamics emerge when a collection of individuals begin to interact. The group may share some characteristic (e.g., living in the same neighborhood), goal (e.g., completing a task at work), or motive for coming or staying together. Formal groups usually meet at a particular time and place to fulfill an identifiable purpose. Usually, formal groups are characterized by limits or structures that define their shared identity and patterns of interaction. Informal groups evolve when individuals who share some space engage in behavior guided by habits, preferences, and norms. As an informal group emerges, members may discern some mutual interdependency. Group dynamics occur in formal groups, such as group counseling, and informal groups, including a collection of associates or peers.

Group dynamics include various mechanisms of change in a group. These dynamics interact with the structure or organization to determine a particular group process. The major group structures are boundary and hierarchy. A boundary is a physical, emotional or symbolic limit that defines who or what is inside a group. This boundary also establishes what is outside or excluded from an identified group. Hierarchy is a structure that distributes power within any system. Hierarchy in group and family systems guides decisionmaking and problem-solving. Literally, the hierarchy of a group can determine who speaks first or who communicates for the entire group. The hierarchy typically reveals leadership, while group boundaries establish alignments of group members into subunits of two (i.e., dyad), three (triad), or more individuals.

A group's structure makes a collection of individuals a real entity or living organism. The boundary that determines who is inside and outside construct the group like a cell. Healthy groups, like living cells, have a semi-permeable membrane that permits nutritious information to pass in and out of the boundary. The exchange of information between or among groups establishes patterns of communication, which in turn define larger or superordinate units. The group boundary or membrane permits the efficient interaction of individual parts. Individuals within the group system take certain roles and perform functions needed to maintain the collection as a living, growing, changing organism.

Typical roles within a group structure include leader, speaker, listener, and member. The leader reminds the group of its identity and purpose, and facilitates the process of change. A speaker in a group is the person who makes a request, disclosure, or another attention-seeking behavior. Most commonly the speaker is seeking some kind of helpful interaction with other individuals. The listener attends to the speaker's message. By conveying respect, empathy, and other dimensions of facilitative communication, the listener encourages the speaker to continue until the person's needs are satisfied. The role of member is shared by all who attend or participate in a formal group. Members provide an audience for the interaction of speaker and listener. They offer a context for decisionmaking and problem-solving, as guided by the leader.

Members may take a myriad of roles in order to accomplish necessary tasks. As certain tasks arise in the group process, members function in the roles dictated by the situation. For example, in group counseling, a speaker may engage in self-disclosure in response to questioning by the leader. Various members take the role of listener, attending to the verbal and nonverbal messages conveyed by the speaker. Certain members may provide direct input (e.g., in the form of information-giving). Others function in their roles by offering feedback, even confrontation. Throughout the process, some group members are highly engaged in communication, while others watch. The leader serves the functions of encouraging participation, summarizing points, reflecting feelings, and otherwise helping to create a shared experience for group members. In general, there are three main functions among group members: providing input, processing information, and producing output.

Input makes up the content of group interactions. Typically, one client will offer input, then another, followed by others, until a theme or focus emerges. In highly structured formal groups, the input may be shaped by an agenda or plan. Within such a group, the topic may be given and tasks may be assigned before the group interaction begins. Even the most structured group tends to produce new input over time as perceptions and understandings change. Thus, group dynamics can alter significantly the nature of the input in ongoing group process. In a less structured group, the group leader may be required to become active to help members identify common interests and proceed toward mutually acceptable goals.

Processing information involves taking the obvious and underlying messages of one or more speakers and developing some shared understanding. Each member brings considerable life experience and a unique history of relationships to the group encounter. Each participant has expectations, preferences, and goals, as well as boundaries that delimit individual understanding and contribution. Some groups, such as juries, process information under very stringent rules and guidelines, including the judge's leadership in the courtroom setting. Other groups must develop their own means and standards for processing information.

Every input produces some output for the group on the whole and particular members. Males tend to be task- and action-oriented, while females seem to be most concerned that feelings are expressed and understood (Hafner, 1986). Most male group members will seek output in the forms of problem-solving and action-planning. Groups in male-dominated business and industry tend to be highly structured, with the goal of moving quickly toward a solution. Therapy groups are less structured, letting outcomes develop slowly through the group process. Teaching and didactic groups are mid-range in terms of structure and movement toward desired output.

Group structures interact with member characteristics and group dynamics to produce input, processing, and output. Members fulfill roles and functions consistent with the tasks at hand and according to the guidance provided by the leader. Boundary and hierarchy determine the limits of membership, theme or focus, and eventual outcome. Successful groups that meet the needs of most members are built upon clear structure. The foundation afforded by adequate structure (e.g., discernible boundaries and leadership) is a prerequisite for group dynamics, which can transform the collective into a powerful force for change.

The three major group dynamics are cohesiveness, validation, and movement. Cohesiveness reflects the "us-ness" or "we-ness," that is, the evolving sense of shared identity and purpose. This dynamic is critical in attracting members to the group and maintaining attendance or regular participation. Typically, greater cohesiveness is associated with similar values and goals. In group counseling, cohesiveness is the major force for working toward desirable changes. In general, cohesiveness is facilitated by pre-existing similarity of group members. For example, the commonalties in appearance and life experience of gang members tend to make this type of group very cohesive. Cohesiveness can be attained in the group process, even when members are dissimilar and have different goals. However, the group leader must facilitate a lot of input and self-disclosure in order to build the cohesion of shared identity.

Validation refers to the evolution of a shared reality or consensus among group members. Although there are facts and empirical realities in the physical world, social interactions are a complex mixture of data, opinions, subjective estimates, and preferences. Two people, even though they are quite close and similar, will experience the same situation differently. The group dynamic of validation provides a means for individual reality testing and movement toward a version of the "real world" that is mutually acceptable among the group members. In most group processes over time, there is a trend toward democratic solutions toward conflicts and differences (e.g., by voting). Such solutions are frequently satisfactory for all; however, each member must compromise. The optimal group will present strong respect for individual viewpoints with sufficient validation of the group position. Powerful group members, including the leader, can influence significantly the validation process.

The third major group dynamic is movement or locomotion. When there is movement in the social field, all particular members are affected to some degree. In order for group process to exist, there must be movement. Yet, not all group movement is healthy or helpful for all group members. The group dynamic of movement was substantial in the mass meetings in Nazi Germany, producing horrific results. Movement can afford beneficial change for members when there is adequate structure and the aforementioned group dynamics are present. Group counseling is a function of the extent to which there is adequate movement to change member behavior. Groups tend to move in terms of content, membership, alignment, hierarchy, and focus. When groups do not move and change, they tend to disintegrate. The leader is responsible for orchestrating the movement of the group, subunits, and individual members. In this manner, the group becomes the vehicle for moving members from a steady state, through change and uncertainty, to a new steady state or life position.

Group leaders must be knowledgeable about structure and dynamics. Individuals who are effective in social situations, making friends and influencing others, seem to have innate skills and awareness for organizing successful, rewarding interpersonal transactions. Most individuals, provided they possess fundamental communication skills, can learn how to interpret group structure and dynamics and facilitate growth-producing movement among members.

Group leadership consists in an array of interpersonal characteristics and communication skills (Table 8.1). Some of the skills are associated with both individual and group counseling (cf. Corey, 1987).

Table 8.1
Group Leadership Skills

Active Listening: Using minimal encourages such as "um-hmm" and head nods

Reflecting: Feeding back to the speaker the basic feeling tone of her or his message

Clarifying: Paraphrasing the remarks of one or more group members in order to sharpen the focus

Summarizing: Organizing fragmented input to obtain a coherent message, frequently at the close of a group meeting

Interpreting: Making tentative attributions of possible meanings to patterns of observed behavior

Questioning: Asking mostly open-ended questions to encourage exploration of the here-and-now

Linking: Encouraging member-to-member conversation to foster greater cohesiveness in the group

Confronting: Pinpointing discrepancies in behavior or disruptive, self-sabotaging influences

Blocking: Setting norms and guidelines such that vulnerable members are protected from power plays and evasive maneuvers

Evaluating: Helping members determine the individual and shared values of group by focusing on group dynamics

Terminating: Ending one group session and bridging to the next, often by assigning homework or asking a member to provide input in the upcoming session

Active listening is associated with any successful transaction. By using minimal encouragement, such as "um-hmm," and receptive body language the leader is able to increase the duration, depth, and relevance of the speaker's message. Reflecting is a group counseling skill intended to capture the feeling tone in group transactions. Clarifying is especially useful in the early stages of group, when it is important to find or maintain a focus. Summarizing is needed in the closing moments of a group experience. Interpreting can be used by skillful leaders to deepen the experience of all members by offering tentative explanations for complex behavior patterns.

Questioning can be used in information processing and focusing during any phase in the group process. The group leader uses linking to facilitate member-to-member communication. By demonstrating commonalties, the leader enhances cohesiveness. Confronting, another group leadership skill, involves pointing our discrepancies and incongruities in individual behavior and disruptive influences among members.

Blocking is an essential skill in group counseling. In active and confrontational groups, leaders block power plays and harmful maneuvers, helping vulnerable members to participate safely. Evaluating is a cognitive skill enabling the leader to demonstrate and teach diagnostic techniques to members. Terminating skills are needed to close a session, end a time-limited group, and help group members say good-bye and take leave.

Group leaders typically present certain characteristics in addition to innate and developed skills. Corey (1987) identified the following characteristics of effective leaders (Table 8.2).

Table 8.2
Characteristics of Effective Group Leaders

Courage: Venturing forth and accepting responsibility, rather than role-playing

Willingness to model: Teaching by example and self-disclosure

Presence: Interacting with others in the here and now with a minimum of countertransference or hidden agenda items

Goodwill: Acting with the best interests of others at heart

Caring: Providing needed warmth and support

Openness: Revealing one's true nature as a participant and leader in the group

Personal power: Possessing adequate congruence and genuineness, as well as assertiveness and charisma

Stamina: Having needed energy and enthusiasm to counteract the draining effects of group member projections and resistances

Willingness to explore: Considering norms and values outside one's cultural group, as well as modeling initiative and adventure

Self-awareness: Being aware of one's goals and purpose in life

Sense of humor: Using humor to release tension and discharge anger

Creativity: Finding opportunities to innovate or express oneself through various modalities

---

Most of the characteristics listed in Table 8.2 are associated with good social adjustment and mental health. Characteristics such as goodwill and caring emphasize sensitivity and capacity for empathy. Several of the traits (e.g., courage, personal power, and stamina) indicate that the leader must have good boundaries and assertion skills. Even a sense of humor has its place in effective group leadership.

Group leadership, along with group dynamics and structure, determine the nature and function of the collective experience among members. While some extroverted individuals may be best equipped constitutionally to lead groups, individuals who present other personalities can learn about dynamics such as cohesiveness and movement, as well as structural variables, including especially boundary and hierarchy. The communication skills of group leaders catalyze the interaction of group structure and dynamics that result in group process.

Group Process

Group process is a series of interrelated stages or phases in the evolution of a group. The following list of stages identifies typical activities associated with each stage (Table 8.3).

Table 8.3
Phases and Stages in the Group Process

Phase/Stage	Representative Activities
Pregroup Phase	Securing informed consent Selecting members Preparing members for participation
Acceptance Stage	Establishing safety and building trust Avoiding premature problem-solving Providing active leadership and high group structure
Transition Stage	Addressing emerging anxiety and anger Neutralizing resistance and projection Dealing with difficult group members
Working Stage	Focusing on the here-and-now Taking risks and trying out new behaviors Exploring unfinished business
Termination Stage	Reducing energy level and emotional investment Focusing on relapse prevention Saying good-bye and preparing for the future
Postgroup Phase	Arranging follow-up and booster sessions Evaluating member and group progress Debriefing between co-leaders

The pre-group stage in the process of group involves many practical considerations. Members must be recruited, then screened, and selected or excluded according to the needs of individuals and the agency or professional providing the services. Generally, members are excluded from most types of groups when they are dangerous, mentally ill, or retarded. However, even individuals with significant communication impairment can benefit from social skills training. The group leader determines the optimal size and composition of the group. Most groups require a "core membership" of at least five persons in order to realize maximum benefits from group participation. Attrition and absences can impede seriously the evolution of group cohesiveness. Other pre-group activities include providing information, rationale, and objectives such that the prospective member can provide informed consent.

Following preparation for group participation, members enter the initial stage of group process, the acceptance stage. There is a life cycle in the evolution of group process. The stage of acceptance is essential to the ongoing development of a group because trust building is the focus. Trust is built by graduated self-disclosure in which revelations of one's true nature are met with acceptance. There is movement toward security and self-acceptance as the leader and group members refrain from jargon, premature advice giving, and excessive interpretation or confrontation. During this stage, the group becomes a "holding environment" (Winnicott, 1964) through the maintenance of adequate structure and active leadership. Structure enables the expression of emotion and containment of inevitable conflicts of interest. The group moves toward the next stage in the process with the emergence of negative affect or an attack upon the leader (Corey, 1987).

The transition stage bridges the period of initial participation and acceptance and the stages devoted to commitment and working toward meaningful behavior change. With the expression of some affect, there is the opportunity to address resistances and conflicts within or between group members. Addressing resistance to change and pinpointing of basic defenses leads to greater risk-taking, openness, and eventually cohesiveness. The transition stage has been described as "kneading the dough to produce a nutritious loaf of bread." If the leader fails to deal with resistances and defenses, the group will stop moving and growing. When the group becomes stuck, there will be an increasing number of drop-outs or individuals who arrive late for sessions.

During the transition stage, members intensify the process of projecting unfinished business from their families of origin onto the leader and other group members. There may be unconscious efforts to replay conflicts and traumas from the past. The leader must maintain an active stance in order to use the structure of group to contain strong emotion. However, the leader moves toward facilitation and passive methods for encouraging movement, especially through self-disclosure. If there is a co-leader, the two can share in decision-making and taking active and passive roles as the process demands. Inevitably, group members tend to become stuck or "type cast" into some predictable roles. Group members collude, or unconsciously agree, to take these roles in order to thwart movement toward change, which can be anxiety provoking. Typical roles of "difficult group members," who take roles and distract attention away from progress toward the next stage, are listed in Table 8.4.

Table 8.4
Roles of Difficult Group Members

The Storyteller: The member who tells stories about persons and places that are irrelevant to the process of group or concerns of current members

The Know-It-All: The member who takes a superior position, giving information and advice, interpreting the behavior of others, generally due to lack of self-confidence and fear of being discovered as inadequate

The Hit and Run Driver: The member who uses unexpected and excessive confrontation of other group members to discharge hostility and protect a vulnerable self

The Victim: The member who attracts the confrontations and attacks of others to remain in a constant state of victimization, avoiding self-reliance and depending upon others for help

The Rescuer: The member who wants to help and to fix others in order to feel better about his or her own wounded self

The Professor: The member who uses logical argument and intellectual maneuvers to avoid self-disclosure and expression of feelings

The Silent Type: The member who hides out on the periphery of group, observing but not sharing because of fear or suspiciousness

The Miser: The member who withdraws or withholds contributions that could be made to the group due to fear of loss or to punish the group leader

The Seducer: The member who uses charm, appearance, or charisma to attract the attention of others and distract the group process

The group member roles described in Table 8.4 become "difficult" when a member is possessed by the role projected onto him or her by other group participants. Then, individuals cannot grow or change; they only enact the roles that possess them. They are also difficult in the sense that such role-taking tends to become very frustrating to the leader and other group members. Exaggerated role-taking must be neutralized in order to progress to the next stage in the evolution of the group.

The working stage of group process involves the strongest group dynamics. Ideally, there is an adequate degree of cohesiveness and consensus, derived from some resolution of conflicts and resistances encountered in the early stages. Less structure is needed and the leader is less active, settling into the role of participant-observer. There is freedom to support and confront group members as needed. Spontaneity and risk-taking are common. In the working stage of group, projections are withdrawn and deeper exploration of unfinished business is possible. If the group is more didactic or task-oriented, then members will be more creative and productive during this stage.

Toward the end of the stage, there is an active spirit of experimentation: trying out new behaviors and roles, in and outside the group. When groups reach this high level of functioning, synergy is produced in which there is more energy or there are more emotional resources available for group consumption than that contributed by the individual members. Most groups do not reach or complete the working stage. Such groups remain somewhat focused on lack, need, or deficiency and, as a result, conflicts continue to arise from the competition for scarce resources.

The termination stage emerges as members consolidate their learning and transfer new skills to the natural environment. The intensity of conflict subsides in stuck groups and the synergy diminishes in working groups. Most members become aware of the need for closure in order for the group process to feel like a nearly complete experience. Termination is very important because each member, including the leader or co-leaders, will be sustaining some losses. Therefore, this stage addresses both separation and potential for future growth. Typically, relapse prevention is a major focus. Members may construct formal relapse prevention or discharge plans. All members are active in planning for follow-up contacts and resources. Resistance to termination may be presented in the forms of crisis or catastrophe, failure to say good-bye, and dropping out.

The postgroup phase addresses both residual member issues as well as concerns in service delivery. If co-leaders were involved, the postgroup phase is an important time for debriefing and venting of feelings. There may be follow-up contacts with group members to evaluate their progress, determine their satisfaction with the group, or arrange "booster sessions." Postgroup sessions should be time-limited and highly focused upon maintenance of treatment gains and transfer of learning, rather than introducing new issues. Some behavioral and psychoeducational groups recycle or start anew after completing some fixed period of group work. Individuals who have not realized maximum benefit or mastery of goals may join subsequent groups. The postgroup phase provides an important opportunity for data gathering and planning for future group efforts.

The phases and stages of the group process refer to the predictable milestones in the evolution of a group over time. Depending upon the nature of the group, activities associated with a given stage may emerge naturally or be instigated by the group leader. Groups of all types evolve over time and present some of the phases and stages of group process. Group counseling is most concerned with movement through the stages toward beneficial therapeutic outcomes. However, any group can be more productive or satisfied when there is some attention to the demands imposed by group process.

While the phases and stages address the transformation of a collection of individuals into a functional group, there are evolutionary forces at work in even a single group meeting. Just as the group process moves from high structure to exploration and returns to structure by the termination stage, a single group session or meeting unfolds according to the demands of group process. In a sense, a single session or meeting of any group is a microcosm of the group evolutionary process. Table 8.5 depicts some tasks and concerns in four hypothetical types of group. These tasks and concerns can last from 75-90 minutes.

Table 8.5
Examples of Group Sessions

Process-Oriented Psychodynamic Group
1. Preparation and invitation
   5 minutes
2. Silence and resistance
   5-10 minutes
3. Emergence of self-disclosure and problem focus
   10-20 minutes
4. Joining and processing
   5-10 minutes
5. Emergence of conflict and tension
   10-20 minutes
6. Resolution of tension, interpretation of process
   5-10 minutes
7. Closing and summarizing
   5 minutes

Problem-Specific Behavioral Group
1. Preparation
   5 minutes
2. Review of homework
   10-20 minutes
3. Practice in group or instruction in a particular coping skill
   20-30 minutes
4. Assignment of homework
   10-20 minutes
5. Closing and summarizing
   5 minutes

Daily Institutional Group for High-Functioning Inmates
1. Orientation and preparation
   5 minutes
2. Setting agenda and "checking in"
   20-30 minutes
3. Addressing individual agenda items
   20-35 minutes
4. Closing and summarizing
   10-20 minutes

Weekly Self-Help or Recovery Group
1. Opening (reading preamble)
   10-20 minutes
2. Making announcements and inviting contributions
   5-10 minutes
3. Discussing a topic or step; listening to a speaker
   20-40 minutes
4. Closing activities (e.g., reciting the Serenity Prayer)
   5-10 minutes

Each of the groups is concerned with opening and closing, moving from high to lower structure, and engaging members in the middle period of the session or meeting. The process oriented and behavioral groups are perhaps the most different, while the institutional and self-help groups are similar. The groups progress from one session to the next, dealing with fundamental group dynamics and process factors.

Group process is a powerful force, transforming a loosely connected assembly of individuals into a functional group, which develops its own identity, reality, purpose, and movement. As the group is transformed by the process, the leader contributes to individual and group progress. Structure, leadership, and sequential stage-related activities facilitate the unfolding of the group process. Groups of all types and purposes are affected to some extent by group dynamics and process. Some factors in group work have been identified as especially important in the evolutionary process.

Essential Components in the Group Process

Yalom is perhaps the dean of group therapists. While his listing of elemental factors for therapeutic experience developed from his experience as an Existential psychoanalyst, the essential components of the group process (Yalom, 1985), listed in Table 8.6, apply in any group experience to some degree. They are most applicable to process-oriented group psychotherapy.

Table 8.6
Essential Components in the Group Process

1. Instillation of hope
2. Universality of member experiences
3. Imparting of information
4. Altruism among group members
5. Repeating themes from one's family of origin
6. Developing social skills
7. Initiating contact with others
8. Overcoming self-defeating behavior patterns
9. Group cohesiveness
10. Corrective emotional experiences
11. Developing a purpose or meaning for life

Hope is a key ingredient in working with any population, especially those separated from home and family. Chronically mentally ill individuals and incarcerated offenders share some of the losses that make change seem impossible and life hopeless. Offenders who participate in the group process regain a sense of community and a stake in conformity. Group counseling is a major modality for instilling hope and catalyzing the change process.

While all group members are unique as autonomous individuals, all share certain fundamental experiences that unite them. All offenders in rehabilitation have experience with families, authority figures, and associates or co-workers. They share the challenge of living and the inevitability of death. As they strive to make sense of a broken life, filled with many losses, focusing on commonalties and universality of life experience helps to build cohesiveness.

Groups are excellent means for imparting information in an efficient manner. Formal group counseling may rarely if ever occur in some correctional case management settings. However, all case managers will come to realize the benefits of sharing and reiterating essential information in groups. When group counseling is appropriate, it is often based on the didactic or psychoeducational model in which the needs of group members are met through information sharing and group learning.

In any group, some members will be selfish or self-absorbed. There is a high probability among offenders that many of the group members will be essentially antisocial or narcissistic. They are not accustomed to sharing in any respect. The lack of empathy is a core problem. Groups present opportunities to learn essential altruism, having some goodwill and taking into account the needs of another person. Yet, group members tend to repeat or replay trauma, arising from childhood neglect or abuse. It is easy to understand why offenders do not trust others and engage in selfish behavior. They perceive scarcity and expect exploitation or violence. Thus, they are inclined to "jump first," or taken advantage of another before they are hurt or exploited. By recapitulating painful themes from one's family of origin, offenders can learn that the worst does not always happen. The group can be viewed as safe, as altruism moves from perceived weakness to strength.

All groups provide opportunities for individuals to learn coping and social skills. By initiating contact with others, taking the roles of speaker and listener, and other techniques, the offender can be socialized. They acquire experiences that contradict self-defeating patterns of behavior. While every offender is not capable of true insight, most members benefit from feedback regarding repetitive patterns of behavior, which interfere with genuine need satisfaction.

The cohesiveness of group creates a safe place to explore the myriad of issues that lead to crime or offender behavior. As noted earlier, the pain and shame of the past tend to teach an offender to avoid nutritious life experiences and engage instead in defensive, self-defeating patterns that inhibit growth. Most offenders are emotionally childlike. Underneath the facade of power and control, there are insecurities, fears, and overwhelming memories. In the safe place of group, some offenders will experience an abreaction or corrective emotional experience. Other group members may participate in this catharsis as energy formerly invested in defensive and deviant behavior is released through intense emotional outlet.

The final component in the group process is an Existential factor. Yalom (1985) was heavily influenced by Existentialist philosophers such as Sartre and Kierkegaard, who addressed the meanings in an individual's life given the inevitability of death. Yalom viewed the group culture as essential in making life decisions. He expanded on the basic goals of Freudian psychoanalysis, "to be able to love and to work," to include the capacity for play, acceptance of self and others, flexible problem-solving, and sharing with others. The group process affords an irresistible opportunity to evolve a set of personal values that make sense out of one's life.

Since correctional case managers are charged with the task of helping offenders avoid relapse by changing their lifestyles, the essential components of the group process will apply for any client. Finding a new purpose in life can be accomplished by individual reflection, counseling, spiritual discipline, career development, family reunification, and other experiences. Group work has been a major modality for accomplishing the general goals and particular objectives of clients in correctional case management.

Group Work in Corrections

Lester and Van Voorhis (1992) described the wide range of group applications with offender populations, including psychodrama, milieu therapy, guided group interaction, and moral development approaches. Group work in corrections was initiated with juvenile delinquents and young adult offenders. Their developmental level and peer group perspective demanded intervention at the group level. For example, Glasser (1965) implemented a Reality Therapy program in the Ventura School for Girls in California. Jesness (1975) implemented group programs for delinquent youth based on either the Transactional Analysis or Behavior Modification models for therapeutic change. Arbuthnot and Gordon (1986) described applications of Kohlberg's moral development model in changing the cognitive development of aggressive delinquents.

Cognitive approaches to group work have been popular, as well. Yochelson and Samenow (1976) identified thinking errors and cognitive distortions justifying criminal activity and deviant lifestyles. They worked with offenders at St. Elizabeth's Hospital, helping them to overcome impulsivity, develop empathy, and practice prosocial behaviors. Gendreau and Ross (1980) heralded the cognitive revolution in corrections, which had earlier affected the mental health disciplines. Cognitive interventions, like behavior modification, use groups to practice social and problem-solving skills. Frequently, the training efforts involve role-playing and videotaping for the purpose of shaping desired behavior through feedback.

Group counseling models developed for most known offender groups, including mentally disordered offenders, sex offenders, and chemically dependent offenders. In many states, community supervision caseloads are specialized according to the special characteristics of offenders. In this case management situation, the correctional professional should consider group interventions ranging from orientation and information giving to regular group therapy sessions.

Conclusions Regarding Group Approaches

Group work is a major, naturally occurring modality for accomplishing the aims of correctional case management. Offenders present delinquent and antisocial behavior due to problems in development and socialization. They may be influenced to commit crime through differential association with criminal peers. Therefore, group interventions are intuitively attractive for clients who need to learn how to relate in a healthy manner to others in the community.

Group dynamics occur when a collection of individuals begin to interact. The case manager needs a basic understanding of the characteristics of formal and informal groups, as well as such group dynamics as boundary and hierarchy. Three major group dynamics are cohesiveness, validation, and movement. The skilled leader can harness the power of group influence by systematically attending to group dynamics and the process of group development.

Group process reflects a series of interrelated phases and stages in the evolution of a group. Initially, high structure and active leadership are required to get a group moving in the desired direction. Later, the leader becomes a participant observer, who uses passive and indirect means for facilitating group development. Essentially, the leader enables the members to learn how to help one another. Relapse prevention, the ultimate aim of correctional case management, is facilitated by providing resources and opportunities to learn coping skills. Then, offenders must apply these skills in such natural environments as their homes and workplaces. The explosion of self-help and recovery groups is testimony to the power of group work in relapse prevention (cf. Hamm, 1992). Family therapy represents a special application of basic group dynamics and systems principles to the problem of relapse in the homes of offenders.

Family Approaches

There are many similarities between group and family therapy modalities. In fact, family treatment evolved from group counseling approaches, especially in Great Britain (Broderick & Schrader, 1991). Both models share an emphasis upon the dynamic interactions among individuals in a system defined by boundaries and hierarchy. In family systems, the leaders atop the hierarchy are the parents. Family boundaries define the marital unit, as well as the nuclear family in the contexts of the extended family and the community. Families evolve like groups; however, the process may extend over generations.

Much of family therapy is concerned with the dyads (e.g., mother-child) and triangles (e.g., father-mother-sick child) formed by alignments of family members. Unfortunately, dysfunctional and unhealthy family systems produce repetitive patterns in family interactions, which are organized to prevent change rather than facilitate growth.

In correctional counseling and case management, families are nearly always involved, even when they are not physically present in a meeting or within an institutional setting. Family members react to arrest, court appearance, and incarceration with a wide range of responses from crisis to sadness to anger. Generally, they experience losses: lost family member, lost income, and lost dreams. Families go through a grieving process as their loved one passes through the criminal justice system. Spouses not only lose their partners, but also they are required to shift abruptly their role in the family system. Children lose essential contact with parents who are incarcerated. In this manner, the children of offenders experience pain and shame, which places them at risk for developing delinquency and criminality. Community treatment of offenders enables the family unit to remain intact. Yet, dysfunctional interactions among family members can trigger relapse or recidivism, resulting in revocation of probation or parole and incarceration.

Clearly, families are affected by correctional interventions. In turn, they influence how well or poorly the offender fares in community supervision and treatment. Therefore, the correctional case manager should possess some basic skills in assessing and treating family systems.

Assessment of Family Systems

It is possible to determine the current status of a family unit, the nature of interactions among members, and the recurrent patterns of behavior that constitute daily family life. Careful observation of interactions among family members, especially in their home environment, provides much information about the status of the family. Interviews with the offender and written exercises, such as the psychosocial history, contribute some data, as well.

The current status of the family is important because of the central focus on relapse prevention in correctional case management. The case manager is concerned with preventing or identifying, then reducing, factors that move the offender toward relapse or recidivism. A rapid means for assessing the current status, as well as the unfinished business of a family, is the genogram.

The Genogram

The genogram is a three-generational map of people and relationships within the family of origin (cf. McGoldrick & Gerson, 1985). The process of drawing or mapping one's family system encourages learning about basic family dynamics. This method is also useful in gaining information about "family scripts" for roles and alignments. Family secrets and forgotten memories may emerge in the process of completing a genogram. Feelings about family members, living and dead, can be identified.

Completing the genogram does not require skill in drawing, although one is free to illustrate or decorate the basic diagram. The client draws circles, squares, and lines to represent individuals and their relationships. A trauma survivor's map of her extended family system might depict an abusive family system over three generations. For example, Meg, a 33-year-old survivor of sexual abuse, could construct a genogram by which she could pictorialize her molestation by her father and older brother, the cold and distant relationship of her father and mother, and the legacy of physical abuse that she handed down to her son and daughters. Although the family system was very abusive, Meg enjoyed a close and warm relationship with her older sister, who was like a mother to her when she was growing up. She can also visually depict this relationship.

Through the use of a genogram, it becomes possible to depict both sides of a family, more than three generations (e.g., by including one's children), and even emotional intensity of relationships by drawing or labeling lines differently. One could show birthdates, anniversaries, and deaths. The offender could provide a lot of additional information by using different colors and shapes in drawing. The use of genograms is very applicable in correctional counseling since many offenders are trauma survivors of various types.

There are many other family assessment techniques, some using graphic displays and others employing narrative accounts of family dynamics. Family systems approaches frequently use analogues such as the circle to depict boundaries and their functions, lines to portray alignments and hierarchies, and triangles to reflect complex emotional relationships. Triangulation is a central construct in family systems approaches to assessment and problem-solving.

Dynamics in Family Systems

Just as in group therapy models, constructs like boundary, hierarchy, alignment, cohesiveness, validation, and movement are important in diagnosing and treating individual problems and relational conflicts. The construct of triangulation is one of the major contributions of the family systems model.

Triangulation refers to the tendency for two individuals who are having some conflict to pull another person or object between them in order to relieve temporarily anxiety and distress. In psychoanalytic approaches to marital and family systems (cf. Skynner, 1981), marriages are viewed as expressions of the principle, "Opposites attract." Attraction to an opposite other is motivated unconsciously to address unfinished business from one's family of origin. Complementarity, the technical term for this form of attraction, predicts approach-avoidance and other conflicts emerging from a marital union based on mutual projections. In order to reduce conflict and anxiety to manageable levels, the couple turns to some person, object, or activity outside their dyad. In the process, triangulation restores the dynamic emotional balance or homeostasis of the overall family system.

Triangulation tends to produce recurrent behavior patterns and emergence of an identified patient, or family member who so obviously has a problem that others are distracted from themselves and preoccupied with the functioning of this person. The identified patient bears the symptoms of the underlying family conflict. As long as triangulation works, the family has little awareness or motivation to resolve underlying difficulties or change their behavior patterns.

A typical manifestation of triangulation involves two conflictual parents and a "sick" child. In this case, the parents are distant or abusive with one another. Their conflicts increasingly threaten the stability of the marriage; therefore, separation or divorce could follow. A sensitive child in the family system absorbs the conflict and anxiety by exhibiting a symptom requiring immediate attention. For example, the child may experience a life-threatening asthma attack in the midst of a parental argument. The parents quit fighting when they hear him wheezing, perhaps rushing him to the emergency room. In this manner the sick child has fulfilled the important functions of keeping his parents together and reducing anxiety in the family system.

A large percentage of delinquents "act out" the conflicts of their parents in order to somehow stabilize the family system. Therefore, it is common in the juvenile justice system to both hold parents accountable and to involve them in their child's treatment. A typical case of neurotic juvenile delinquent behavior may help to illustrate.

Vicki, 14-year-old white female from Beverly Hills is placed in juvenile hall after eloping from a psychiatric hospital where she resided for eight months. Her history of offenses includes running away, curfew violation, and shoplifting. Vicki has been apprehended 10 times for shoplifting makeup and clothes, with friends and alone. Her parents divorced when she was five and her mother remarried an attorney, who has been a father to Vicki. Within the last two years, since she reached puberty and entered adolescence, Vicki's parents have been arguing about the extent of involvement in his law practice. Vicki's mother feels lonely and fears that one day her husband may leave her, just the way her former husband deserted her for another woman. Vicki was triangulated into the troubled marital relationship in order to hold them together. Whenever her father and mother come to juvenile hall or a psychiatric hospital to visit, the family system is "reassured," as they hope for a better future together.

Bowen, one of the pioneers in the family treatment of schizophrenia at the National Institute of Mental Health, was concerned with the unhealthy triangles formed by distant parents and symptomatic children. Bowen described how parents perpetuate emotional problems, even across several generations (Aylmer, 1986). According to the Bowen family systems model, individuals are programmed by their families of origin to pursue or avoid close relationships. Parental triangles are established to transmit the unresolved multigenerational issues to the next generation. For example, a man who grows up in a family triangle consisting of a distant, critical father and an overinvolved, smothering mother (who may be trying to get her relationship needs met through her son), develops an "emotional allergy" to close relationships with women. Correspondingly, a woman growing up in another parental triangle with an absent, idealized father and an overdemanding, critical mother seeks an "emotional addiction" to distant, unavailable men (Aylmer, 1986:110). This form of complementarity will result in the wife becoming a pursuer and the husband a distancer in the relationship. To have a semblance of closeness in an overall distant, unemotional marriage, a child may be triangulated, becoming an identified patient and receiving the family legacy of needy, pursuing women and unavailable, distancing men.

Family triangles have profound effects in the lives of offenders. Most of the aforementioned patterns apply to delinquents and adult offenders. However, the general public and many correctional professionals are predisposed to focusing upon crime as an individual problem. The development of the relapse prevention model taught important lessons regarding the salience of family issues in relapse. Correctional professionals are aware increasingly of the importance of relationships in the adjustment and compliance of offenders in community and restrictive settings.

Incarcerated offenders tend to become preoccupied with the behavior of family members in the "free world." A typical jailhouse theme is the dilemma of the cheating wife. An inmate suspects his wife or girlfriend is cheating on him. Initially, he tries to maintain surveillance and some illusory sense of control by encouraging friends and family members to watch and report her daily activities. Before long, the inmate is forced to acknowledge emotionally the futility of such efforts. He begins confronting her directly, telling her what to do, where to go, and how to lead her life. Obviously, this pushes her away from him, as she struggles to maintain autonomy. As she pulls away, the inmate redoubles efforts to control, creating a vicious cycle or "negative feedback loop," which continues until one partner refuses contact with the other.

Although the immature behavior may hold little interest for correctional officers, the behavior of angry, distressed inmates is a central concern. Noncompliance, insubordination, and fighting may follow from family conflicts such as the aforementioned vicious cycle. Generally, inmates who maintain some stable relationships with spouses or partners, children, and family members will realize better adjustment in jails and prisons. This perspective is translated into correctional facility policies regarding such matters as contact and conjugal visits, as well as innovations in child rearing within institutional settings (cf. Durham, 1994).

A related issue in institutional corrections is the effect of parental deprivation upon the development of children. Offspring of offenders are considered a population at risk for the pathogenesis of offender behavior. Therefore, some facilities allow young children to have extended contact with their mothers, who are incarcerated. There is awareness, as well, that the lack of relationship with a father perpetuates the intergenerational transmission of pain and shame resulting in criminality (cf. Wilson & Herrnstein, 1985). Thus, parenting education and training may have a place in correctional counseling and case management, not only for the families of identified delinquents, but also for children thought to be at risk for developing behavior problems.

Family triangles figure prominently in community corrections as well. The savings realized in community versus institutional corrections and the gains made by family members justify careful attention to family problems. Obviously, such problems as unemployment, poverty, and hunger can be addressed directly by the case manager who brokers services and advocates for community assistance in such cases. The correctional case manager may choose to involve family members in intake, orientation, assessment, intervention, and other stages in the process. Family systems interventions are especially relevant among chemically dependent offenders, which accounts for the greatest increase in the correctional population (Durham, 1994).

Triangles play roles in the onset and treatment of chemical dependency (Stanton & Todd, 1982). Using the Bowen family systems model (Aylmer, 1986), a conflictual couple, struggling with closeness, may triangulate an object or process, such as drinking alcohol to excess. In this manner, alcoholism is symptomatic of an underlying family disease process. Typically, an over-functioning spouse enables and protects the under-functioning alcoholic spouse from the consequences of problem drinking. As long as the "drunk" is the spouse's problem, then the partner has no need for genuine introspection. The martyred spouse appears to be forced to assume the overly adequate role by the problems created by the under-functioning partner. However, the key to diagnosing and treating this hypothetical case may actually involve removing the "cover" afforded by the alcoholism and exploration of the highly functioning family members' need to control.

In contemporary times, the dilemma of over- and under-functioning partners has been described as co-dependency. Codependency is a relational problem in which one partner lives for and through the other, losing one's identity and freedom in the process (Schaef, 1987). Both offenders and their partners present co-dependency, which can easily result in relapse and recidivism. Characteristics of co-dependent partners are listed in Table 8.7.

The characteristics of a co-dependent person focus attention on an individual, which is in some respects a violation of family systems thinking. However, it is sometimes valuable to consider the needs and characteristics of a partner, who seems to "benefit" from the problems of a family member. Co-dependent partners should become involved in treatment, including the self-help or recovery group movement. For example, participation of a co-alcoholic partner in Al-Anon can reduce or eliminate some of the person's attempts to enable, rescue or punish the offender, who resists perceived control by drinking and being arrested.

The review of family systems dynamics highlighted the importance of viewing "sick" behavior, including criminal conduct, as an expression of underlying needs and conflicts. Although family systems approaches to treatment are most relevant in interventions with delinquent youth, the constructs of

Table 8.7
Characteristics of the Co-Dependent Person

1. An over-developed sense of responsibility. It is easier to be concerned with others than to be concerned for oneself.

2. Avoiding feelings from a traumatic childhood. One loses the ability to feel or express feelings because it hurts too much.

3. Isolation from people and fear of authority figures.

4. Dependent upon approval and excitement (crisis). Loses one's identity in the process.

5. Frightened by angry people and any personal criticism.

6. Living from the viewpoint of a victim. Survivors are attracted to abuse in forming love and friendship relationships.

7. Judging oneself harshly and having a low sense of self-esteem.

8. Terrified of abandonment. One will do anything to hold onto a relationship, resulting from living with people who were "never there" emotionally.

9. Experiencing guilt feelings when standing up for oneself instead of giving in to others.

10. Confusing love and pity and tending to "love" people who can be "rescued."

11. Covering up one's own addiction to eating, sleeping, working, shopping, gambling, and so forth.

12. Reacting to life rather than acting. Guessing at what is normal.

13. Having difficulty relaxing or having fun.

14. Being extremely loyal even in the face of evidence that loyalty is undeserved.

15. Fearing failure, but sabotaging one's success.

complementarity and triangulation definitely apply in the daily lives of adult offenders. Although family systems treatment has evolved to the place where it is widely accepted in such fields as medicine, mental health, and education, family therapy is rarely encountered in correctional settings.

Family Work in Corrections

Family therapists have treated successfully a wide range of lifelong (e.g., schizophrenia or alcoholism) and life-threatening (e.g., violence or diabetes) conditions (Broderick & Schrader, 1991). In fact, one of the pioneers of family therapy, Minuchin, developed structural family therapy to help impoverished, inner-city families deal with the acting out behavior of juveniles (Minuchin, Montalvo, Guerney, Rosman & Schumer, 1967). However, family systems approaches are rare in correctional settings.

Most family treatment programs are offered to families whose delinquent children have come into contact with the juvenile justice process (Van Voorhis,

Braswell & Morrow, 1992). There may be a tendency among criminal justice professionals to view family therapy as an attempt to excuse offender behavior or shift responsibility away from the perpetrator. The realities in the evolution of criminal conduct (Blackburn, 1993; Wilson & Hernnstein, 1985) substantiate that offender behavior is a complex, multifaceted phenomenon in which genetics, early life experiences, family life, education, neighborhood friends, and society play some role. It is possible to hold the perpetrator accountable for his or her behavior (i.e., moral responsibility), while addressing family factors in etiology (i.e., causal responsibility) and treatment.

Recent reviews of the status of marital and family therapy (Atwood, 1992; Gurman & Kniskern, 1991; Jacobson & Gurman, 1986) indicated that the delinquent and conduct problems of youth can be treated successfully. However, family therapists may tend to minimize the significance of criminal "acting out" behavior, viewing their families as basically normal or typical. Social learning approaches to the treatment of delinquency (e.g., Patterson, 1982; Stumphauser, 1987) have demonstrated good results. In addition, the social learning methods, which focus upon training parents to apply sound discipline and become behavior change agents at home, are more compatible with criminal justice etiology. Nevertheless, structural and strategic forms of family systems therapy have demonstrated efficacy with juveniles and adults (Van Voorhis, Braswell & Morrow, 1992).

Family therapy can be used to neutralize denial, pinpoint problem behavior, improve marital communication, reduce stress, and prevent relapse. Special programs have been developed for chemical dependency, incest and family violence perpetrators. Family programs are offered in correctional institutions to assist in reintegration and reduce relapse potential (Van Voorhis, Braswell & Morrow, 1992).

Conclusions

Offenders, although sometimes isolative and secretive, usually belong to some groups that exert considerable influence over their behavior. All offenders are born into some type of family unit. They tend to suffer above-average rates of neglect and abuse in their families of origin. Individuals predisposed to become offenders fail to identify with their fathers, who tend to be absent, critical, or emotionally unavailable. Therefore, future offenders enter adolescence without a stable sense of identity or life direction. They have not internalized norms and ethics, and they lack or lose their stake in conformity. Many youthful offenders fall under the influence of older and stronger peers who encourage them to participate in acting out behaviors. All of the aforementioned characteristics, derived from Wilson and Herrnstein (1985), have clear group and family implications. Group and family approaches to correctional counseling and case management present significant promise to intervene in the evolution of offender behavior. Yet, group and family approaches are not well understood or accepted among criminal justice and correctional professionals.

Group and family approaches are effective and efficient modalities for addressing predictable problems with relapse prevention. Group and family therapy enable the offender to address self-sabotaging, recurrent behavior patterns arising from dysfunction in the family of origin. Many problems, such as alcoholism, are perpetuated over generations by the processes of projection and triangulation. What is left unfinished by one direction is passed on to the next, creating an intergenerational legacy of pain and shame. Group approaches provide opportunities to resolve interpersonal conflicts and learn new behaviors in a safe environment, which affords a kind of surrogate family. Self-help groups are especially potent in providing for surrogate family life. Family approaches provide real and symbolic opportunities for changing interactional patterns in marital and family relations. Co-dependency, triangulation, and vicious cycles not only interfere with individual development, but also, contribute profoundly to the emergence of relapse.

Both family and group approaches are based on systems-thinking. The systems model asserts that individual behavior cannot be understood in isolation. There is always a group context, with levels and layers of contribution from the family of origin to one's current associates. The dynamics of systems must be understood in order to pinpoint problems and plan for intervention. The relapse prevention model informed correctional professionals about the salience of family factors in recidivism. Now, family therapy promises exciting new approaches for reconceptualizing offender behavior.

Correctional case managers need to know what to anticipate with families when working with any offender. Having some knowledge of group and family work, the case manager is better prepared to understand denial, minimization, noncompliance, and other forms of resistances. By working with offenders in groups, the correctional case manager, who has leadership skills and specialized knowledge, can catalyze latent family and group dynamics, shaping the client away from the criminal career toward recovery. Family members and peers can become collaborators with the offender in meaningful lifestyle change. By addressing family issues, the case manager has some opportunity to contribute to prevention of criminality in high-risk populations. Although the prevailing ideology in criminal justice favors punishment over rehabilitation, prevention through effective group and family work may prove to be attractive on financial and humanitarian grounds.

References

Atwood, J.D. (ed.) (1992). *Family Therapy: A Systemic-Behavioral Approach*. Chicago, IL: Nelson-Hall.

Arbuthnot, J. & D. Gordon (1986). "Behavioral and Cognitive Effects of a Moral Reasoning Development Intervention for High Risk Behavior-Disordered Adolescents." *Journal of Consulting and Clinical Psychology*, 54:208-216.

Aylmer, R.C. (1986). "Bowen Family Systems Marital Therapy." In N.S. Jacobson & A.S. Gurman (eds.) *Clinical Handbook of Marital Therapy* (pp. 107-150). New York, NY: Guilford

Blackburn, R. (1993). *The Psychology of Criminal Conduct: Theory, Research and Practice*. Chichester, England: John Wiley & Sons.

Broderick, C.B. & S.S. Schrader (1991). "The History of Professional Marriage and Family Therapy." In A.S. Gurman & D.P. Kniskern (eds.) *Handbook of Family Therapy*, (Vol. 2) (pp. 3-40). New York, NY: Brunner/Mazel.

Corey, G. (1987). *Groups: Process and Practice* (Third Edition). Pacific Grove, CA: Brooks/Cole.

Durham, A.M. (1994). *Crisis and Reform: Current Issues in American Punishment*. Boston, MA: Little, Brown & Co.

Gendreau, P. & R. Ross (1980). *Effective Correctional Treatment*. Toronto, CN: Butterworth.

Glasser, W. (1965). *Reality Therapy: A New Approach to Psychiatry*. New York, NY: Harper & Row.

Gurman, A.S. & D.P. Kniskern (eds.) (1991). *Handbook of Family Therapy*, (Vol. 2). New York, NY: Brunner/Mazel.

Hafner, R.J. (1986) *Marriage and Mental Illness: A Sex Roles Perspective*. New York, NY: Guilford.

Hamm, M.S. (1992). "The Offender Self-Help Movement as Correctional Treatment." In D. Lester, M. Braswell & P. Van Voorhis (eds.) *Correctional Counseling* (Second Edition) (pp. 211-224). Cincinnati, OH: Anderson Publishing Co.

Jacobson, N.S. & A.S. Gurman (eds.) (1986). *Clinical Handbook of Marital Therapy*. New York, NY: Guilford.

Jesness, C.F. (1975). "Comparative Effectiveness of Behavior Modification and Transactional Analysis Programs for Delinquents." *Journal of Consulting and Clinical Psychology*, 43:758-779.

Lester, D. & P. Van Voorhis (1992). "Group and Milieu Therapy." In D. Lester, M. Braswell & P. Van Voorhis (eds.) *Correctional Counseling* (Second Edition) (pp. 175-191). Cincinnati, OH: Anderson Publishing Co.

McGoldrick, M. & R. Gerson (1985). *Genograms in Family Assessment*. New York, NY: Norton.

Minuchin, S., B. Montalvo, B. Guerney, B. Rosman & F. Shumer (1967). *Families of the Slums*. New York, NY: Basic Books.

Patterson, G. (1982). *A Social Learning Approach: Coercive Family Process*. Eugene, OR: Castalia.

Schaef, A.W. (1987). *When Society Becomes an Addict*. San Francisco, CA: Harper & Row.

Skynner, A.C.R. (1981). "An Open-Systems, Group Analytic Approach to Family Therapy." In A.D. Gurman & D.P. Kniskern (eds.) *Handbook of Family Therapy* (pp. 39-84). New York, NY: Brunner/Mazel.

Stanton, M. & T. Todd (1982). *The Family Therapy of Drug Abuse and Addiction*. New York, NY: Guilford.

Stumphauser, J. (1987). *Helping Delinquents Change: A Treatment Manual of Social Learning Approaches*. New York, NY: Haworth.

Van Voorhis, P., M. Braswell & B. Morrow (1992). "Family Therapy." In D. Lester, M. Braswell & P. Van Voorhis (eds.) *Correctional Counseling* (Second Edition) (pp. 155-174). Cincinnati, OH: Anderson Publishing Co.

Wilson, J.Q. & R.J. Herrnstein (1985). *Crime and Human Nature*. New York, NY: Simon & Schuster.

Winnicott, D.W. (1964). *The Child, the Family and the Outside World*. London, England: Penguin.

Yalom, I. (1985). *The Theory and Practice of Group Psychotherapy*. New York, NY: Basic Books.

Yochelson, S. & S. Samenow (1976). *The Criminal Personality: A Profile for Change* (Vol. 1). New York, NY: Jason Aronson.

Chapter 9

Relapse Prevention

Introduction

While the topic of relapse prevention has received increasing attention in the mental health field, it is a central concern of corrections. Reduction of risk for recidivism is the primary goal of any correctional intervention. Correctional case management addresses the needs of individual offenders and identified classes or groups in order to prevent or delay re-offense. Classification of offenders contributes to prediction of recidivism and direction in treatment planning.

Relapse prevention is a separate treatment component in therapy for mental health problems. Psychotherapy targets specific problems or symptoms arising from emotional disturbance or mental disorders. Counseling interventions address problems in daily living by removing obstacles to ongoing development and fostering a meaningful lifestyle. Relapse prevention in psychotherapy and counseling is concerned with maintenance of treatment gains after the formal termination of the intervention or therapeutic relationship. In recent years, treatment of addictive behavior, including chemical dependency, extended the scope of relapse prevention well beyond basic programming for maintenance. The writers believe that the methods which have evolved in recent years in relation to relapse prevention for persons with addictive behaviors, such as substance abusers, holds great promise and utility value for relapse prevention with most types of offenders that correctional case managers are likely to encounter.

Relapse rates are unacceptably high in cases of addictive behavior. The field of behavioral medicine evolved in large part to solve problems with relapse and noncompliance with follow-up regimen in patients presenting alcoholism, obesity, cigarette smoking, heart disease, and other lifestyle disorders (Davidson & Davidson, 1980). For example, in spite of overwhelming scientific evidence and expert opinion against smoking, three out of four individuals who stop smoking will return to the habit within one year of intervention (Shiffman, Read, Maltese, Rapkin & Jarvik, 1985). The majority of alcoholics who stop drinking following treatment will relapse, often within the first 30-90 days (Marlatt, 1985). The lessons from behavioral medicine teach practitioners that even those who successfully complete a treatment program will be at risk for relapse when the structure afforded by the intervention is removed. The severity of public health and addiction problems demanded a comprehensive approach to relapse prevention.

A comprehensive approach to relapse prevention takes into account the powerful motivational forces implicit in addictive behavior and lifestyle disorders. It is clear that addictive behavior is a function of the immediate reinforcers associated with ingesting mood-altering chemicals. Addictions provide potent gratification of numerous needs of individuals who have difficulty in tolerating frustration and discomfort. Yet, reliance upon addictive behavior interferes with development of coping and social skills, as the addict increasingly orients his or her whole lifestyle around opportunities to secure and use alcohol, drugs, or another mood-altering substance or activity (e.g., compulsive overeating).

Behavioral medicine, public health, and addictionology have by necessity identified non-disease factors in chronic illness and relapse. Family members, friends, and coworkers in daily life may actually contribute to relapse. While attempts to escape from negative emotional states constitute a major intrapersonal determinant of relapse, interpersonal conflicts at home and work figure prominently in recidivism as well. By trying to help or monitor the addict, a co-dependent family member or employer can unintentionally trigger a chain of events leading to relapse.

Relapse Prevention

Relapse Prevention (RP), a cognitive-behavioral model for decreasing risk of recidivism (cf. Marlatt & Gordon, 1985), has been applied with a wide range of health problems, especially addictive behaviors (Donovan & Marlatt, 1988). Since nonchemical addictions, such as compulsive eating or working, are treated within the relapse prevention model (Marks, 1990) and chemical dependency is viewed as compulsive behavior (Lee & Oei, 1993), it is likely that a wide range of life problems, including criminal behavior, fit an addictive-compulsive behavior model.

Hodge (1991) proposed that any experience that produces intense emotion and manipulates general arousal level can become addictive. Apter (1989) provided a reversal theory describing, among other phenomena, the addictive nature of rapid changes in arousal and mood state. Solomon's (1980) opponent-process theory of addiction observed that compensatory changes in the body in response to contact with an addictive substance or activity conditions a wide range of symptoms to environmental cues or triggers. Therefore, traditional problems in chemical dependency, such as withdrawal, tolerance, and craving, may be less a function of underlying biological variables and more a consequence of conditioning and expectancy. Recently, Hodge (1991) suggested that crime should be considered an addictive behavior, which can be treated through the relapse prevention methods.

The Relapse Prevention Model

Marlatt (1978) initially developed the Relapse Prevention (RP) model to address cravings for alcohol and loss of control in alcoholics. He synthesized the growing cognitive-behavioral literature, identifying both skills deficits and information processing problems in the pathogenesis of addictive behavior. For Marlatt, relapse prevention was a self-management approach that targeted the maintenance stage of the habit-changing process. For him, the goal of relapse prevention "was to teach individuals who are trying to change their behavior how to anticipate and cope with the problems of relapse" (1978:3). According to the RP model, there are common determinants in the relapse process across addictive behaviors.

There are interpersonal and intrapersonal determinants of relapse shared by alcoholics, smokers, heroin addicts, compulsive gamblers, and dieters. Interpersonal determinants, which accounted for 44 percent of relapses in the original study (Marlatt, 1985:37-40), consisted of interpersonal conflicts at home or work, social pressure to engage in addictive behavior, and positive emotional states afforded by situations (e.g., having a birthday or sobriety anniversary). Intrapersonal determinants (56% of relapses in the sample), included negative emotional states, negative physical states, positive emotional states (arising intrinsically or spontaneously), testing personal control, and urges and temptations. Negative emotional states contributed most to the understanding of relapses across problem areas with 35 percent of all individuals attempting to reduce anxiety, depression, or dysphoria through addictive behavior.

The aforementioned intrapersonal and interpersonal determinants of relapse constitute high-risk situations. Provided an individual has adequate, nonaddictive coping responses or resources, relapse can be avoided, even in risky situations. Possessing adequate coping skills to resist urges and avoid lapses in high-risk situations produces increased self-efficacy or sense of perceived power and control. Having few or no coping responses contributes to a chain of events that leads eventually to relapse.

Cognitive-behavioral determinants of relapse were originally identified by Marlatt (1985). The writers have developed their own cognitive-behavioral model which is in accordance with the work of Marlatt, but which also includes components derived from the authors' professional experience. The model may be viewed, descriptively, in this manner:

1. Abstinence, which is the goal of relapse prevention, reflects a set of expectations related to self-efficacy. The addict anticipates positive results from ongoing abstinence and attributes the outcomes to personal efforts.

2. Lifestyle imbalance involves the perceived deprivation and sense of constraint associated with addictive overcontrol and resulting "cognitive claustrophobia."

3. Apparently irrelevant decisions, also called subjectively unimportant decisions (e.g., Steen, 1993), are set-ups or choices that appear to be reasonable, yet actually increase risk or access to opportunities to engage in addictive behavior.

4. High-risk situations include negative emotional states, which the addict will try to avoid, and interpersonal conflicts arising at work or home. These risky situations demand coping responses such as relaxation, social skill, problem-solving, and conflict resolution. When coping responses are not available in the behavioral repertoire, the chain of events in the relapse process leads to a lapse.

5. A lapse or slip involves fantasy, reflecting unresolved issues in the person's development and compensatory solutions. Fantasies also include mental rehearsals of addictive behavior. Lapses lead to ritualized behavior or repetitive habits associated with urges and cravings.

6. Finally, a lapse elicits justification for addictive behavior, as well as rationalization and denial. These cognitive errors move the individual closer to addictive acting out or externalizing behavior.

7. The "abstinence violation effect" is the final pathway to relapse. The abstinence violation effect involves a series of errors and misattributions. Since the addict violated self-imposed norms for abstinence in the lapse, he or she takes responsibility for the failure, gives up, and engages in self-deprecation. When there are no coping resources available, the addict experiences the problem of immediate gratification. An addict has overlearned that compulsive behavior produces positive mood states or relief from rapidly accruing distress. However, participation in the fully blown relapse episode elicits shame, or a deep, internalized sense of essential badness or worthlessness. This shame feeds overly perfectionistic standards for abstinence and heightens the constraint or overcontrol, which maintains the addict's lifestyle imbalance.

Imbalance in the Criminal Lifestyle

Lifestyle imbalance among offenders refers to the relative absence of healthy, growth-producing experiences and excess of either addictive overcontrol or release. The offender in rehabilitation trades the known gratification of a hedonistic lifestyle for the unknown rewards of an honest approach to life that has probably been ridiculed in the past. Boundaries are imposed by the correctional system, limiting access to opportunities for criminal or addictive acting-out behavior. These boundaries separate the recovering offender from the powerful motivational forces of the criminal lifestyle. However, these exclusive boundaries do not teach an offender new ways of approaching life. In order for a correctional intervention to succeed, the offender must learn how to use structure imposed by the criminal justice system, while he or she acquires the skills and boundaries that define a new lifestyle.

The correctional case manager actively assists the client in exploring and restructuring the lifestyle. Initially, assistance takes the form of prescribing some mandatory exclusive boundaries, such as abstaining from the use of alcohol or other mood-altering substances and refraining from contact with criminal associates. Mandatory boundaries, such as those contained in a probation agreement, naturally elicit some resistance from the correctional client. Therefore, rapport and trust building will be important functions at this stage in the correctional case management process. Slowly, the client will come to understand the value of exclusive boundaries in reducing risk of relapse. However, the offender will also experience loss and yearning for the "highs" of the old lifestyle.

The case manager assists the client in reclaiming normal adjustment, while anticipating the loss, boredom, and emptiness. There is a tendency in correctional case management to impose excessive boundaries for long periods of time without addressing the underlying losses. Lengthy probation or parole agreements with multiple terms or stipulations may in fact represent the correctional system's contribution to early relapse. Certainly, the correctional worker will act to protect the community's interests by carefully monitoring compliance with such terms as having no contact with victims, possession of weapons, or participation in crime. However, other exclusive boundaries may be negotiated in the case management process. The goals of boundary-setting are to move from external structure to self-monitoring, and from exclusive to inclusive boundaries.

Many losses are produced when an offender, by legal mandate or personal choice, excludes most persons, places, and things from the emerging lifestyle. Some new, healthy options can eventually fill the void created by abstinence. In the interim, the offender will need considerable assistance to avoid apparently irrelevant decisions, high-risk situations, and lapses.

Research on relapse prevention with a wide range of addictive behaviors (cf. Donovan & Marlatt, 1988) identified overcontrol in the lifestyle as a precursor to addictive release or acting out. In effect, some recovering addicts react to losses by imposing even more control (or having others exert more external control) than needed to maintain abstinence. The Relapse Prevention model addresses this phenomenon by programming relapse on a small scale. For example, a compulsive overeater who has imposed an overly rigid food plan consisting of a long list of "forbidden foods" may be encouraged to eat one brownie (formerly forbidden) under supportive therapeutic conditions. The overeater learns to use coping skills and avoid self-defeating cognitive distortions by realizing that one bite of a forbidden food does not lead inevitably to relapse. Obviously, the correctional case manager cannot program or condone criminal lapses. However, there are naturally occurring slips, such as having contact with "forbidden" persons, which can be addressed in the therapeutic relationship. Similarly, the client must be able to freely discuss urges, cravings, and fantasies, without threat of immediate sanction, in order to avoid relapse. The client and case manager work together to maintain useful boundaries, rather than imposing arbitrary or overly restrictive boundaries that actually contribute to relapse.

Eventually, the client and case manager can turn their attention from the exclusive to the inclusive boundaries that define the new lifestyle. The recovering addict or offender typically resists external control, experiences losses, tries novel activities, and then embraces a new identity. At this stage in the process, correctional case management involves introduction of new options. The client may pursue additional education or job training, look for rewarding employment, establish healthy relationships, and explore new leisure activities. Leisure has been sacrificed in most criminal lifestyles. Even in the midst of great hedonism, there is a lack of genuine recreation. People, places, and things are used by addicts and offenders to avoid the pain and shame of the past. Normal, healthy leisure activities involve self-expression through individual and group endeavors. Success in leisure (e.g., a delinquent youth gaining recognition in a midnight basketball league), compensates for losses in the suddenly empty lifestyle. The recovering client gains relaxation and other coping skills, as well as enhanced self-efficacy. Thus, leisure programming and therapeutic recreation are important components in relapse prevention as the offender moves from a shameful past to a new, healthy future.

Establishing inclusive boundaries is an exciting process because it enables exploration of strengths, assets, and preferences. The correctional case manager helps the client find his or her place in the evolving lifestyle. However, this process may still feel as though one is trying to pull the offender out of a shell. While exploration of leisure and recreation typically emerges in the ongoing relationship, other important facets of a healthy lifestyle need to be included. Inclusive boundaries may incorporate changes in nutrition and health practices; relationships with family members, co-workers and friends; creative and self-expressive outlets; and spiritual practices and disciplines.

Changes in spirituality are common among offender populations. While there are "jailhouse conversions," motivated primarily by the desire to avoid consequences, many offenders earnestly reflect upon the costs of the criminal lifestyle and become aware of spiritual needs. Incarceration in the penitentiary was intended originally to facilitate reflection and conversion. The correctional case manager can contribute to the natural evolution of spirituality by initially mandating and later encouraging participation in a self-help or recovery group based on the Twelve Steps of Alcoholics Anonymous.

Relapse Prevention and Recovery

Dozens of self-help groups have been formed from the Twelve Steps and Twelve Traditions. Two of the groups, Narcotics Anonymous, and Sex Addicts Anonymous, along with Alcoholics Anonymous, serve large numbers of addicted offenders in fellowships across the United States. Each of the groups is self-sustaining and operates on the basis of anonymity or strict confidentiality. These self-help or recovery groups are dedicated to the maintenance of abstinence and eventual attainment of serenity through a progressive spiritual growth process.

Although avoidance of relapse or reoffense is the goal of both the cognitive-behavioral model of relapse prevention (Marlatt & Gordon, 1985), and the recovery movement, Twelve Step groups de-emphasize self-efficacy and focus upon "powerlessness" and reliance on a power greater than oneself. The steps described in Table 9.1 clearly indicate the process of recovery.

Table 9.1
The Twelve Steps of Alcoholics Anonymous

1. We admitted we were powerless over alcohol—that our lives had become unmanageable.

2. Came to believe that a Power greater than ourselves could restore us to sanity.

3. Made a decision to turn our will and our lives over to the care of God *as we understood Him.*

4. Made a searching and fearless moral inventory of ourselves.

5. Admitted to God, to ourselves and to another human being the exact nature of our wrongs.

6. Were entirely ready to have God remove all these defects of character.

7. Humbly asked Him to remove our shortcomings.

8. Made a list of all persons we had harmed, and became willing to make amends to all of them.

9. Made direct amends to such people wherever possible, except when to do so would injure them or others.

10. Continued to take personal inventory and when we were wrong promptly admitted it.

11. Sought through prayer and meditation to improve our conscious contact with God, *as we understood Him*, praying only for knowledge of His will for us and the power to carry that out.

12. Having had a spiritual awakening as the result of these steps, we tried to carry this message to alcoholics, and to practice these principles in all our affairs.

The initial steps in the recovery process are devoted to turning over control of one's life to God or a Higher Power. Atheists and agnostics participate in the program by choosing Higher Powers such as nature, the overall self-help group, and the accumulated wisdom of sage members or "old timers" (Grateful Members, 1977). Middle steps address character defects and personal shortcomings that interfere with personal growth. Later, the recovering addict makes amends or offers restitution to those harmed by the previous addictive behavior. The stepwork in the recovery process culminates in advocacy, by which the message of this spiritual program is carried to others. In this manner, the program is self-sustaining.

Newcomers in recovery are encouraged to regularly attend meetings in which members share aspects of their lives, without fearing judgment or interpretation. The group meetings are chaired or moderated by one member, although the groups are essentially leaderless. The process of each group meeting is guided by materials provided by headquarters for the organizations, as well as publishers such as Compcare and Hazledon. Meetings include open discussion, step study, and testimonial activities. However, members are discouraged from "cross-talk," which could involve one member giving another member advice, interpretation, or problem-solving. The structure afforded by the resource materials, meeting guidelines, and the 12 traditions reduce the likelihood that the leaderless meetings will become some type of pseudo-therapy or harmful application of group dynamics.

A typical recovery group meeting begins with the chairperson asking various members to read from program materials, which describe the 12 steps and traditions, how the program works, and selected guidelines. Then, the chair introduces a topic for consideration; a speaker, who provides a testimonial; a step for study, perhaps using the "Big Book" (the original text of Alcoholics Anonymous) or step workbooks; or a plan for members to volunteer self-reflections and disclosures. The group meeting concludes with prayer or collective recitation of recovery slogans or meditations.

The slogans of Twelve Step meetings convey conventional wisdom and short-hand reminders of what is important in recovery. Recovering addicts become mindful of these principles in daily life. The following slogans have been used in sexual addiction recovery (cf. *Hope and Recovery*). (Table 9.2.)

The HALT acronym in the fourth item affords a rapid self-test for estimating relapse risk. For example, "Am I hungry, angry, lonely, or tired?" If the answer is affirmative for any condition, the recovery person will be wary about making decisions, fearing potential relapse. Recovering addicts who have learned not to trust their distorted thinking seek feedback from other members before making major decisions, such as altering one's boundaries. One of the most important sources for feedback and support is the member's "sponsor."

Since recovery groups are not conducted by professional therapists, it is important to provide adequate structure to correct any excesses that could arise from individual members and their dynamics. In the recovery movement, the relationship of a member and his or her sponsor is an essential means of struc-

Table 9.2
Slogans in Recovery

1. *One Day at a Time*. It is possible to maintain sobriety in the here and now. One is responsible for recovery only today, or even for just one hour at a time. Preoccupation with the past or future elicits addictive thought patterns.

2. *Easy Does It*. Recovery is a slow, lifelong process. This slogan reminds the addict and co-addict to be tolerant and respectful of the natural course of change.

3. *Be Gentle With Yourself*. Pushing oneself relentlessly to achieve is an expression of addiction. Nonaddictive coping requires relaxation, rest, fun, and balance in the overall lifestyle.

4. *H.A.L.T.* These four conditions frequently signal risk for relapse: Hunger, Anger, Loneliness, and Tiredness. Recovery requires good physical and emotional health.

5. *First Things First*. Addicts will try to do everything at once. To combat perfectionism, it is important to make recovery the first priority in every decision.

6. *Act As If*. In order to continue participation in the recovery process, it is useful to counteract doubt by "acting as if" the program will work for you. With experience comes faith because you will see that you actually are recovering.

7. *If It Works, Don't Fix It*. This slogan addresses two problems in relapse: grandiosity and perfectionism. Since the program has worked for thousands of persons, it is the addict, not the program that needs to change. Accept things the way they are.

8. *This Too Shall Pass*. Believing that negative emotional situations will change insures that life is tolerable. This hope makes coping possible. Also, there is no situation so bad that acting out wouldn't make it even worse.

9. *Let Go and Let God*. This slogan reminds the addict to stop fighting and surrender concerns to the Higher Power.

10. *To Thine Own Self Be True*. Since the heart of recovery is honesty and recognizing personal value, the setting of boundaries should reflect personal rather than societal needs.

11. *Live and Let Live*. Each person has his or her own Higher Power and program of recovery. The addict focuses on working one's own program and respects the rights of others to find their own way.

12. *Keep It Simple*. Addicts and co-addicts thrive on crises and complex, unsolvable problems. The Twelve Steps remind one of the value of simplicity in daily life.

13. *There But For the Grace of God Go I*. Addicts are troubled by the desire to compare and control. Humility comes from recognizing the commonalities in the addictive process.

ture and guidance. The member, especially someone new to the self-help program, will consult regularly (perhaps daily) with the sponsor. This affords an opportunity to vent feelings, receive instruction about the program, and secure feedback about boundaries and lifestyle changes. Unlike a therapy relationship, contacts with the sponsor and recovery group members are frequently informal, even social. Most recovery meetings conclude in the clubhouse and reconvene in a local coffee shop or café.

The goals of relapse prevention are well served by participation in a Twelve Step group. Addiction is perceived by members as a chronic, deadly illness, requiring daily attention throughout the lifespan. The lifestyle is reorganized around safe boundaries as members learn from sponsors and old timers "what works." Cognitive distortions and triggers for relapse are identified through self-reflection, meditation, and practical application of slogans. New members find a strong, mature support network, as well as many resources for changing the lifestyle. Typical resources used during the initial term in the program include the family tree or life history, powerless and unmanageability inventories, step guidelines or worksheets, daily meditations, character defect checklists, affirmations, and reading lists (cf. Carnes, 1989).

Relapse Prevention and the Offense Cycle

Each addict or offender has a unique pattern of thoughts, feelings, and actions that converge on relapse. Yet, there are sufficient commonalities among certain classes of offenders to identify predictable sequences or cycles. Emerging from the cognitive-behavioral model of relapse prevention, there is a generic cycle of offense, which should be investigated thoroughly in correctional case management. The cycle of offense moves in a clock-like fashion leading to relapse:

Shame→Triggers→Feelings→Fantasies→Urges→Rituals→Distortions→Lapse, and so forth.

Triggers include interpersonal conflicts at home and work, as well as idiosyncratic symbols or reminders of past traumas. Feelings that contribute to relapse are primarily negative affective states such as fear and anger. However, any strong emotion can increase relapse risk. Fantasies emerge to compensate for feelings of loss or emptiness, to indirectly express anger and passive rage, to manage stress and anxiety, or to bolster a fragile ego. When fantasies persist, urges build. The urges may be experienced as cravings, preoccupations, or strong yearnings. Concurrent with the emergence of urges are rituals, the characteristic habit patterns that increase access to opportunities for reoffense or relapse. Rituals include getting into the car and driving to the old side of town, making contact with former associates, and walking past areas where lapses occur. In addition, rituals can involve unusual gestures and complex behavior patterns particular to the individual addict or offender.

While cognitive distortions permeate the thought process of the addict or offender, certain errors in thinking hasten relapse. Some of the typical distortions take the form of covert self-statements: "One last time," "I deserve some fun," or "No one is going to tell me what to do." Distortions facilitate or justify acting out of underlying conflictual or traumatic feelings. In this manner feelings are not expressed directly. Instead, undetected or undisclosed needs fuel a lapse or slip. During the lapse, the person perceives failure and experiences hopelessness. Low self-efficacy and lack of coping skills at this juncture may lead to a full-blown relapse. Following a slip or relapse, the addicted offender accumulates additional shame or internal feelings of emptiness and unworthiness. The accumulation of shame increases the likelihood that persons, places, and things will act as triggers for the next offense cycle.

Relapse Prevention Plan

As the offender and correctional case manager become familiar with the individual's cycle of reoffense, the two can work together on a plan to prevent relapse. Ideally, the terms of the treatment plan or probation/parole contract reflect boundaries needed to avoid relapse. The relapse prevention plan should not become an arbitrary exercise. Rather, the plan should be an application of a sophisticated understanding of the dynamics of relapse in an individual case. The following items in Table 9.3 represent basic terms in a relapse prevention plan.

Table 9.3
Relapse Prevention Plan

1. List emotional and interpersonal triggers.
2. Identify high-risk situations for you.
3. Specify nonaddictive coping resources.
4. Describe apparently irrelevant decisions made in the past.
5. Identify some lapses you have experienced.
6. Write names and telephone numbers of persons you could call for help.
7. Record plans for modifying your work life for better balance.
8. Record plans for modifying your leisure life for better balance.
9. Record plans for modifying your social life for better balance.
10. List meetings and groups you will attend.
11. State your present exclusive boundaries.
12. State your present inclusive boundaries.
13. State your present relationship boundaries.
14. Record probable consequences of relapse.

The relapse prevention plan includes terms derived from both the cognitive-behavioral and recovery models. While there can be conflicts between professional service providers and self-help groups, because of implicit conflicts in the two models, the recovering offender can be encouraged to partake of the best of both worlds. Most offenders will require some therapy and recovery program participation in order to avoid relapse.

Conclusions

Relapse prevention has received increasing attention in correctional counseling and case management. While relapse prevention can be a separate treatment component, it is addressed typically throughout the correctional case management process because reoffense is unacceptable. There are numerous similarities between offender behavior and addictive behavior. In fact, crime can be considered an addiction. Addictionology has provided methods and resources for reducing risk of relapse.

The Relapse Prevention (RP) model of Marlatt and his cognitive-behavioral colleagues emphasizes the cognitive distortions, expectancies, and habit patterns in the cycle of offense. The recovery or self-help movement emphasizes the need for lifestyle change and lifelong spiritual development. Unlike the RP model, the recovery model is based on attributions of powerlessness. The cognitive-behavioral model focuses upon the development of positive self-efficacy and expectancies of self-control, even in high-risk situations. The recovery model recommends strict boundaries and avoidance of "slippery situations" in order to maintain abstinence. Both models recommend a variety of activities to move from high external structure to greater self-management. Relapse prevention activities and resources include life histories, checklists, groupwork, and feedback. The offender and correctional case manager work together to construct a relapse prevention plan reflecting relapse dynamics and individual needs.

References

Apter, M.J. (1989). *Reversal Theory: Motivation, Emotion and Personality*. London, England: Routledge.

Author (1987). *Hope and Recovery: A Twelve Step Guide for Healing from Compulsive Sexual Behavior*. Minneapolis, MN: CompCare.

Carnes, P. (1989). *A Gentle Path through the Twelve Steps: A Guidebook for all People in the Process of Recovery*. Minneapolis, MN: CompCare.

Davidson, P.O. & S.M. Davidson (eds.) (1980). *Behavioral Medicine: Changing Health Lifestyles*. New York, NY: Brunner/Mazel.

Donovan, D.M. & G.A. Marlatt (eds.) (1988). *Assessment of Addictive Behaviors*. New York, NY: Guilford.

Hodge, J.E. (1991). "Addiction to Crime." *Issues in Criminological and Legal Psychology*, 2:92-96.

Grateful Members (1977). *The Twelve Steps for Everyone Who Really Wants Them*. Minneapolis, MN: CompCare.

Lee, N.K. & T.P.S. Oei (1993). "Exposure and Response Prevention in Anxiety Disorders: Implications for Treatment and Relapse Prevention in Problem Drinkers." *Clinical Psychology Review*, 13:619-632.

Marks, I. (1990). "Behavioural (Non-Chemical) Addictions." *British Journal of Addiction*, 85:1389-1394.

Marlatt, G.A. (1978). "Craving for Alcohol, Loss of Control, and Relapse: A Cognitive-Behavioral Analysis." In P.E. Nathan, G.A. Marlatt & T. Loberg (eds.) *Alcoholism: New Directions in Behavioral Research and Treatment* (pp. 271-314). New York, NY: Plenum.

Marlatt, G.A. (1985). "Relapse Prevention: Theoretical Rationale and Overview of the Model." In G.A. Marlatt & J.R. Gordon (eds.) *Relapse Prevention* (pp. 3-70). New York, NY: Guilford.

Marlatt, G.A. & J.R. Gordon (eds.) (1985). *Relapse Prevention*. New York, NY: Guilford.

Shiffman, S., L. Read, J. Maltese, D. Rapkin & M.E. Jarvik (1985). "Preventing Relapse in Ex-Smokers: A Self-Management Approach." In G.A. Marlatt & J.R. Gordon (eds.) *Relapse Prevention* (pp. 472-520). New York, NY: Guilford.

Steen, C. (1993). *The Relapse Prevention Workbook for Youth in Treatment*. Brandon, VT: Safer Society Press.

Chapter 10

Issues in Correctional Case Management with Ethnic Minority Offenders

Introduction

The purpose of this chapter is to help sensitize the potential correctional case management counselor to some problems and issues that may impinge upon successful correctional case management intervention with ethnic minority persons. Having knowledge about various ethnic minority individuals and groups in our society heightens the ability of the correctional case manager to become a more successful counselor because awareness of other cultures results in more culturally informed and perhaps more effective correctional case management. Culturally informed counseling is also important because it avoids standard explanations for human behavior and conventional strategies for counseling with offenders. Conventional methods for counseling with offenders have been, for the most part, derived from psychological, psychoanalytic, social learning, and biosocial theories concerning human behavior. These theories place less emphasis upon social factors in personality development. We believe that understanding social factors with respect to ethnic minority offenders is a vital dynamic in successful case management counseling with ethnic minority offenders. This point is in keeping with Goffman's (1961) idea that social behavior was shaped by the interaction among social norms, values, and roles within the environment.

What the authors propose to do in this chapter is to present some information from sociological and anthropological sources concerning cultural awareness and community learning that may help direct case management correctional intervention with ethnic minority persons and groups into more positive rehabilitation directions. In essence, we argue in this chapter for a kind of case management correctional counseling that includes cross-cultural knowledge, understanding, appreciation, and sensitivity. Four major themes that apply to correctional case management counseling with ethnic minorities will be presented:

1. Racism and most of its manifestations.

2. Ethnicity and ethnic minority status.

3. Some important issues with respect to ethnic minority families, and religious and spiritual beliefs and practices.

4. Some techniques for more ethnic-sensitive correctional case management interventions with ethnic minority offenders.

Barriers to Effective Correctional Case Management Intervention: Racism and its Kith and Kin

Understanding attitudes about racism with respect to its specific meaning as well as its generic manifestations is, by far, a necessary condition in order to promote effective case management correctional counseling. It is important to explore some commonly held attitudes about the self and the other person.

The term "attitudes" is a very difficult social science construct to comprehend. The authors are inclined to favor a social-psychological construction of the term. In the sociological sense, keeping with the ideas of Thomas and Znaniecki (1927), attitudes and values are thought to both coexist and be interdependent at the same time. In this sense, attitudes refer to an individual's tendency to react to certain social values in either a positive or negative way. In the psychological sense, Newcomb (1968) describes attitudes as residues from one's developmental experiences which influence how one interprets current situations and persons, and which also determine how one behaves toward current situations and persons. The social science literature is replete with all sorts of descriptions and definitions of the term. By way of summary, attitudes may be conceptualized as irrational belief systems and ideologies. We will continue, now, to examine a number of these concepts encompassing racism per se, discrimination, prejudice, stereotyping, powerlessness, oppression, and exploitation.

Racism

In its most specific form, racism is a system of beliefs which maintain that one racial group is superior to another. It is essentially an ideology because it is factitious and propagandistic. People who are racists seek to proselytize others in order to draw more converts to the belief system. It is commonly used to justify discrimination against one group or another. Quite commonly, the discrimination becomes institutionalized because a particular out-group may be denied an opportunity of access to social and economic goods or services because they are alleged to be inferior by a more dominant in-group.

Discrimination

Discrimination derives from racism. It is composed of two elements: a distorted cognitive process that maintains, without affirmative evidence, that one group of persons is inherently inferior to another; and, second, an affective or emotional element manifested by personalized dislike of a person of a different race. Discrimination can perhaps be more easily seen than defined. It often becomes visible when there is competition among groups for scarce resources. In this sense, one group, in the competition for resources, may view another group as a threat for certain resources. Some ethnic groups are larger or more powerful than others. Because of this, they may control more of the access to social and economic goods and services than smaller, less powerful groups. Often, this results in a differential social stratification by way of race, gender, and ethnicity, and, additionally, sometimes by sexual orientation, disability, and age. This results in a lack of access to social, educational, and economic opportunity structures for some groups. Parolees, for example, and especially those who have committed sexual crimes, often encounter discrimination when they re-enter a community. These limitations may be thought of as institutional barriers.

The notion of institutional barriers to social and economic mobility for certain groups is very well described in the sociology literature. The idea of institutional barriers has persisted as an important explanation of social disorganization and deviancy, including criminal behavior, beginning with the work of Durkheim (1951) and the theory of "anomie." Anomie is widely cited in the criminology literature as an explanation for deviancy. Anomie explains deviancy as the product of estrangement from society by certain individuals and groups because of the contradiction that appears to exist between the tendency of society to deify material success as the "American dream," coupled with a limitation of means to attain that success. Merton (1957) expanded upon this theory and used it to explain social organization and disorganization in terms of various patterns of deviancy and conformity. Cloward (1959) building upon Merton's work, conceptualized one form of criminal deviancy, illegal drug use, as a pattern of individual adjustment in the form of "retreatist" behavior, or, on a group basis, as the development of a retreatist subculture, as a response to the goals-versus ends societal contradiction.

Prejudice

Prejudice is primarily affective. That is, it is composed of emotions and feelings about other persons or groups which color these groups in an adverse, unfavorable, and sometimes sinister or ominous light. For example, prejudice is apparent when one group is unable to deal with their own unfavorable attitudes about another group and, instead, blames the other group for their own problems and difficulties. It is a form of scapegoating. Heffernan, Shuttlesworth, and Ambrosino (1992) characterized prejudice as values that were learned through socialization. These values become incorporated into the persona of the individual and become a part of their value system.

Stereotyping

Stereotyping is a type of distorted cognitive process. It involves making deductions or drawing inferences or conclusions from the specific to the general when a lack of connection or association is not demonstrable. More precisely, it involves noting one unfavorable characteristic or trait in a specific individual and concluding that all such persons that make up that group have the same trait. It is usually preceded by the word "and" and includes the word "are," such as: "and all women (African Americans, Hispanics, and so forth) are (insert derogatory label or trait)." It is a kind of simplistic and pejorative labeling that passes for more rigorous categorization and classification systems based upon more generally empirical or recognizable traits among groups. It leads to a belief that persons in certain groups usually act or respond in certain characteristic ways. It is based upon a process of illogical deduction and results in false predictions about behavior.

Powerlessness

Powerlessness and oppression are constructs that are generally derived from the literature on conflict theory. Conflict theory is associated with the work of Marx (1967). Marx, in his major work *Das Kapital*, suggests that as workers give up their labor and the products that they make to capitalists, they lose a sense of control (powerlessness) over their labor and over these products. For Marx, this results in an estrangement or alienation from society. More contemporaneously, the work of Fanon (1963) may provide a substantive basis for understanding these ideas. For Fanon, powerlessness and oppression could be understood in terms of the historical and current dialectical or interaction between Colonial and Third World countries; a relationship characterized by economic exploitation and social and psychological intimidation, control, and oppression. For example, in applying these ideas, people on welfare might be described as being the victims of a national "welfare colonialism" which uses the economic power of the welfare check to manage and control behavior in order to maintain the societal status quo.

Powerlessness, then, refers to power imbalance between and among various individuals and groups of individuals. On the micro or interpersonal level, it can be used to explain differences in status and role relations between, for example, a husband and wife, or a parent and child. In the sense in which it is used in this chapter, it refers to the fact that some groups have more social, psychological, economic, or political power to impact and access opportunity systems, and to obtain valuable goods and services vis-à-vis other groups. Ethnic minority groups, by and large, have historically had less power of various kinds to control their own destinies by impacting their biopsychosocial environments.

Oppression

Oppression is a very difficult construct to understand. On the external level, it refers to the actions taken, either directly or indirectly, by one group to prevent or hinder another group from gaining access to important and valuable psychological, social, political, economic, and educational opportunities and services. However, oppression has a more human or personal dimension.

Oppression can be used, with respect to managing the interactions between majority and minority groups, in order to obtain conformity and obedience to majority culture norms and values. It can be used to maintain a societal status quo. As Baxter (1992) conceptualized it, on the psychosocial level it refers to a process inherent in society through which people are directed toward conformity and obedience in their behavior. It is, in particular, most apparent in modern, technologically driven societies, and, especially in the workplace. It occurs when individuals are redirected away from opportunities, via their work, to meet some of their self-fulfilling or self-actualizing psychological needs. What occurs instead is an obsession with organization efficiency in order to maximize the attainment of economic goals. It can especially result in self or personal alienation when technological and economic values conflict with personal and psychological values.

Exploitation

Exploitation refers to a process whereby one group appropriates and misuses the skills, talents, resources or energies of a subordinate group in order to advance the interests of the majority group. It usually involves maneuvers and manipulations to gain social, economic, or political power over another group. It can also take the form of co-option. Co-option is a process whereby a dominant group, through persuasion, manipulation, or coercion causes a member or members of an opposing group to become assimilated or absorbed into the majority group, thus helping to stifle discord or protest. Acculturation, or the adoption of the central cultural and social values of the majority culture by an ethnic minority person, is another form of co-option. Sometimes acculturation is incomplete. When this occurs, an individual is often "marginalized" or caught between the interface of the dominant and minority cultures. Urbanized American Indians who sometimes spend a weekend at a "sweat lodge" on a reservation, or who, when imprisoned, insist on access to native religious services, are examples of this phenomena.

Ethnicity and Ethnic Minority Groups

The usual caveat is in order here when presuming to describe common characteristics of groups of any type: groups are comprised of individuals of various sorts. Their characteristics range across a wide spectrum. However, social science research has identified some characteristics which, in the aggregate, tend to co-vary with specific ethnic minority groups. Understanding what some of these major characteristics are is an important requisite for professional case management correctional counseling. Before proceeding to describe some of these characteristics, however, it is important to define two terms: ethnicity and ethnic minority.

Ethnicity

Ethnicity refers to a group of individuals who share in a common a set of values, traditions, and a social and cultural history and experience, not held in common with other persons with whom they interact. In other words, ethnicity refers to the cultural features of a specific group. Unlike racial differences, ethnic differences are culturally driven and are not genetically based. DeVos (1975) holds that the ethnic identity of a group consists of their subjective or symbolic or emblematic use of any aspect of their culture for the purpose of separating or distinguishing themselves from other cultural groups. Some of these cultural aspects commonly include religious beliefs and practices, language, common ancestry, similar place of residence or birth, national origin, and a sense of historical continuity of the group. Mindel, Habenstein, and Wright (1988) describe how ethnic groups work to maintain their ethnic identification and solidarity. They point out that ethnic groups do this as the families socialize their members into the culture through exposure to family lifestyles and activities. Community celebrations of cultural and religious holidays and family gatherings are means for promoting and developing cultural awareness and solidarity.

Ethnic Minority

There are many groups and subgroups of ethnic minority persons in the United States. What distinguishes the term for the purposes of effective correctional case management practice is the extent to which a particular ethnic minority group is at risk, or believes itself to be at risk, or at social, political, or economic disadvantage with respect to other groups or to the larger society. In interpreting Wirth (1945), a renowned sociologist, the term refers to persons who regard themselves as being the objects of collective societal discrimination. This is probably the most succinct definition of the meaning of the term.

More specifically, ethnic minority persons or groups that are at risk in our society generally have several distinguishing characteristics. The most commonly observed distinction is skin color. Usually, African Americans, Asian Americans, and Native Americans can be distinguished in this way from other persons in society. However, it is generally true, but not always true, that persons of color comprise ethnic minority groups at risk. There are many confounding cultural variables. As Lum (1986) noted, name and language are also important characteristics. For example, many African Americans have Africanized their names although most carry European names. Many Latinos are named after ancestors or close relatives, while others have Anglicized their names. Asian Americans sometimes combine an English first name with Asian middle and last names.

Other distinguishing characteristics of this group might include religion and language. Racial differences, such as skin color or other physical characteristics, as well as social and cultural differences, such as religion and language, are visible differences. These differences are often aggregated and become group characteristics that are often viewed in a pejorative manner by the majority culture. Thus, a stereotyping occurs since individuals' characteristics become less important than the characteristics of the group of which the person is a member. This can lead to collective discrimination.

There are a number of other distinguishing characteristics of ethnic minority groups at risk as well. One such difference is group solidarity or cohesiveness. As Jenkins (1981) notes: "Black people believe that no matter what your basic differences may be with fellow Blacks, you must stand together in a common cause" (1981:77). Of course, although there are a number of distinguishing characteristics of ethnic minority groups, deviations from value orientations, such as racial loyalty, are sometimes breached. A notable example was the testimony Anita Hill presented against the nomination of Clarence Thomas for Supreme Court Justice during his United States Senate hearing. Nevertheless, in many ethnic minority groups there is often the feeling of being in the presence of "our own kind," as well as an affinity for other persons of the same group. Quite often marriage within the same group is encouraged. Group solidarity represents an ethos of the common ancestry, common traditions, and common values. Persons are born into these groups. Even if they are descended from interracial parentage, the ethnic minority ancestry is often viewed as the key determinant of group membership.

DeVos and Romanucci-Ross (1975) describe this kind of group solidarity or cohesiveness as "mutuality." For these researchers, mutuality means that activities that are carried out within the group are based upon parallel or concerted behavior and a bond of mutual trust. Ethnic minority groups, in terms of their intragroup interactions, tend to emphasize cooperation and minimize competition unless the competition is directed at individuals or groups outside the ethnic group. In other words, ethnic groups at risk tend to create a wall of solidarity against what they consider to be discrimination or oppression. In addition, they collectively strive toward what they view as independence, liberation, and autonomy.

Finally ethnic minority persons and groups can be understood from the standpoint of a social systems perspective. Individuals, groups, and institutions as social systems do not exist in a vacuum. They interact in a three-way relationship. As Anderson (1981), while interpreting and applying some of the theoretical work of Maslow (1970), and Erickson (1963) describes it, an individual's personality system consisting of his or her needs, wishes, and desires; the group's milieu, spirit, or mood; and, an institutions's roles and expectations converge in our society and culture. Each system affects the other systems and is, in turn, affected by the other systems. Therefore, racial, cultural, and ethnic differences have importance and meaning for the ethnic minority persons and groups as they interact with other individuals and groups, and especially as they interact with social institutions, such as the criminal justice system. Norton (1978) calls this a "dual perspective." For her, ethnic minority persons and groups can be understood as simultaneously having a dual perspective or world-view about life. She believes that ethnic minority persons who are at risk or at some particular disadvantage in our society tend to consciously and systematically perceive, compare, interpret, or understand the attitudes, behaviors, intentions, and values of other majority individuals and groups and the larger society through the filters of their immediate family and community systems.

Gomez and Cook (1977) in discussing mental health services and Chicanos, view the dual perspective as an interplay between the Chicano and majority cultures which affects their use of these types of services. As they view it, "Cultural conflict results from Chicanos' attempts to accommodate both the 'Mexican' and the 'American' cultures" (1977:10). The writers believe that this dual perspective is an important and defining characteristic of ethnic minority persons and groups, and is an important consideration in delivering effective case management correctional services.

Ethnic Minority Family, Religious, and Spiritual Beliefs and Practices

We have chosen to focus upon the family and religious and spiritual beliefs and practices of ethnic minority persons because we believe that these are the most important social factors with respect to understanding and working with ethnic minority offenders. It is also helpful that the social science research literature appears to contain a larger amount of empirical data concerning these areas. This is especially true with respect to the literature about ethnic minority families.

However, before proceeding, the issue of assimilation versus multiculturalism needs to be addressed. This issue is, and has been, under considerable debate in our society almost since its inception. Important advocates for the assimilation perspective, such as Schlesinger (1993), argue that American culture and society is an ideal that came about through the assimilation and integration of various ethnic minority groups into American society. Ethnic group values and traditions are important and need to be celebrated and maintained. He notes that American society is, after all, a melting pot of various cultural strains. On the other side, multiculturalists seem to oppose assimilation and integration and argue, instead, for the recognition and acknowledgement of the importance of each group's cultural values and tradition. Some of them believe that an ethnic minority person's psychological well-being and self-esteem are tied to the historical understanding and current link that they have with their own cultural and racial roots. This is the ideological rationale for bicultural and bilingual programs in schools, and for Afro-centric education programs. The point that is often made by proponents of multiculturalism is that each culture is important and is of equal value, and needs to be maintained and fostered as separate strands in the American societal mosaic. Advocates of either position often accuse the others of racism.

It can be observed that some groups hold on to their cultural values and traditions very closely. With other groups, the hold is more tenuous. However, the writers believe that what is important for a clinician or correctional counselor with respect to any sociocultural hypothesis about society is the understanding that no one is culture-free. Mayo (1991) underlines the importance of this point by stating that "ethnicity is more than distinctiveness defined by race, religion, or national origin. Conscious and unconscious processes that fill a deep psychological need for security, identity, and continuity are involved" (1991:318). Or, as Devore and Schlesinger (1986) have pointed out, although one's ethnicity can be a source of identity, strength, and group solidarity, it can also be a source of conflict, strife, and discord. What is most important is the present and the emotional meanings that we attach to the reality of our current circumstances. This is the key point for correctional counselors.

Before describing some of the more important family, and religious and spiritual values and beliefs among ethnic minority groups and individuals, it should be re-emphasized that ethnic minority groups are very diverse. We do not maintain that the values and beliefs that we will present are characteristic of all members of these groups. There are many exceptions. However, in order to deal with this topic from a social science perspective, we have to look for common characteristics, patterns, and trends. This is an exercise in reductionistic thinking. The generalizations that emerge from this process represent aggregate characteristics that research methodologies suggest have a goodness of fit for most ethnic minority persons. There are other considerations as well that impinge upon efforts to clearly describe the characteristics of ethnic minority persons and groups. These considerations include geographical proximity to the mother culture, and immigration history and status.

Ethnic minority persons who have only recently entered this country maintain closer ties with the mother culture. Hispanics who live along the southwestern border between the United States and Mexico have a close proximity to Mexico and thus maintain closer cultural and language ties. In fact, some of these persons maintain dual citizenship. By contrast, the self-described Spanish of northern New Mexico can trace their ancestral roots to pre-colonial America. Many of the traditions of colonial Spain can be found in their culture intermingled with American Indian traditions. In addition, one should understand that many ethnic minority persons are also bicultural and/or bilingual. They are in the process of trying to combine two different cultural systems. When we use terms such as "ethnic minority group" we are essentially using a term that represents an umbrella under which many subgroups can be placed. For example, the term "Latino" can include Mexican Americans, South and Central Americans, and Mexicans, as well as persons from various Caribbean areas, such as Cubans, Dominicans, Puerto Ricans, and so forth. However, the term "Hispanic" seems to have a more limited scope. It principally refers to Mexican Americans. Similar difficulties exist with terms such as "Asian Americans."

Religion is also not a definitive factor in delineating members of ethnic minority groups. Although the great majority of Hispanics are Roman Catholics, because of missionary work many Hispanics are fundamentalist Protestants.

Language is also not a principal determinate of ethnic minority status. The Cajuns of southern Louisiana and the Hispanics of the southwestern United States use dialectical and provincial forms of the original mother language. Northern New Mexicans use an archaic form of Spanish. In Hawaii, many native Hawaiians speak "pidgin English" which is a blending of Hawaiian, English, Portuguese, and several Asian languages (cf. Reinecke, 1969).

The federal government, in its zeal to classify and categorize various groups within American society for demographic purposes, has contributed to the difficulty of defining ethnic minority groups. The principal difficulty with federal efforts comes about through its attempts to classify ethnic minority persons and groups by their geographic regions or by the country from which they immigrated. In addition, the problem is further compounded because an individual may become a member of an ethnic group by self-proclamation. The difficulty in classification based on country of origin or geographic region can be seen in the federal government's definition of the term "Hispanic." As the term is used, it can refer to any individual whose origin is from Mexico, Cuba, Puerto Rico, Central or South America, or from another Spanish culture, regardless of race (Office of Management and Budget, 1978). This definition is based on the supposition that all of these people have a common Spanish culture, regardless of race. Of course, these geographical areas represent many different cultures and races. In an important work, Castex (1994) gets at the problem with this type of classification system. For her, it represents an attempt to create "an ethnic group in a dialectic with the state" and, for Hispanics, as a process that "was bidirectional, involving state institutions and those so ascribed, to identify, control, and provide needed services to members of the new group" (1994:289). She states that this kind of classification system has been applied to African Americans and American Indians as well. It may very well be that the rationale for the use of these kinds of omnibus classification systems is political rather than demographic.

The Family

It is important to define the term family before discussing ethnic minority families. Definitions of the term are very inexact and usually ethnocentric. In order to get at its best meaning, one should define it in terms of its characteristics. Robertson (1979) provides a cumbersome but excellent definition: "the family is a relatively permanent group of people related by ancestry, marriage, or adoption, who live together and form an economic unit and whose adult members assume responsibility for the young" (1979:316).

There is a great deal of social science research literature concerning ethnic minority families. Jenkins (1981) was a pioneer with respect to providing insights about the structure and function of African American families. He described the African American family structure in terms of a vertical hierarchy of parental authority and control. In spite of the fact that today many African American families are single-parent matriarchal families, the historical pattern was patriarchal, with the father as the principal parental authority and the recipient of obedience from the mother and the children.

Research suggests that ethnic minority families serve as a vehicle for the socialization of their children into their culture. This is often done through the family milieu and lifestyle. It also is accomplished via participation in many types of community activities (Mindel, Habenstein & Wright, 1988). For example, the celebration of Martin Luther King Day serves to bring pride in their ethnic heritage to African Americans, reiterates their social and cultural history, and emphasizes the notion of pan-Africanism and links to the mother country.

Family structure is also very important to Asian Americans. Lum (1986) has noted that Asian American families have historically underscored the importance of the family and its structural relationships. For example, in Chinese American families, the family becomes the source of identification of the self. The family is also the primary reference group. The family provides social support and psychological identity for its members. More specifically, Lum states that: "It (the Chinese American family) exerts control over interpersonal conduct, social relations, and occupational and marital selection" (1986:64). Family structure is also an important socialization force in Japanese American families. Japanese Americans place a great deal of importance upon cohesiveness, mutual aid, and cooperation among family members. It is expected that the older members will be obeyed and respected. This is especially true with respect to the patriarch of the family (the oldest male). In Japanese American families, as well as with most ethnic minority families, it is expected that the younger members will take care of the aged members. Mutuality, cooperation, and cohesiveness are factors that also characterize Filipino, Korean, and Hawaiian American families. A number of other cultural values concerning the family, noted in Japanese American families, seem to apply across other Asian American groups as well. These values are: obedience to family rules and roles, enryo or self-effacement, a sense of fatalism, hiya or the avoidance of shame, and respect for authority (Browne & Broderick, 1994). Lum (1986) would add to this list the use of indirect communication, and personal and sexual modesty.

In Hispanic families, a configuration of parental authority, with the father at the apex of a vertical structure, is normative. With this pattern, the authority of the father is maintained through respect (respecto) and obedience. Model children respect and obey their fathers. The ideal wife is acquiescent and compliant. Respect and obedience to the father as the patriarch is the model for child development and socialization. Achieving an understanding of ethnic minority family structures, and the status and role relationships in these family structures, can inform correctional case management offender rehabilitation efforts because it allows the case manager to target his or her counseling energies toward the most influential change agents in the family system in order to enlist the family in efforts to rehabilitate the offender.

One cannot venture very far in an examination of the literature about Chicano or Hispanic families without encountering the term "machismo." An understanding of this concept is very helpful in understanding Hispanic family structures and intra-familial relationships. In its literal meaning machismo alludes to the masculine ideal of domination and sexual potency. However, it means much more than that. In a more culturally specific sense, it refers to certain beliefs and values concerning the normative aspects of the male role: maintenance and support of the family, protector of the children and the wife, and defender of the honor of women. Paradoxically, however, the term also refers to men who are sexually aggressive, tend to dominate women, and are sexually hyperactive. In many instances, the sex roles of Hispanic males have been more commonly, and stereotypically, subsumed under these kinds of antisocial behaviors. This has often resulted in a pejorative depiction of Hispanic males in popular literature and in the media as the "macho man" or as participants in gang violence.

"Marianismo" is an important concept that must be understood in order to define the sex role of wives and mothers in Hispanic families. In Hispanic folk culture, marianismo is a characterization of the ideal personality of women. Across the literature on the subject, this ideal woman is emotional, kind, instinctive, whimsical, docile, compliant, vulnerable, and unassertive. She has a higher status in the community if she has children. The roots of marianismo reside in Roman Catholic theology. In Roman Catholicism, the Virgin Mary was both a virgin and a madonna. She was a virgin and angel, thus a subject of worship. Because of this, she was, in the religious sense, spiritually better than men (Comas-Diaz, 1988). Therefore, marianismo alludes to the expectation that the ideal wife and mother is required to be immaculate and spiritually superior to men. This translates into a kind of sex-based role behavior in which the ideal woman is expected to suffer without complaining, and to place the needs of her husband and children before her own wishes and desires. In some Hispanic families it is also important to understand the corresponding female role of the "madre" or grandmother. She is often the key person with respect to carrying out the duties of child-rearing, socialization, and discipline when the parents are not present.

Hispanic folk cultural families consist of extended family and kinship systems. This characteristic allows for reciprocal self support and interconnectedness among the members. This kind of family system is, in essence, a natural support system or "compadrazo." Compadrazo refers to the kinship network that interconnects the godparents and the godchildren ("padrinos" and "ahijados"). This linkage occurs at the baptism of the child. The godparents are expected to have a role in the socialization and development of their godchild. If something adverse should happen to the parents of the child, godparents are expected to support and care for their godchild. These interconnected systems, which consist of parents, children, godparents, and godchildren form a kind of mutual support system in which the godparents become co-parents ("compadres") for the child. This type of support system often reduces or eliminates the need for social welfare service. Correctional case managers need to understand the importance of the compadrazo.

American Indians are very difficult to characterize on a group basis because there are so many different tribal groupings and even subgroups among tribes. The Ojibwa of the Lake Superior region, the Seminoles of Florida, the Cherokees of Oklahoma, and the Tegua of Texas have many common social and cultural characteristics, but also have many dissimilar characteristics. In general, common family characteristics among American Indians include a strong sense of responsibility and obligation toward the family and the tribal group, family and tribal loyalty, cohesiveness, and inter-tribal cooperation. Extended kinship systems also seem to be to be the norm, and non-competition among family and tribal members is held in importance. Non-interference in the personal matters and situations of other persons is also valued. Increasingly, however, American Indians are relocating to urban areas. When their family groups are examined in urban settings, most of their distinctive "Indian" characteristics seem to diminish. For example, it is difficult for an Apache child to maintain the tradition of long hair among males when public school dress codes prescribe a different standard. Other examples can be cited with respect to dress, food items, and religious practices.

Religion and Spiritualism

Religion may be defined as a system of spiritual beliefs and practices that help people understand and cope with the issues of life and death. For ethnic minority persons, however, religion fills many other needs.

The African American church has historically held a place of major importance in the lives of African American families. In planning for social welfare service in African American communities, the support and cooperation of the churches must be considered. For more than 300 years, African American churches have provided a place where African Americans could find sanctuary from the hostile white world and escape from the stress of racism (Frazier, 1963). Frazier believed that the African American church was important in the lives of African Americans not only because it provided a place for spirituality and sanctuary but because it was also a place where individuals and families would find "a structured social life in which the Negro could give expression to his deepest feelings and at the same time achieve status and find a meaningful existence" (1963:44). Staples (1976) states that the church filled the need for refuge from a hostile and racist white world. He notes that African American churches have helped African Americans deal with the detrimental forces of racism, while providing a means for reducing stress and tension. In addition, he stated that the African American church has also "given credibility to cultural heritage, validated the worth of Black people, and provided for the future" (1976:32). We also know that African American churches provided a base and the leadership for the civil rights movement of the early 1960s.

Although evangelical protestantism has made some inroads, Roman Catholicism has endured as the principal and dominant religious ideology among Hispanics. Every barrio seems to have a church. In Hispanic communities, the church is the hub of religious activities, but is also the center for social and cultural activities and ceremonies. The priest, or padre, is an important religious figure and symbolic father figure in Hispanic neighborhoods. He is responsible for the religious leadership of the community and he is interconnected with most of the educational, social, and cultural activities and programs that occur in the neighborhood. In these kinds of communities, it is important to establish a professional linkage with the priest in order to enhance case management services with offenders.

In many Hispanic communities, especially those that are closer to the mother country, several Roman Catholic beliefs and practices have been blended and combined with various folk cultural ideas. The religious synthesis that has resulted has come about through a fusion of certain American Indian and African beliefs with Catholicism. Borrello and Mathias (1977) describe religious customs in some Puerto Rican American communities as a blending of certain Roman Catholic practices with African and Caribbean Indian beliefs. They refer to this phenomena as "santeria." The center for the practice of santeria seems to be the local herbal medicine store or folk medicine pharmacy ("botanica"). Along with herbal medicines, these stores sell santerias or religious images ("santos"), icons, blessed ornaments, and artifacts that have spiritual significance and magical powers. Botanicas are important because they serve as locations for folk medical remedies as well as for religious worship. These kinds of stores may be found in all sorts of ethnic minority neighborhoods, for example in Chinese, Vietnamese, and Salvadoran American neighborhoods. Some Chinese Americans, for example, attribute magical and spiritual properties to various kinds of herbs, such as ginseng. Products derived from deer antlers are also thought by some Chinese Americans to contribute to sexual virility. The senior author of this book encountered a Chinese American family that was treating their developmentally disabled son with ginseng. They believed that the plant had medical and spiritual properties.

There are a number of other spiritual beliefs and practices that are important for many Hispanics. One of the most important of these is "curanderismo." Gomez and Cook (1977) describe "curanderos" and "curanderas" as folk healers. They state that these folk healers are sometimes believed to have received their power to heal from God. Curanderos and curanderas, therefore, are religious or spiritual healers.

The notion of curanderiso is closely related to another belief, "espanto" or "susto." Susto, the more common term, refers to a process by which an individual's soul can be lost or stolen by someone else. This can happen through a magical process or ritual involving a magically inspired fear, or by an evil hex ("mal puesto" or "brujeria"). Sometimes hexes occur because of romantic jealousy or envy ("envida") by a former lover (Gomez & Cook, 1977). Susto may symptomatic of certain kinds of mental health disorders, principally chronic depression and some psychosomatic reactions.

Gillin (1958), an anthropologist, has provided some important insights about susto derived from field research in Guatemala. He stated that the Guatemalans he observed believed that susto was caused by the loss of the soul that escaped during a magical fright. When the soul is lost, a person remains in a state of religious limbo, and can never achieve salvation and go to heaven. While observing the work of a courandero, he noted that the curandero combined Indian methods of massage, imitative magic, and suggestion, with confession, in order to return the stolen soul to the patient. The connection to Roman Catholicism is clear.

For Gillin, susto was always connected to physical illness or other abnormal conditions of the body, including psychological abnormalities. He stated that "magical fright is manifested in a person by symptoms of depression, withdrawal from normal social activity and responsibility, and signs of a temporary collapse of the ego organization" (1958:354).

A closely related belief is that of "mal ojo" or evil eye. In many rural Hispanic communities the mothers of infants hide or shield the faces of their children from the view of outsiders, and especially from the view of non-Hispanics. This belief centers upon the notion that the soul of a child could be captured through the magical process of mal ojo by an outsider who gazed admiringly upon the child. It is important for case managers to consult with curanderos and curanderas if they are working with offenders who believe that they are affected by susto and hexes.

American Indian beliefs, as a religious system, can be best described as animism. In this type of religious system, magical spirits are thought to exist and to occupy the world. They can become present in the world in the form of people. They are also present as inanimate objects and things. As inanimate objects they may take on the appearance of rocks, mountains, rivers, valleys, and so forth. They can also take the form of material forces such as the rain, snow, and the wind. In some cases, they can take an animate form such as a deer, a bird, or a bear.

Their religious and spiritual belief systems view life as a partnership between people, animals, things, and the forces of nature. Facets of nature and the phenomena of natural and physical forces can be seen in all aspects of their life. Nature inspires and directs their belief system and shapes much of their personal and group behavior.

In the opinion of the writers, a great deal of insight about American Indian religious beliefs and practices, which has direct implications for correctional counseling, can be seen in the work of Boyer (1964). Boyer was a psychoanalyst who conducted clinical research among the Mescalero Apaches of New Mexico. In one of his major findings, he determined that these Apaches viewed religion as an indistinct and enigmatic spiritual power. On occasion, this power entered into the natural world. When this force entered the world, it inhabited inanimate objects and gave these objects the ability to become animate objects. Many of these inanimate objects were tools and implements. But they could also be mountains, rocks or other natural objects. These spiritual forces would appear, in a physical or human form, usually during a dream or while an individual was in a trance. At this point, supernatural powers were given to him. The appearance of the spiritual power in a physical or human form parallels the Hispanic folk cultural belief concerning susto or magical fright.

The recipient of these powers could use them as a means to achieve good or evil outcomes. Shamans or tribal priests directed their supernatural powers toward good purposes. Boyer stated that "This power has no intrinsic attribute of good or evil; its virtue is its potency" (1964:523). Therefore, in a religious context, the shaman would use his magical power to work with other supernatural powers, witches, and the ghosts of the dead toward positive outcomes for an individual or for the tribe. This is particularly evident in healing ceremonies for physical illnesses. The shaman also had another important magical power. He could, through spiritual ceremonies and rituals, mediate with other supernatural powers, beings, or witches that the tribe or any of its members may have offended (Boyer, 1964).

Today, many urban and rural American Indians engage in various kinds of religious and spiritual ceremonies. These ceremonies are designed to put people in contact with supernatural and spiritual forces. In this way, spiritual and magical healing may be obtained. Quite often the ceremonies are community-based, and American Indians and non-American Indians participate. Examples of various ceremonies include powwows, sweat lodges, dream and vision sessions, dancing, rhythmic drumming, and chanting. Medicine men may also be contacted during these ceremonies concerning physical illnesses.

With respect to American Indians and, to a lesser degree, with Hispanics, and with some Asian Americans, and Hawaiians and Pacific Islanders, religious and spiritual beliefs and practices generally include animism, myths and rituals, magic, witchcraft, divinations, the magical treatment of illness, death, ghosts, ancestor worship, shamans and priests, and ritualism and taboos (cf. James, 1904; Lessa & Vogt, 1958; Pukui, Haertig & Lee, 1972).

It is also important for correctional case managers to understand the role of religion and spiritual values among Asian Americans. Asian Americans comprise a large and very diverse group. It is not possible to comment about all of the religions and spiritual belief systems among the various groups. We will direct our efforts toward some of the major religions of Asian Americans. These include: Hinduism, Buddhism, and Confucianism.

In Christian theology, mankind was created by God in his own image. Mankind, however, is imperfect, but through faith, words, and deeds, mankind can be perfected and achieve salvation. Hinduism does not have a parallel with

Christian ideas about original sin and the fall from grace. Mankind is not alienated from the Deity because of personal or human failings such as sin. In Hinduism we all mirror God. Mankind contains divine power. In order to attain perfection, a person must act on their divine nature. Campbell (1959) interprets this idea to mean that a person expresses his or her divine nature by bringing "the spontaneous activity of his mind stuff to a state of stillness and he will experience that divine principle within him which is the very essence of his existence" (1959:57). The divine power within us is our sense of independence, intellect, rationality, and self-worth. Divine power is manifested by living the life of a world and material-renouncing ascetic. Living an ascetic lifestyle releases the God-like power within us.

Bouquet (1961) comments that for those who practice Hinduism, the events of human life lack singular importance. Life is a circular and unending journey through the world. Those who follow the path of the ascetic are looking after their spiritual welfare. Bouquet states that in Hinduism "self-denial is better than self-indulgence, the suppression of passion and desires is better than their gratification" (1961:147).

Self-perfection is achieved when we act in harmony with others persons. This will result in a harmonious world, thus mankind will be perfected. This last point represents an intrapersonal and intergroup dynamic with respect to understanding and counseling many types of Asian American offenders.

Buddhism began as a reform movement within Hinduism. Buddhism does not acknowledge any deities or supernatural powers that could help mankind overcome the vicissitudes of human existence. The essence of Buddhism is contained in a view about the meaning of life termed "The Eightfold Path." This view of life consists of "Four Noble Truths." Correctional case managers can enhance their effectiveness in working with some Asian American offenders if they understand these four truths.

The first truth exemplifies the reality that life consists of suffering and that the cycle of life is full of events that cause unhappiness. Some of these events include separation from loved objects, and failure to obtain one's desires. The second truth describes the source of unhappiness. It is caused by selfish urges and desires for pleasure, worldly existence, and affluence. The third truth contains the optimistic message that selfish desires and urges can be destroyed. The fourth truth describes how selfish urges and desires can be destroyed, and how happiness can be achieved. This is accomplished by following The Eightfold Path, which consists of these behaviors: right views, right aspirations, right speech, right conduct, right livelihood, right endeavor, right mindfulness, and right meditation (Braden, 1954; Ringgren & Strom, 1967).

In an analogy to Buddhism, the problems of offenders reside in their fixation upon selfish needs. Selfish cravings can be destroyed and happiness can be achieved if an offender follows The Eightfold Path. The elements in The Eightfold Path correspond well with cognitive-behavioral counseling approaches. The Twelve Step Alcoholic Anonymous support group approach also seems to have much in common with the steps in The Eightfold Path.

Confucianism is considered to be both a philosophy and a religion. The importance of understanding Confucianism cannot be understated for the case manager who wants to be able to work effectively with Asian Americans; especially Chinese Americans, as well as with many Southeast Asian refugees.

As a religious and philosophical system, Confucianism informs its practitioners about how to achieve a righteous life style. Its primary difference from Christianity is encompassed by the term "hsiao" or piety. Hsiao refers to the religious idea that those who are now living are interconnected with their ancestors as well as with the institutions of society (Ringgren & Strom, 1967). Those who are now living must live a good and virtuous life so that the interconnections among the ancestors, living persons, and societal institutions can be strong and viable.

Confucianism represents the essential teachings of Confucius, who was renowned as the greatest of Chinese philosophers. His teachings include the following points (Braden, 1954):

1. Human nature is good and evil is unnatural.

2. People have free will and can choose their own conduct and behavior.

3. Virtue is a reward in itself.

4. People do not refrain from evil conduct because of the fear of punishment.

5. And, in a remarkable similarity with Christianity, "do not do to others that which you do not want them to do to you."

Confucianism contains several important elements for correctional case mangers. First, it emphasizes the importance of self-understanding and personal introspection into our conduct and behavior. Second, it causes us to understand the importance of valuing the feelings and needs of other people. And, third, Confucianism seems to be telling us, through its belief about the ladder among ancestors, living people, and society, that we can all learn from other persons and from other experiences.

Correctional Case Management and Ethnic Minority Offenders

From our examination of some of the research about ethnic minority families and their religious and spiritual belief systems, several pervasive themes have emerged that merit consideration by correctional case managers. We believe that an understanding of these themes can result in more effective and more ethnic-sensitive case management with ethnic minority offenders:

1. The significance of the history, traditions, and ceremonies of ethnic minority groups in the formation of an individual's personal identity.

2. The role of the family as a system for the socialization and acculturation of individuals into the culture of the group.

3. The importance and meaning of the role relationships in ethnic minority family and the kinship systems.

4. The value that various religious and spiritual beliefs and practices hold for ethnic minority persons and groups.

5. The impact of the historical experiences of ethnic groups, especially experiences involving racism, because these experiences are frequently used by ethnic minority individuals as a means to screen and test the behavior, actions, and motives of other groups.

6. The concept of the dual perspective. The dual perspective requires a delicate sociocultural balancing act. Ethnic minority persons derive energy, identity, security, and a sense of group cohesiveness from their ethnicity. At the same time, their ethnicity creates personal tension and role strain as they attempt to accommodate their ethnic identity values with the majority cultural values without becoming culturally marginized or perceived as having sold out to the majority culture.

We now come to a discussion and analysis of some techniques for effective correctional counseling with ethnic minority persons. These techniques can support and enhance the correctional case management process, roles, and techniques that were discussed in Chapters 6 and 7.

The Importance of Problems in the Current Context

It is important to focus on a present rather than future time orientation when counseling with ethnic minority offenders. The immediacy of their problems must be addressed. It may not be feasible or possible to obtain a complete diagnostic and assessment picture. Furthermore, there are few reliable, culturally relevant and culturally specific assessment and diagnostic tests. In many cases, the problems that ethnic minority offenders present are often related to the effects of socioeconomic and environmental forces such as poverty, unemployment, lack of education, cultural and religions differences, and language barriers. The case management approach needs to be highly focused, time-limited, and crisis-oriented. The planned change interventions should be directed at obtaining concrete or tangible services, such as public welfare assistance, job training, education, housing, medical, or other direct social services; therefore, generalist case management intervention techniques are usually in order.

The Viability of Psychotherapeutic Methods

We do not maintain that ethnic minority persons cannot benefit from psychotherapeutic approaches. Generally speaking, most ethnic minority persons (and, lower socioeconomic class persons of all types as well), have had little acquaintance with or exposure to psychotherapeutic methods for problem solving. Psychotherapies are idiosyncratically Western-culture specific in nature. In addition, these approaches work best with clients who have adequate education levels, and good verbal skills and language abilities. Other counseling approaches, such as social learning, reality therapies, and cognitive therapies, may not be effective with ethnic minority persons either. We have observed in our counseling work that non-racial/ethnic minority offenders seem to relate more easily to therapeutic techniques that involve an exploration of traumatic incidents in one's developmental history, reflection upon that history, and development of insight derived from that exploratory and reflective process. In short, our experiences suggest that the use of traditional kinds of helping approaches with ethnic minority offenders may be highly problematic and therapeutically non-productive.

Nevertheless, there are a number of folk cultural practices that appear to be analogous to psychotherapies. The work of Gomez and Cook (1977), provides examples of many of these practices. One of the most important of these practices is called "platicando." Platicando is based upon a highly personalized counselor-client relationship. The relationship contains strong elements of acceptance of the other person, or empathy, by the counselor. The counselor is viewed as the personal helper for the client. This phenomena is referred to as "personalismo." Among Hispanic clients, personalismo is readily evident by their strong preference for a particular counselor. In platicando, the method that is used to deal with problems of life that originate from social and environmental stress is also called personalismo.

As a counseling system, platicando incorporates the use of advice-giving and conveying information for problem solving. However, Gomez and Cook see it as more than just advice- and information-giving. They believe that as the relationship progresses, it can become a supportive therapy. As the relationship evolves, the focus may shift from coping with problems in the social and physical environment to dealing with the client's feelings about the problem, his or her reactions to the problem, and upon effective and ineffective ways used in the past to cope with problems. In essence, platicando can evolve into a relationship therapy.

We believe that what might ultimately be most helpful, in the therapeutic sense, with ethnic minority offenders, is a kind of ethnotherapy. By this we mean correctional counseling efforts that focus, when necessary for problem solving, upon race, culture, and ethnicity. There are several ways this can be accomplished.

To begin with, feelings can be explored when the offender is asked questions that require personal reflection and consideration, for example: "What was it like for you growing up in the barrio?", or "Do African Americans feel differently about this country than white persons?", or "How do you feel about having to deal with a white counselor?", or "Do you think that I, a white person, can understand you and your problems?"

It is important to discuss issues of race and ethnicity with ethnic minority offenders; however, one should not become fixated about race and ethnicity. The case manager should engage the offender whenever he or she perceives or believes that issues about race and culture that affect the counseling relationship or impact on the offender's ability to engage in problem-solving have not been dealt with. Solomon (1976) is very insightful about the genesis of this problem. She feels that it is very threatening for many counselors to deal with racial issues, especially if the issues may lead to confrontation. Instead, many counselors prefer to withdraw or avoid racial and cultural issues. The admonition for correctional counselors is simply that issues of race and ethnicity must be engaged if the offender has distorted or misinterpreted the behavior of the counselor with respect to such issues.

It is important to remember that many ethnic minority persons feel that they are powerless to deal with social and environmental forces that are affecting them. Some African Americans, in particular, feel that they are living in a hostile and destructive white world over which they have little control. Brill (1978) notes that many ethnic minority persons deal with these kinds of problems by adopting learned helplessness as a mechanism of defense. She feels that in these kinds of situations the counselor will have to help these clients develop and maintain feelings of personal adequacy so that they can cope with destructive environments.

Most importantly, she notes that the counselor "will have to deal first with the feelings involved and must expect that these feelings will be dumped on them as representatives of the destructive society with which these vulnerable people must cope" (1978:183). Whether we agree or disagree with Brill's characterization of our society, reality tells us that ethnic minority offenders often feel that they are the victims of a destructive society. In any case, case managers must deal with their feelings about this issue.

Empirical research directed at evaluating the success of therapeutic outcomes comparing same or different clients and counselors with respect to the variables of race and ethnicity has not been conclusive. The writers believe that, regardless of racial variable in the counselor to client relationship, two key factors are associated successful correctional counseling with ethnic minority offenders. First, the correctional counselor (regardless of his or her race, gender, or ethnic minority status) has to be perceived as being believable. The ethnic minority offender has to feel that the counselor can make a difference in their lives. This is the issue of the credibility of the counselor. The second point is more obvious: the ethnic minority offender must believe that the correctional counselor is knowledgeable about and sensitive to their ethnic minority background.

We agree with Norton (1978) that the issue of the dual perspective is at the core of accomplishing effective psychotherapy or counseling with ethnic minority persons. The concept of the dual perspective suggests that the way to effectively work with ethnic minority offenders through correctional case management lies in dealing with the sense of personal fragmentation and identity loss and crisis that they may be experiencing as their ethnocultural foundation increasingly become marginalized through interactions with the dominant societal values and culture. Modification, accommodation, or change in deviant patterns of behavior by the offender may be accomplished through the counseling process if the case manager would, as Comas-Diaz (1988) recommends, use "ethnocultural identification [to help] the patient manage cultural values, negotiate transitional experiences, and cope with identity readjustment in an alien cultural environment" (1984:340).

Some Folk Cultural Mental Health Practices

There are a number of folk cultural beliefs, principally in Hispanic communities, that are analogous to mental health or psychotherapeutic treatment approaches. Much more research is needed to identify and describe these beliefs. In this section of the chapter, we will discuss two of these beliefs: "espiritismo" and "simpatico." It is important for correctional case managers to understand these kinds of beliefs. In some instances, a case manager might want to incorporate them into the treatment plan via a referral to various ethnic "mental health" practitioners.

Several of these folk cultural mental health beliefs are inseparable from the religious beliefs and spiritual practices that were previously discussed. Of primary importance is the folk cultural belief of espiritismo. An understanding of espiritismo is important when working with Hispanic offenders and it is especially important when working with Puerto Rican offenders. The "espiritista" is a spiritualist, medium, or fortune teller. She usually gives advice about life, love, and fortune. In addition, a great deal of her activity centers upon psychosomatic problems and illnesses. She can be described as a folk or street psychiatrist. It may become necessary to consult with her in order to understand the relationship between the physical and psychological difficulties that an Hispanic offender may be experiencing.

Simpatico is also an important Hispanic folk culture mental health dynamic. Simpatico is akin to a personal code of conduct. It is the idea that a person should always remain personable and pleasant in terms of interactions with other people. This is especially true in terms of interacting with non-Hispanics. It values the importance of avoiding confrontation, dissension, and disagreements. The notion of seeking consensus rather than conflict in intergroup relationships is held in importance. Evidence of simpatico can sometimes can be inferred by the behavior of clients who appear to be stoic, passive, dependent, and lack affect or demonstrable emotional feelings. These persons are often prone to suppress feelings, especially feelings of anger, hostility, and frustration.

In working with offenders who appear to have these kinds of characteristics, sometimes a warm, positive, and supporting relationship, particularly a highly personalized one, may be effective. However, the demands of the criminal justice system often require the correctional case manager to deal with their clients in a more candid and confrontational way. It is frustrating for the correctional case manager to work with offenders who exhibit these kinds of behaviors. Usually, very little therapeutic progress is made. A proper decision about how to work with them can only be made after an extensive assessment and diagnostic process has been completed. This is particularly important since their behavior may be a facade that is masking a serious or life-threatening depression.

Distinctive Mental Health Problems

There is some evidence to suggest that ethnic minority persons have a prevalence of certain types of mental health problems (Comas-Diaz & Griffith, 1988). Ethnocultural religious systems and values, as well as folk cultural beliefs, appear to influence how many ethnic minority persons perceive life, and how they deal with the vicissitudes of life, including pain, suffering, and death. Some ethnic minority persons are very pessimistic about life. American Indians, in particular, have often been described as being stoic and fatalistic about life. In addition, they are often wary and skeptical of white counselors.

Depressive illness seems to be common among members of most ethnic minority groups. Depression is often followed by withdrawal, isolation, and suicidal ideations. Sometimes, threats about self-destruction or self-injury are made. In some instances, self-destructive actions, such as suicide, may occur. Depressive illnesses often occur when feelings of anger and frustration have been repressed and internalized. Sometimes these feelings break out and become expressed by personal or group acts of violence. For example, the 1991 riots over the Rodney King episode in Los Angeles have been attributed to "Black rage."

Depression and suicide seem to be prevalent among Southeast Asians. Many Southeast Asians also have somatization symptoms. This is evidenced by the presence of physical problems that may be related to memories of tragic events in their lives that have been repressed and suppressed. Most of these events concern incidents related to the war in Vietnam and to their subsequent status as refugees and immigrants in a new country.

Substance abuse, and particularly alcoholism, is prevalent among many ethnic minority persons. American Indians have a long-documented history of difficulties with alcohol. Some ethnic minority families, particularly Hispanic families, tend to cover-up substance use among their members. They prefer to handle these matters within the family and kinship network (Royce, 1990).

With respect to ethnic minority persons, perhaps these special types of mental health problems can be best understood when framed in a sociological context. For this, we need to turn to Durkheim's (1961) theory of anomic suicide. Anomic suicide comes about because the nature of our modern, technologically driven society requires the acceptance, integration, and manifestation of certain majority culture values that may be fundamentally different from the values of many ethnic minority persons.

This is particularly true with persons who are geographically closest to the "mother" country, and who are more recent immigrants. It may also be true with respect to native or indigenous American groups. The most egregious examples of the impact of today's industrial, technological, and entrepreneurial values upon folk cultural values has been upon American "native peoples" such as American Indians, Alaskan natives, and Hawaiians. This phenomenon is nowhere clearer than in Hawaii with respect to native Hawaiians. For example, Hawaiian cultural values are associated with family and group relationships ("ohana"), mutual support groups ("hui"), deference to others, respect for elders ("kupuna"), a preference for working out problems and meeting personal needs within the family ("ho'oponopo"), and native religious practices and forms of spiritualism ("kahuna"). These values are often in direct contrast with American social and economic values that stress materialism, aggressiveness, competition, and individualism (Mokuau & Matsuoka, 1995). Consider, also, the current trend by some American Indian tribes to enter into the business of casino gambling on their lands. There are a number of important implications related to reconciling tribal cultural values with the casino business (sometimes referred to by American Indians as the "new buffalo"); especially, the long-term effects upon their children and their culture.

These are some of the special mental health problems that the writers have observed in their practice with ethnic minority persons. In most cases, these kinds of issues present counseling situations that are beyond the expertise of most professionals. In these instances, it becomes important to recognize the problem, refer the offender for a proper medical, psychological, and psychiatric work-up, followed by referral to a specialized mental health practitioner or to a relevant outpatient service agency. Perhaps treatment by the use of medications may be indicated. In many cases, inpatient hospitalization or institutionalization in a mental health center or psychiatric hospital may be recommended.

Conclusions

The purpose of this chapter was to bring to the consciousness of case management correctional counselors some information about the characteristics of major ethnic minority groups in this country in order to help them deliver more ethnically and culturally sensitive correctional counseling services. The information in this chapter is intended to supplement the information about roles and case management intervention techniques previously discussed in the book.

We do know that an understanding of racism, and its related and associated manifestations, is important for effective correctional case management. It is important to understand what is meant by the terms ethnicity and ethnic minority. We have chosen not to enter the debate concerning assimilation versus multiculturalism. This is a subject that is currently in contention in our society. But, it is important to remember that every person, minority status notwithstanding, has a culture. Their cultural values and experiences hold important meanings for the individual. They may hold even more important meanings for ethnic minority offenders. This seems especially to be the case with respect to certain ethnocultural values and patterns such as the role of the family, and the religious and spiritual values.

We discussed some techniques that could be used to enhance the effectiveness of correctional counselors in working with ethnic minority offenders. We described why it is important for case managers to remember that psychotherapeutic approaches, as well as other traditional approaches, such as social learning, reality-based therapies, and cognitive therapies, are generally not productive with ethnic minority offenders. What seems to come closest in effectiveness with this population are Rogerian, client-centered, humanistically oriented types of approaches. More precisely, counseling methods that stress friendship, empathy, understanding, and are highly personalized seem to be most effective.

Similarly, we believe that there are a number of folk cultural beliefs, especially among Hispanic populations, that need to be understood in order to become an effective case manager. Some of these beliefs, such as platicando, are analogous to supportive and sustaining procedures used in mental health counseling. A particular link can be made with some of the case management generalist roles described in Chapter 6. We also discussed two folk cultural beliefs, espiritismo and simpatico. Espiritismo can inform correctional practice by helping the case manager understand the association between physical and psychological illnesses. Similarly, simpatico alerts the case manager to the possible presence of repressed and suppressed feelings that may be masking a serious or life-threatening depression.

At the end of this chapter we discussed some special mental health problems of ethnic minority persons. Although many of the problems were derived from our counseling experiences, there is research support concerning their prevalence among ethnic minority persons. Ethnic minority persons appear to have a high prevalence of depressive illnesses, suicide, and substance abuse and dependency. Many of them appear to be pessimistic, stoic, or fatalistic about life. It seems that they often have to repress anger and aggression. Others exhibit somatization symptoms.

In short, in this chapter we addressed the central question of counseling with offenders who have become culturally marginalized, or who suffer from the strain of trying to harmonize very different cultural values. The best answer, from the perspective of these writers, seems to lie in Comas-Diaz' (1988) suggestion that we must help people manage their cultural values, and use these values in order to help them deal with changing passages and transitions in their lives. Many folk cultural values and beliefs can be utilized, often in conjunction with more traditional counseling methods, to help ethnic minority offenders understand and cope with the problems of daily life, and with what they may perceive as a malevolent, destructive, and unfriendly world.

References

Anderson, J. (1981). *Social Work Methods and Process*. Belmont, CA: Wadsworth Publishing Co.

Baxter, B. (1982). *Alienation and Authenticity*. London: Tavistock.

Borrello, M.A. & E. Mathias (1977). "Botanicas: Puerto Rican Folk Pharmacies." *Natural History*, 86:64-73.

Bouquet, A.C. (1961). *Comparative Religions*. London: Cassell.

Boyer, L.B. (1964). "Psychoanalytic Insights in Working with Ethnic Minorities." *Social Casework*, 45:519-526.

Braden, C.S. (1954). *The World's Religions*. New York, NY: Abingdon.

Brill, N. (1978). *Working with People: The Helping Process*. (Second Edition). Philadelphia, PA: J.B. Lippincott.

Browne, C. & A. Broderick (1994). "Asian and Pacific Island Elders: Issues for Social Work Practice and Education." *Social Work*, 39:252-259.

Campbell, J. (1959). "Hinduism." In J.E. Fairchild (ed.) *Basic Beliefs* (pp. 54-72). New York, NY: Sheridan House.

Castex, G.M. (1994). "Providing Services to Hispanic/Latino Populations: Profiles in Diversity." *Social Work*, 39:288-296.

Cloward, R. (1959). "Illegitimate Means, Anomie and Deviant Behavior." *American Sociological Review*, 24:164-176.

Comas-Diaz, L. (1988). "Cross-Cultural Mental Health Treatment." In L. Comas-Diaz & E.H. Griffith (eds.) *Clinical Guidelines in Cross-Cultural Mental Health* (pp. 337-361). New York, NY: John Wiley & Sons.

Comas-Diaz, L. & E.H. Griffith (eds.) (1988). *Clinical Guidelines in Cross-Cultural Mental Health*. New York, NY: John Wiley & Sons.

Devore, W. & E.G. Schlesinger (1986). *Ethnic-Sensitive Social Work Practice* (Second Edition). Columbus, OH: Merrill Publishing Co.

DeVos, G. & L. Romanucci-Ross (1975). "Ethnicity: Vessel of Meaning and Emblem of Contrast." In G. DeVos & L. Romanucci-Ross (eds.) *Ethnic Identity: Cultural Continuities and Change* (pp. 363-390). Palo Alto, CA: Mayfield Publishing Co.

DeVos, G. (1975). "Ethnic Pluralism: Conflict and Accommodation." In G. DeVos & L. Romanuccci-Ross (eds.) *Ethnic Identity: Cultural Continuities and Change* (pp. 5-41). Palo Alto, CA: Mayfield Publishing Co.

Durkheim, E. (1951). *Suicide*. New York, NY: The Free Press.

Fanon, F. (1968). *The Wretched of the Earth*. New York, NY: Grove Press.

Frazier, E.F. (1963). *The Negro Church in America*. New York, NY: Schochen Books.

Goffman, E. (1961). *Asylums*. Garden City, NY: Doubleday Anchor.

Gomez, E. & K. Cook (1977). "Chicano Culture and Mental Health: Trees in Search of a Forest." *Monograph No. 1, Centro Del Barrio*. San Antonio, TX: Worden School of Social Service, Our Lady of the Lake University.

Erickson, E. (1963). *Childhood and Society*. New York, NY: W.W. Norton & Co.

Gillin, J. (1958). "Magical Fright." In W.A. Lessa & E.Z. Vogt (eds.) *Reader in Comparative Religion*. Evanston, IL: Patterson.

Heffernan, J., G. Shuttlesworth & R. Ambrosino (1992). *Social Work and Social Welfare: An Introduction* (Second Edition). St. Paul, MN: West Publishing Co.

James, G.W. (1904). *Indians of the Painted Desert Region.* Boston, MA: Little, Brown, & Co.

Jenkins, S. (1981). *The Ethnic Dilemma in Social Services.* New York, NY: The Free Press.

Lessa, W.A. & E.Z. Vogt (eds.) (1958). *Reader in Comparative Religion.* Evanston, IL: Patterson.

Lum, D. (1986). *Social Work Practice and People of Color: A Precess-Stage Approach.* Monterey, CA: Brooks/Cole Publishing Co.

Marx, K. (1967). *Das Kapital.* New York, NY: International Publishers.

Maslow, A.H. (1970). *Motivation and Personality* (Second Edition). New York, NY: Harper & Row.

Mayo, J.A. (1991). "Culture Adaptive Therapy: A Role for the Clinical Sociologist in a Mental Health Setting." In H.M. Rebach & J.G. Bruhn (eds.) *Handbook of Clinical Sociology* (pp. 309-322). New York, NY: Plenum Press.

Merton, R. (1957). *Social Theory and Social Structure.* New York, NY: The Free Press.

Mindel, C.H., R.W. Habenstein & R.W. Wright Jr. (1988). "Family Lifestyles of America's Ethnic Minorities: An Introduction." In C.H. Mindel, R.W. Habenstein & R.W. Wright Jr. (eds.) *Ethnic Families in America* (Third Edition) (pp. 1-14). New York, NY: Elsevier.

Mokuau, N. & J. Matsuoka (1995). "Turbulence Among Native People: Social Work Practice with Hawaiians." *Social Work*, 40:465-472.

Newcomb, T.M. (1968). "On the Definition of Attitude." In M. Jahoda & N. Warren (eds.) *Attitudes* (pp. 22-24). New York, NY: Penguin Books.

Norton, D.G. (1978). *The Dual Perspective: Inclusion of Ethnic Minority Content in the Social Work Curriculum.* New York, NY: Council on Social Work Education.

Office of Management and Budget (1978, May 4). "Directive 15: Race and Ethnic Standards for Federal Statistics and Administrative Reporting." *Federal Register*, 43:19269.

Pukui, M.K, E.W. Haertig & C.A. Lee (1972). *Nana I Ke Kumu (Look to the Source)* (Vol. 2). Honolulu, HI: Hui Hanai.

Reinecke, J.E. (1969). *Language and Dialect in Hawaii.* Honolulu, HI: University of Hawaii Press.

Ringgren, H. & A.V. Strom (1967). *Religions of Mankind.* Philadelphia, PA: Fortress Press.

Robertson, I. (1979). *Sociology.* New York, NY: Worth.

Royce, J. (1990). *Alcohol Problems and Alcoholism: A Comprehensive Survey.* New York, NY: The Free Press.

Schlesinger, A. (1993). "Stop Pulling America Apart." *The American Legion*, 135:28-29,70-71.

Solomon, B.B. (1976). *Black Empowerment: Social Work in Oppressed Communities.* New York, NY: Columbia University Press.

Staples, R. (1976). *Introduction to Black Sociology.* New York, NY: McGraw-Hill.

Thomas, W.I. & F. Znaniecki (1927). *The Polish Peasant in Europe and America* (Vol. 1). New York, NY: Knopf.

Wirth, L. (1945) "The Problem of Minority Groups." In T. Parsons, E. Shils, K.D. Naegele & J.R. Pitts (eds.) *Theories of Society* (Vol. 1) (pp. 309-315). Glencoe, IL: The Free Press.

Chapter 11

Ethical Issues

Introduction

This chapter is directed at a consideration of some major ethical issues with respect to case management correctional counseling. The issues that will be addressed are not fundamentally different from those faced by all sorts of mental health counselors. What is different is a matter of emphasis. Since correctional case managers work in community-based settings, the emphasis will be upon those ethical issues that, in the judgment of the writers, present problems and pose challenges for case managers in these kinds of settings. Before one can examine various ethical issues in case management correctional counseling, some background information about the field of criminal justice in general, and American corrections in particular, which have implications for ethical issues, has to be considered. It is important to have background information with respect to: education for the profession; certification or licensing; and the public sector nature of the work.

Background

Correctional counseling is not an organized profession in the same way that other "counseling" professions, such as psychology, social work, educational counseling and guidance, or rehabilitation counseling are. Although much of social science theory blends across various academic fields, most social science-based disciplines can lay claim, largely with some justification, to a body of knowledge that is distinctly theirs. Criminal justice, with the possible exception of the field of penology, is not at the point in its development wherein it can make such a claim. Within criminal justice, the field of correctional counseling is a case in point. Most of the theoretical concepts and practices in this field are derived from psychology, sociology, social work, or educational counseling and guidance. Schrink (1992) reinforced this point when he described how hiring practices for correctional counselors have improved during the last 20 years. He noted that: "For entry-level counseling positions, most corrections departments now require at least a BA/BS degree in some relevant major such as a social/behavioral science, criminal justice/criminology, social work, or counseling" (1992:42-43). From this statement, one can infer that there is no generally agreed upon educational process to prepare students for work in this field, and that there is very little agreement about which areas of education to stress: understanding human behavior or understanding criminal law and criminal justice systems. Cast in another light, this is a recapitulation of the rehabilitation versus punishment and control model of criminal justice argument. In terms of understanding how professions grow and develop, this is the issue of: whether the field (the institution, the agency, the practice arena) shall take precedence concerning the nature of educational content for the preparation of correctional counselors, or whether acadamia, with its commitment to the principles of social and behavioral science research, shall take precedence. In addition, there are related educational controversies concerning levels of acceptable educational preparation for the field (undergraduate or graduate), the relative importance of staff training versus academic education, and the role and importance of continuing education for ongoing training and education. Because of these disputes and controversies, the field of corrections lacks a coherent philosophy or ideology that could serve as a base for its ethical principles.

Certification or licensing is another factor that needs to be considered when we examine the issue of ethical principles and correctional case management. Certification is a type of regulation of professional practice that affords to the holder of a particular type of academic degree and/or educational preparation an exclusive and legally protected right to the use of a particular title. For example, in some states a practitioner could not hold himself or herself out to the general public as a "social worker" unless that individual had completed a course of university studies which followed a generally agreed upon curriculum accredited by that profession's state or national professional accreditation body. Sometimes there are additional requirements concerning completion of a practicum, supervision, and a certification examination. Licensing, by contrast, is a more highly regulated process. It is the formal and legal regulation of practice by statute law. It functions to control access to both a title and to define the areas of practice competency and jurisdiction. Like certification, licensing requires the completion of an approved curriculum. In addition, it usually requires the completion of supervised internship or practicum, work experience, and a passing score on a professional examination. Licensing allows more possibilities for independent or private practice, consultation, and financial reimbursement from third party sources. Indications of licensing may be noted by a title, such as: "licensed professional counselor" or "clinical psychologist."

In any case, certification and licensing are attempts to standardize practice by levels of competency, educational preparation, supervision, and experience. Codes of professional ethics are intrinsic to certification and licensing. These codes are, at least pro forma, designed to protect consumers of the service. This is an important public service feature since most clients have no method for evaluating the professional competence, character, and honor of a practitioner; nor do they have a ready means for evaluating the efficacy of his or her services. Codes provide protection by providing ethical guidelines for professional practice, and by regulating and controlling the relationship of practitioners with respect to their clients, staff members, colleagues, and employers. A code of ethics can also compel appropriate professional behavior by the imposition of sanctions and discipline upon its members, including the use of civil law remedies. Lowenberg and Dolgoff (1982) are correct in maintaining that all modern professions have codes of professional ethics. This is a singular deficiency with correctional counseling. Simply put, because correctional counseling does not have formal certification or licensing bodies, adherence to standards of practice and ethical principles are difficult to enforce. However, ethical codes reflect values; they do not give guidance or advice concerning the right courses of action that a correctional case manager should take.

Of course, many practitioners who are titled as correctional counselors meet the membership criteria of their respective national professional associations, such as the American Psychological Association, the American Personnel and Guidance Association, or the National Association of Social Workers. Membership in these organizations generally allows them to become licensed in states that have licensing requirements. Unfortunately, correctional counselors who do not have a background in the traditional counseling disciplines do not have this advantage.

In any case, as Clear and Cole (1994) point out, there is an important consequence with respect to a discrepancy between ethical standards and correctional work. Using the example of attorneys and physicians, they note that the ethical requirements for these professionals are clear and operate through a strong client-to-professional privilege. They state that by contrast, such a privilege is not clear for correctional personnel and that as a result, issues about ethical standards are inclined to be resolved by litigation rather than by utilizing standards promulgated by professional organizations.

The third factor that should be understood in terms of ethical issues and correctional counseling is the public sector context of the work. Correctional counselors are primarily local, state, or federal government employees. They are members of various civil service systems. Upper-level correctional personnel, such as administrators, are commonly political appointees. Quite often, the civil service requirements for correctional counseling positions are based on general, objective examinations. These types of examinations tend to measure intellectual traits rather than the kinds of attitudes, values, skills, and knowledge that correctional counselors should have in order to do a good job. In terms of personnel selection, correctional counselors should at least be subjected to the thorough and sophisticated process that many law enforcement officers go through. As Meyer (1992) has suggested, an ideal selection process ought to include interviews with supervisors and psychologists; a thorough life history, physical health, mental health, substance abuse, and employment history check; a psychological evaluation including projective testing; and, most importantly, tests of situational responses wherein role-playing is used to measure the candidate's reaction to simulated real-life situations.

The political appointment of correctional administrators is also an area of concern. Such appointees tend to reflect the political ideologies of those in power at the time. This opens up the possibilities for political corruption, influence peddling, and cronyism. Although many professionals in correctional counseling would wish otherwise, it is true that crime and justice are essentially political issues. In their seminal work about the relationship of politics and criminal justice, Klonoski and Mendelsohn (1970) asserted that the legal system functioned as a subsystem of the political system. Their contention was that certain political elites, rather than the courts alone, were involved in the process of allocating justice. As they viewed it: "The system's basic legal mission is to place the stamp of legitimacy on the allocations of benefits and penalties produced by the operation of the political system" (1970:xviii-xix). If this characterization of the legal system is generally true, then one can understand how difficult it might be to develop, maintain, or promulgate ethical principles and standards for correctional counselors since they are an intrinsic part of governmental legal systems; systems that appear to be highly influenced by local politics.

There are, of course, professional organizations that embody the interests and needs of correctional counselors. These organizations include the American Correctional Association (ACA), and the American Probation and Parole Association (APPA). The ACA has developed national accreditation standards for correctional personnel who work in prisons, jails, and in community settings. The APPA has also worked to improve the professional standards of correctional personnel. Much of the thrust for improving professional standards in corrections has also been provided by the National Institute of Corrections. However, these organizations have chiefly educational, research, and training missions. They also function somewhat like trade unions and advocates for increases in salaries, improvements in working conditions, and also for expansion of health and retirement benefits for their members. Furthermore, these organizations are large, umbrella-like associations and represent a wide variety of professional, academic, and lay persons who are interested in corrections. There may be little commonality between participants in these organizations who are interested in correctional counseling versus those who view the function of corrections in other ways. In short, there are ideological splits and differences. What may be needed is an independent national association to represent the interests of correctional counselors, per se. This sort of organization could deal with the issues of education, training, supervision, certification or licensing, and a code of ethics for correctional counselors.

Ethics

An operational definition of ethics is needed before we examine ethical principles and issues with respect to correctional case management in community-based settings. In order to define the term, one needs to employ a bit of reductionistic thinking by differentiating ethics from two other terms that the writers have often used in this book: "values" and "norms."

Values may be defined as sets of widely held and socially shared social and cultural beliefs. Values are central to any society and are highly regarded, esteemed, and respected. Of course, values are generally socially and culturally defined, specific, and relevant, and, therefore, vary among different societies and groups. Robertson (1979) expands this definition by adding that values are philosophical and abstract. Furthermore, he clarifies the distinction between values and norms by stating that norms are the behavioral rules or guidelines that flow from values, and prescribe how people should react and behave in certain situations.

Ethics, on the other hand, has to do with questions concerning what is good or bad, or right or wrong. Ethics involves issues of morality and morally right conduct. Ethics refers to very abstract and general concepts that guide one's moral reasoning with respect to deciding what is right, what ought to be done, and what is one's obligation or duty (Bales & Henle, 1989). Bruhn (1991) establishes the point more clearly: "Ethics is concerned with questions of right and wrong, of duty and obligation, of moral responsibility" (1991:99). This is the essential difference. Values are conditioned by external or outside factors such as our socialization process, experiences, and by our membership in particular social, cultural, or ethnic groups. By contrast, we contend that our ethical orientation is primarily psychologically constructed. That is to say, it is personal and internal. It may be influenced by our socialization process, experiences, and developmental history, but, ultimately, it develops aside from (or, perhaps, in spite of) these factors. It is analogous to the construct of the super ego, it is our consciousness of good and evil. It is not so much predetermined as it is determined; in other words: you do not have to be a prisoner of your developmental history.

It becomes activated when we respond to problematic situations by taking an ethical stand. To take a stand means that we can determine our own right course of action. Frankl (1969) a renowned psychiatrist and father of "logotherapy," who survived the Nazi concentration camp at Auschwitz, crystallized the meaning of ethics by his belief that mankind was not pan-determined. He felt that individuals did not simply exist, but could, instead, take stands or become self-determined, especially when issues of good or bad were concerned. Frankl believed that: "Man does not simply exist, but always decides what his existence will be, what he will become in the next moment" (1969:206). May (1967) extended the definition of ethics to its furthest dimension with his analogy of the differences between men and animals. He believed that people had the potential, if not the actuality, to become "ethical animals." For May, mankind could balance out the need for immediate gratification against future consequences; especially bad consequences. This would come about if an individual could obtain a consciousness of himself or herself. This consciousness could guide them so that they would be disinclined to choose bad courses of action because of the downstream consequences these actions could have on themselves, but especially because of the impact of their actions upon other persons. Consciousness comes about when a person can "imagine himself into someone else's needs and desires, can imagine himself in the other's place . . .

therefore will act to . . . make his choices with a view of the good of his fellows as well as himself" (1967:150). May often spoke of this phenomena as the "I and thou" or "love thy neighbor" paradigm.

The issue concerning ethical dilemmas has usually centered on the absolutist versus relativism positions. This issue cannot be easily settled (Bayles & Henley, 1989). However, the authors maintain that in the main, given the nature of their work and the kinds of institutionalized structures in which they work, correctional case managers should try to rely upon absolutist rather than relativistic standards of morality for resolving ethical dilemmas. We believe that, in most cases, clear principles exist for resolving ethical dilemmas within correctional settings. As with Frankl and May, we believe that there is an absolutist core that guides moral reasoning and determines ethical principles: it is conduct derived from actions based upon an internalized and determined moral core.

We will now proceed to discuss and describe ethical issues of concern for correctional case managers. There are three general areas of professional work wherein ethical issues arise. These areas include: the realm of counseling with the offender or with his or her family or significant others; the arena of agency policies, programs, and services; and the context of working relationships with other staff members and professional co-workers.

In Chapter 3, we discussed some professional paradoxes that correctional case managers encounter. To reiterate, paradoxes are situations faced by correctional counselors wherein general or public opinion appears to be the controlling ideology with respect to an issue in criminal justice. For example, a primary opinion is that offenders are not capable of being rehabilitated. This view is paradoxical for most correctional counselors because it is contrary and contradictory to their experiences with helping offenders. Paradoxes impinge upon the professional domains of counselors because they are value-laden. Ethical issues in correctional case management are closely related to professional paradoxes, but are fundamentally different on one dimension: they touch upon areas of personal morality and right conduct. Ethical issues in correctional case management are usually framed as dilemmas rather than as paradoxes.

A dilemma refers to a problematic situation in which two or more alternatives are presented for resolution, but neither alternative is particularly satisfactory or appealing. Sometimes the dilemmas are really "Hobson's choices." This means that there is only one alternative, and that alternative is often a very difficult one to act upon. We shall now discuss some central ethical issues for correctional case managers from the standpoint of the ethical dilemmas that they present. What we have chosen to emphasize are certain dilemmas that, in our experience, case managers are almost certain to face when working in community-based correctional settings. We do not pretend that these dilemmas are not faced by most, if not all counselors of various sorts. Nor do we maintain that they are easy to resolve.

Ethical Dilemmas in Working with Offenders

Case managers in community-based settings often encounter a set of common ethical dilemmas when providing counseling to some offenders. These dilemmas pertain to: confidentiality; informed consent; impact of the intervention; and, angry, hostile, and aggressive offenders.

Confidentiality

A primary ethical dilemma in case management correctional counseling is that of the confidentiality of the relationship. Confidentiality is never an absolute in correctional counseling. By virtue of having been adjudicated, offenders lose many civil rights. This is essentially true even in instances of deferred-adjudication. Records and evaluations are very often open to scrutiny by outside sources. More protection of the confidentiality of records occurs in community-based settings, however, all records can ultimately be subjected to judicial orders for exposure. Correctional case managers do not generally enjoy the status of privileged client-to-counselor communications. In addition, criminal offenders pose unique problems due to the fact that they must adhere to certain judicial criteria in order to remain in community settings.

The difficulty with the issue of confidentiality resides in the fact that it is very difficult to maintain either an absolutist position: "I will maintain confidentiality no matter what," or a relativistic position: "I will maintain confidentiality except for information that is destructive to you, to me, or to other people." Schrink (1992) is correct in maintaining that the correctional counselor needs to work out his or her personal statement about confidentiality. We feel that the correctional case manager cannot guarantee confidentiality. In fact, such a guarantee, in addition to being naive, may present an opportunity for manipulative and deviant behavior by some offenders. Although confidentiality cannot be guaranteed in correctional settings, the case manager can detail those areas of confidential exchange that he or she is comfortable with and can realistically guarantee. However, the offender needs to understand that contingencies may arise, or crises may develop, which may abrogate certain guarantees. In any case, we believe that the case manager has an obligation to release confidential information that has either been shared or revealed by an offender, or by a collateral source, if that information poses a threat to another person or to the offender.

Informed Consent

Another major ethical dilemma that correctional case managers often face when working with offenders is that of informed consent. We know that even a highly intelligent and educated person may not really be able to voluntarily consent to participate in a service, such as correctional counseling, because they may not be able to understand all of the implications of the choices that are presented to them. With many offenders, their intellectual and cognitive abilities are often impaired. As much as we try to gain informed consent, it remains very problematic as to whether they are aware of the choices that they are making and the consequences that are attendant with various choices.

Typically, when working in mental health settings or in social service agencies, a counselor would not implement a treatment plan unless the client had the intellectual, physical, emotional, and knowledge bases to be able to both understand the treatment plan and to make a voluntary, rational, and informed choice regarding participation in therapy. The same is not necessarily true in correctional settings. Offenders are essentially non-voluntary clients who have been coerced, remanded, or "sentenced" to treatment. Much of their behavior is already non-voluntary because it has been circumscribed by judicial orders in terms of the conditions of their probation or parole. In some cases, the issue of informed consent is problematic because offenders will volunteer to participate in special or experimental programs with the hope that such participation will reduce or shorten the time span of their judicial orders. In some cases volunteering may just be another way to "con" the correctional counselor. In extreme cases, some offenders may be willing to accept abhorrent remedies in order to absolve their criminal sentences. For example, some offenders may voluntarily participate in experimental trials of new drugs. Recently in Texas, an interesting judicial dilemma came about when a chronic sexual offender proposed to the court that he was willing to undergo physical castration in lieu of imprisonment. The dilemma of informed consent for the case manager is thus: what can we make of the rationality of informed consent when we are dealing with offenders since they are non-voluntary clients and are therefore not in a position to make informed and voluntary choices?

The writers believe that case managers can personally deal with this dilemma only if three conditions are apparent. The first condition concerns the information or data base of the offender. An offender must be presented with a complete knowledge base concerning the program or service that is being considered. This means that the offender must be informed about the treatment goals, the techniques and procedures that will be used, and about any risks that may be associated with the treatment. Second, the offender must have sufficient intellectual, physical, and emotional capacity and ability to understand the choices that he or she is being asked to consider. And, third, the offender must be willing and motivated to participate in the program and service on the basis of what appears to the offender to be in his or her best interest. This choice has to be theirs, but it may be abrogated if the choice is irrational, socially unacceptable, or manipulative in nature. If these three conditions maintain, then the case manager may be able to feel that the offender has made an informed and rational choice.

Impact of the Intervention

A dilemma that is confronted almost daily by correctional case managers is that of not being clear, or of being uncertain, about the effect that the counseling efforts will have upon the offender. This is a dilemma that other mental health counselors struggle with as well. Uncertainty comes about because human beings are very complex and are likely to react to encounters with other persons in a myriad of ways. It is also a consequence of the fact that as professionals we often have to act without having all of the facts and data concerning the offender that we would like to have.

The answer to this dilemma is to understand that correctional case managers, like other types of mental health professionals, are often in situations where they must make professional decisions based upon limited, incomplete, or fragmented data. Professional persons often have to act on a crisis basis. This may be understood by way of an analogy to another crisis-based profession, medicine. We usually think of medicine as a science. However, it is not an exact science. Many a healthy appendix has been removed because the patient's symptoms mimicked appendicitis. Being uncertain, but being impelled to act, often because of a crisis, is part of the ethos of being a correctional case manager. We can personally resolve this dilemma if we are comfortable with the fact that we have the professional competence and expertise to support our methods of intervention with the offender, and moreover, that our expertise and competence is as good or better than other intervention choices or means that are available to the offender at the time. Therefore, we must make sure that our counseling efforts are guided by research-validated and effective treatment methods and theories. We must also be clear with our clients about the outcomes of treatment; we need to convey to them a reasonable and sensible representation of what they can expect. In addition, we need to document and maintain records concerning the process of our work with them. Finally, we must be very careful about making "personal" recommendations to the offender, for example, making suggestions or giving advice about matters that are external to the professional treatment or therapeutic goals, but which can have a major bearing or effect upon the client's life. For example, we should not make suggestions about medical care, marriage or divorce, how to deal with an in-law, and so forth.

Angry, Hostile, and Aggressive Offenders

A final dilemma that correctional case managers sometimes face in counseling with offenders is that of how to deal with the dangerous client. Many of the offenders that we encounter will express hostility and anger, and may appear to be potentially aggressive. It is extremely difficult to predict when anger and hostility may erupt into aggression and lead to physical danger or destruction. There is very little research data to allow us any comfort in bei able to predict aggression and dangerousness. However, some research h emerged that is very informative.

Much of the early work about this topic was performed by Megargee (1976). He provided us with some important information concerning the general predictor variables of violent behavior. These included personality factors, situational factors, and the interactions between the two. Monahan (1981) compiled a list of predictor variables of aggression; these included: the age of the offender, particularly those up to age 35; male gender; membership in socially or economically disadvantaged groups, including membership in a minority group; lower levels of education; low levels of intellectual functioning, plus a fragmented school or vocational education history; and, a history of substance abuse, such as the use of "hard" drugs and/or alcohol. We also know from the clinical literature that certain developmental traumas, such as an historical experience of physical abuse, chronic neglect, or sexual abuse may be reliable predictors of aggression and dangerousness. In addition, Kutzer and Lion (1984) have summed up a list of mental disorders associated with violent behaviors. These disorders included: thought disorders, affective disorders, behavior disorders, organic dysfunctions, and situational reactions. Most of us who are involved in mental health or correctional work also know from experience that offenders who are depressed, suicidal, or confronting various crises or emergency situations have a heightened potential for aggression toward self and others. This is precisely why police officers consider calls concerning domestic relations disputes to be highly dangerous. More recently, Toch and Adams (1989) conducted an important descriptive research study derived from a large-scale demographic base of convicted offenders. From their study, they were able to distinguish among types of violent offenders who had histories of mental health problems versus those who did not have such histories. From their analysis of offenders with mental health problems, they concluded that those who were more most violence-prone had these kinds of attributes: exhibited symptoms and problems at an early age, and were subsequently institutionalized at an early age; had a history of a series of institutional placements; lived a marginal and migratory existence that included numerous brushes with the law; had multiple problems, particularly emotional problems that were worsened by substance abuse and that seemed to impact upon their social and mental competence; and, most importantly for community-based correctional counselors, their study suggests that offenders with the aforementioned types of characteristics had a high potential for reoffense, including violent reoffense, and a limited potential for successful community adjustment. Finally, the work of Stuart, et al. (1981) should be recognized since it contains some important information about social learning approaches to the prediction, management, and treatment of violent behavior exhibited by various kinds of clients.

There are some courses of action that the case manager may take to deal with the potentially aggressive offender. We present the following commandments in order to deal with the ethical dilemma of working with a potentially violent offender. First, it is important to take preventive actions. Obviously, common sense and intuition are good guides concerning social and physical environments that might pose danger. Second, there are other very important preventive actions that the case manager should take. Start by reviewing the records of an offender, paying particular attention to any history containing demographic or psychological factors, such as those described in the previous section of this chapter, that research suggests may be associated with violence or assaultive behavior. Third, carefully review any medical, psychiatric, or psychological evaluations and assessments that may indicate the potential for violent or dangerous behavior. Fourth, do not hesitate to obtain any additional experiential or subjective information, or even impressions, from colleagues who may have previously worked with the offender, and from any persons who are significant in the life of the offender. Fifth, work closely with your supervisor by sharing impressions and information as your work with potentially aggressive offenders progresses.

As with any other human phenomena, the ability to accurately predict violence and dangerousness is very limited. Monahan (1984) himself has raised some serious issues with respect to the accuracy of predictor variables of violence and dangerousness. Therefore, it is always better to err on the side of caution. However, we also need to understand that, as a basic rule, many offenders will characteristically express anger and hostility. Often, their anger and hostility, although directed at us, may instead be expressions of how they feel about their situations and circumstances. Sometimes, the anger and hostility is an expression of the guilt that some of them feel about the nature of their offense; this is particularly true with respect to sexual offenders. In other cases, the anger and hostility is a means that they are using in order to manipulate and control us so that we will respond to their desires and wishes. Sometimes anger and hostility are used in an attempt to get us to lose control by responding with anger. Both of these kinds of reactions are characteristic of offenders who are antisocial personalities. As long as our encounters with offenders are characterized by verbal exchanges and interactions, aggressive potential is probably low. Generally, all verbalizations are meaningful. In fact, allowing or even encouraging anger-based verbalizations may be therapeutic. This is because of its cathartic effect. In some cases, we might channel their anger and hostility into a therapeutically productive medium, such as various forms of activity group therapy, role-playing, encounter groups, or support groups. However, we need to become alert to verbalizations that appear to be evolving into physically aggressive actions toward the self or other persons. In such instances, the use of physical structure (including medication) to manage and control behavior, may be indicated.

Ethical Dilemmas with Respect to Agency Policies, Programs, or Services

Case managers often have to deal with a number of ethical dilemmas that come about because of the structure and function of the agency in which they work, or because of how the programs and services of the agency are administered. In many cases, the counseling process and the direction of treatment is significantly impacted, and often impaired, by the nature of the management and operation of the agency. Some of these dilemmas include lack of resources, job standards and the needs of the offender, and putting your value system on hold.

Lack of Resources

An ongoing dilemma in correctional counseling has to do with the issue of resources; both physical resources and professional resources. This dilemma is compounded by the large caseloads and heavy burden of paperwork that correctional case managers experience. In reality, agencies are never fully funded nor fully staffed. Nor are they likely to be fully funded or staffed in the future. Correctional counselors are being asked to do more with less and less. This problem is usually never addressed or controlled for when correctional programs or services are being evaluated with respect to their outcomes; instead, cost:benefit analyses seem to rule.

The dilemma comes about because of the nature of limited resources. Limited resources create the traditional "zero sum game" phenomenon. There are risks and rewards with this kind of economic allocation system. Economists frame this as the "guns versus butter" dichotomy. As a consequence, when working with offenders, the case manager often has to choose, as best he or she can, between those offenders who they think can best use professional help or resources versus those who they think cannot. They have to apply resources equally when, in many cases, directed resources could produce greater dividends with some offenders rather than with others. Traditional community correctional programs, such as judicial-based probation and parole work, consist of undifferentiated programs and services that tend to spread out the resources evenly. By contrast, differentiated community correctional programs, such as community administered intermediate sanctions, tend to target programs and services toward offenders who, on the basis of various types of case classification schemes, seem to have higher potential for modifiability of behavior. Our discussion at this point may seem reminiscent to the reader of the dilemma faced by the protagonist in the film *Schindler's List*. Metaphorically speaking, as in the film, the correctional case manager may be assigning some potentially treatable clients to a therapeutic concentration camp.

To resolve this dilemma, the case manager must remove himself or herself from situations in which they may be forced to make choices that benefit one group at the expense of another. Usually, one has to endure these kinds of work situations for a period of time so that, with the accumulation of experience, one is able to move into an occupational niche in correctional counseling that offers a more limited caseload and affords more face-to-face contact with offenders. Attaining a higher level of education, particularly graduate education, may accelerate this progression. Obtaining employment in correctional programs that administer community-based sanctions often allows the case manager access to an occupational niche that contains opportunities to engage in more treatment-focused efforts with offenders. Some of these types of settings include: home confinement programs, community service programs, intensive probation supervision caseloads, and day reporting centers. Some types of boot camps and restitution centers may also fit this mold. And, in some cases, private minimum security prisons also afford the opportunity for work in intensive treatment units.

Job Standards and the Needs of the Offender

A dilemma that correctional case managers frequently must face has to do with conflicting expectations and requirements of the job versus the needs of the offender. This is the archetypal role conflict of the counselor as therapist cum disciplinarian. He or she must try to balance the importance of maintaining a therapeutic relationship with the offender against the imperative to manage and control behavior. This phenomenon represents a major difference between correctional counseling and traditional types of mental health counseling. This issue is more prominent in institutionalized settings since these kinds of places are primarily oriented toward risk management and control. In community-based correctional settings, there is some degree of balance between control and management of behavior, and meeting the idiosyncratic needs of the offender.

This is not an easy dilemma to resolve. We believe that case managers can come to grips with this dilemma if they understand that sometimes with offender populations it becomes necessary to use stringent and coercive means to manage and control behavior. This course of action is acceptable as long as these measures follow and are in accord with the agency's policies, rules, and regulations, and as long as they do not violate local, state, or federal laws and directives. Although such means are often harsh, they are often necessary. It seems that we are being forced to save offenders from themselves. As correctional case managers, we should remember that sometimes offenders need to experience failure in order to bring them to the crisis point that might force them to make effective use of the counseling process. For example, a chronic alcoholic may not be amenable to help until he finds himself lying down in the gutter, dead drunk, and on the verge of death. Recovering alcoholics often state that they were not able to marshall emotional energy to seek help until their drinking had spiraled upward to a deadly crisis point. At the point of the crisis they realized that they had a choice of getting help or dying.

Putting Your Value System on Hold

Another dilemma is worth noting. Sometimes, a correctional counselor has to put his or her value system, common sense, or intuition "on hold" with respect to a particular program or service. We have seen programs or services that didn't work before, appearing again like old wine in new bottles. Déjà vu. We remember that they didn't work before, but we have to try them again against our better sense of judgment. We wonder at the absurdity of certain innovations. For example, consider the wisdom of locating a halfway house program for substance abusers in a building that was donated to the program when that building is across the street from a 24-hour bank automatic teller machine (ATM) station, and one block away from a drive-through liquor store. The usual way to deal with this kind of dilemma is to try to change an incorrect set of beliefs by the use of persuasion and logical and rational arguments. Correctional case managers, however, are not usually in a position wherein they have sufficient administrative power to change misdirected and misguided decisions. It is particularly vexing to go against decisions that reflect certain expediences, principally those that are economically or politically driven.

In these kinds of situations, a case manager's best reaction, in the opinion of the writers, is to try to "suspend judgment." This means that we have to realize that we have no effective power to control the decision-making process, that the possibility exists that our opinion may be incorrect, and that we must resolve to be comfortable with the belief that sometimes better programs or services rise, like the proverbial phoenix, from the ashes of poor or misdirected ones. Unfortunately, sometimes we must become "pollyannas" and suspend our better judgment through a process of irrepressible optimism that everything will turn out for the good. Suspension of belief is often a key to survival in criminal justice bureaucracies. The other course of action is to resign your position. That may be the "best" personal course of action to resolve this dilemma. However, as with all ethical dilemmas that case managers will face, the act of resignation forecloses upon the possibility of being a "player" in the correctional arena, now or in the future. Perhaps a nefarious remark attributed to the late President Nixon is apropos here: "outlive your enemies."

Ethical Dilemmas and Professional Working Relationships

Case managers also face a number of common ethical dilemmas that arise in the course of their work through interactions between themselves and staff members or other colleagues. Three areas will be explored in this section of the chapter: wrong-doing, deception, and relationship issues. Several caveats are in order when dealing with the ethical dilemmas that we will discuss in this part of the chapter. They are:

1. Be sure that you have complete and accurate records and sources of documentation.

2. Consult with your supervisor.

3. Consult with administrative personnel in your human resources department, since personnel in these kinds of

departments are usually responsible for ensuring the agency's compliance with local, state and federal laws, regulations, procedures, and programs.

4. Consult with the attorney assigned to your agency. In some cases, the attorney that you may need to consult with may be located at the state or federal level.

Wrongdoing

In the opinion of the writers, Reamer (1984) gets at the essence of the issue of wrongdoing with his statement that the practitioner has: "The obligation to obey laws, rules, and regulations to which one has voluntarily and freely consented" and that this obligation "overrides one's right to engage voluntarily and freely in a manner that conflicts with these laws, rules, and regulations" (1984:34). We cannot overemphasize this point: a case manager must adhere to and act in accordance with the agency's policies and procedures, and his or her behavior must also conform to local, state, and federal regulations and laws.

There are numerous forms of wrongdoing in all types of counseling work. In the opinion of the authors, several that can pose ethical dilemmas for case managers in community-based correctional settings can be cited. Consider the following examples:

1. Counseling with an offender in the agency while also working with the offender (for remuneration) as a private practice client.

2. Referring an offender, for a fee or for some other source of economic value, such as fee-splitting or quid-pro-quo referrals, to another agency or practitioner for services.

3. Collecting and compiling confidential information about offenders that can be used for personal or monetary gain, or that can be used to manipulate, control, exploit, or "blackmail" the offender.

Many additional examples of wrongdoing could be cited as well. Some of these issues would include: having sexual relations with clients, loaning them money or borrowing money from them, having them perform private work for you, and so forth. All of the examples cited illustrate professional wrongdoing and, in addition, could result in legal liability for damages to the counselor and/or the agency with respect to malpractice.

Dealing with ethical dilemmas when issues of professional wrongdoing are apparent are, in the opinion of the writers, straightforward or absolute. The case manager must "blow the whistle" on colleagues or staff members who violate the laws, rules, or regulations which govern the agency. This is not just an issue of morally right conduct, it is an issue of legal obligation, as well. We cannot turn a blind eye to violations of law, even at the highest levels, in an agency. In some situations, reporting these kinds of violations can be done anonymously. In others, they must be directly confronted. Fortunately, in most civil jurisdictions, statute laws have been enacted to protect "whistle-blowers."

Deception

Deception has to do with willfully and premeditatedly misleading a client, or other colleagues or staff members. Deception can take many forms. One form of deception involves failing to report concerning wrongdoing by other employees. This is often accomplished by rationalizing that the deception "was in the best interest of the agency." Or, sometimes, deception is practiced in order to cover up the behavior of an incompetent employee because we are sorry for them, or because we are concerned that a greater harm might come to them or to their family if we revealed the rule violation. The behavior of many "burnt-out" or otherwise impaired employees, such as an alcoholic or substance-abusing counselor, has been covered over by the misdirected concerns of their co-workers.

Another form of deception involves false credentials. From time-to-time, one encounters colleagues who fraudulently claim educational or professional credentials that they do not possess; or, they misrepresent their credentials. Such persons have the potential of posing harm to their clients unless their deception is dealt with.

Schrink (1992) refers to another type of deception which he calls "conning the client." This means being less than completely open and honest with the offender. Often, it takes the form of making misleading statements about the course and process of the counseling relationship. It may take the form of presenting deceitful information about the outcomes of the counseling. Or, it may take the form of deceitfulness by interpreting so-called "agency rules and regulations" in order to influence, coerce, or control the offender. Another form of conning involves what Sheafor, Horejsi, and Horejsi (1988) call "dumping clients." This refers to a method of dealing with difficult clients by referring them to another counselor or to another agency. In most cases involving conning the client, the deception is usually a kind of purposeful avoidance by the counselor. It consists of various kinds of maneuvers that are used to shield the counselor from the stress and strain of the regimen of correctional work, and from the vicissitudes of such work. There is a great deal of literature to support the notion that "burn out" may impair functioning at work (Bernstein, Roy, Srull & Wickens, 1988). The writers believe that burn out may be also predictive of a tendency to engage in deceptive behaviors with clients and other workers.

In cases concerning the violation of agency rules, regulations, or procedures, the choice is clear: we must report the behavior. Other areas can be treated more subtly. In some instances, we believe that the best way to approach these kinds of ethical dilemmas is to first discuss them with the staff member or colleague in question. Often, these kinds of problems can be worked out or resolved at that level. Perhaps an impaired colleague could be persuaded to seek counseling in the form of participation in a stress management program. Most agencies have recourse to mental health and counseling programs for such employees, especially for those who, sometimes as a consequence of their work regime, may have reacted by abusing drugs or alcohol, by exhibiting marital discord and conflict, or by developing physiological symptoms. In some work settings "quality circles" are available. Quality circles consist of groups of employees and managers who meet on a regular basis to discuss the operations of the agency and how production and efficiency could be improved. Although quality circles developed in order to deal with contentious issues between management and labor in industrial settings, in the opinion of the writers, it may also have a natural application to human services agencies. The use of mediation and dispute resolution models for consensus-building, and the use of outside human relations consultants, are also viable means to resolve some of these human personnel issues. Ultimately, however, it may be necessary to consult with your supervisor concerning these kinds of improprieties if they continue to persist.

Relationship Issues

There are numerous relationship issues that arise in the course of employment in an agency that create ethical dilemmas. Relationships that can be characterized as "personal," that is to say, go beyond friendship and become romantic and sexual, are the most problematic. With respect to personal relationships and correctional case management, we believe that it is especially important to understand the issue of sexual harassment.

Sexual harassment is generally thought of as behavior that includes making unwanted and unwelcome sexual suggestions or proposals, seeking or soliciting sexual services, or the use of verbal or physical communications which, implicitly or explicitly, contain suggestive sexual messages. Sexual harassment is a problem in the workplace because it may force someone to believe that they must submit or tolerate the harassment in order to obtain or continue in employment. Sexual harassment is also a problem because it can interfere with an individual's job performance by creating a work atmosphere that is intimidating, inhospitable, or humiliating. Sexual harassment is also a problem because submission or rejection of sexual favors or requests might be used as a basis for hiring, promoting, or dismissing employees.

At its core, sexual harassment is based upon exploitation. As such, it exploits an imbalance in a psychosocial "power" relationship between individuals in order to obtain a sexual service or favor. The imbalance in the power relationship generally results from differences between individuals based upon role and status. For example, a supervisor may use power of his or her position with respect to managerial and administrative control over the employee for leverage in order to obtain a sexual favor. Or, a counselor may use the power of the counseling relationship, especially the psychological elements inherent in a relationship with a dependent and emotionally fragile client, in order to obtain a sexual service. Most instances of sexual harassment involve females as the victims.

Sexual harassment should be a clear and unambiguous issue for correctional case managers. With respect to civil law, it is illegal by virtue of Title VII of the Civil Rights Act of 1964. It may also be a criminal law violation under state penal codes. It is strictly prohibited by the policies and regulations of agencies. There is, in the opinion of the writers, no ethical dilemma with respect to clear violations of policies and laws concerning sexual harassment: all such violations must be reported. Toward this end, agencies are required to develop, maintain, and disseminate such policies. Sexual harassment policies usually include: a statement regarding the purpose of the policy; definitions of sexual harassment; management and supervisory and nonmanagement and nonsupervisory responsibilities concerning implementation of the policy; complaint procedures; provisions for confidentiality; the investigative process; the review and determination process; types of sanctions; and, procedures for false charges. It should be noted that agencies also have in place similar laws, policies, rules, and procedures with respect to personnel issues concerning violations of civil rights and human rights. There are also various federal and state legislative acts and codes concerning nondiscrimination that pertain to equal employment opportunity and civil rights.

Ethical dilemmas in terms of relationships with staff or colleagues are more likely to arise in relation to what has been euphemistically referred to as "consensual relationships." Generally, most agencies are not predisposed to address the issue of consensual relationships among their employees. However, a correctional case manager who enters into a consensual relationship with a staff member or a colleague should be aware of several possible negative implications of such behavior. First, if the relationship is unbalanced or unequal, for example, between a counselor and a clerical person, then the opportunity for exploitation is probably present, and the possibility for sexual harassment may be present. Second, such relationships may create the appearance of a conflict of interest. Other employees may feel that some individuals are being treated better than others because of the relationship. Personal relationships often blind one to the faults of another. Other persons in the work environment may view the consensual relationship as being adverse to their best interests. Third, consensual relationships may cause one of the partners in the relationship to feel that they cannot be candid with the other partner with respect to job performance. It may cause them to feel that they must "take sides" with their partner with respect to situations in the work environment. Often, they may feel compelled to change their work behavior or to change jobs. Finally, if a consensual relationship falls apart, anger, bitterness, and resentment may surface. This might affect the working environment, and may evolve into an issue of sexual harassment.

There are no easy answers concerning the ethical dilemma of consensual relationships in work settings. The only answer that we proffer is that the case manager who contemplates entering into such a relationship should be clear about its implications, and recognize that his or her behavior is a matter for which they may become personally responsible.

Conclusions

The purpose of this chapter was to help the correctional case manager understand some of the major ethical issues that arise in the course of his or her counseling practice. In addition, the writers presented some suggestions for dealing with ethical dilemmas via a consideration of ethical principles.

The writers began by noting that correctional counseling is not an organized profession. There is no general consensus about educational and experiential preparation for a career in this field; nor is there any general consensus about whether academic institutions or the agency should "lead out" in terms of education and training. The issue concerning the major ideological thrust of correctional counseling is very likely to remain unresolved: is it to be rehabilitation or is it to be management and control of behavior? In addition, there are no specific correctional counseling professional organizations per se that could influence the field, especially with respect to ethical codes for practice. Issues concerning ethical behavior are usually determined by courts and litigation, rather than through professional codes or civil statutes that license or otherwise control the conduct of the practitioners.

The writers also presented an operational definition of ethics. Ethics were defined as having to do with issues of good or bad, and making decisions based upon morally right conduct. Morally right conduct was described as an absolutist position with respect to issues of good or bad. Right conduct was referred to as a consciousness of the self that took into account the effect of one's actions upon the self, the other person, and the long-term consequences of one's actions and behavior. Thus, ethics are internally or psychologically constructed. By contrast, values and norms are socially constructed, and reflect and embrace widely held cultural values, and determine how we should act in a societal context.

Ethical issues in correctional counseling are generally framed or presented as ethical dilemmas when case managers confront them in community-based correctional settings. Some of the most important and common ethical dilemmas when working with offenders were described. These included: confidentiality; informed consent; impact of the intervention; and the phenomenon of angry, hostile, and aggressive offenders. Ethical dilemmas concerning agency policies, programs, or services were also presented. These consisted of: lack of resources, job standards versus the needs of the offender, and putting your value system on hold. Finally, ethical dilemmas and professional working relationship were discussed. These included wrongdoing by staff members or colleagues, deception, and relationship issues.

References

Bayles, M.D. & K. Henley (1989). "General Introduction: The Importance and Possibility of Ethics." In M.D. Bayles & K. Henley (eds.) *Right Conduct: Theories and Applications.* (Second Edition) (p. 1-14). New York, NY: Random House.

Bernstein, D.A., E.J. Roy, T.K. Srull & C.D. Wickens (1988). *Psychology.* Boston, MA: Houghton Mifflin.

Bruhn, J.G. (1991). "Ethics in Clinical Sociology." In H.M. Rebach & J.G. Bruhn (eds.) *Handbook of Clinical Sociology* (pp. 99-123). New York, NY: Plenum Press.

Clear, T.R. & G.F. Cole (1994). *American Corrections* (Third Edition). Belmont, CA: Wadsworth.

Frankl, V. (1969). *Man's Search for Meaning: An Introduction to Logotherapy.* New York, NY: Washington Square Press.

Klonoski, J.R. & R.I. Mendelsohn (1970). "Introduction." In J.R. Klonoski & R.I. Mendelsohn (eds.) *The Politics of Local Justice* (pp. xiii-xxii). New York, NY: Little, Brown.

Kutzer, D.J. & J.R. Lion (1984). "The Violent Patient: Assessment and Intervention." In S. Saunders, A.M. Anderson, C.A. Hart & G.R. Rubenstein (eds.) *Violent Individuals and Families: A Handbook for Practitioners* (pp. 69-86). Springfield, IL: Charles C Thomas.

Lowenberg, F. & R. Dolgoff (1982). *Ethical Decisions for Social Work Practice.* Itasca, IL: F.E. Peacock.

May, R. (1967). *Man's Search for Meaning.* New York, NY: The New American Library.

Megargee, E. (1976). "The Prediction of Dangerous Behavior." *Criminal Justice and Behavior,* 3:3-21.

Meyer, R.G. (1992). *Abnormal Behavior and the Criminal Justice System.* New York, NY: Lexington Books.

Monahan, J. (1981). *Predicting Violent Behavior.* Beverly Hills, CA: Sage Publications.

Monahan, J. (1984). "The Prediction of Violent Behavior: Toward a Second Generation of Theory and Policy." *American Journal of Psychiatry,* 141:10-15.

Reamer, F.G. (1984). "Ethical Dilemmas in Social Work Practice." *Social Work,* 28:31-35.

Robertson, I. (1979). *Sociology.* New York, NY: Worth.

Schrink, J. (1992). "Understanding the Correctional Counselor." In D. Lester, M. Braswell & P. Van Voorhis (eds.) (Second Edition) *Correctional Counseling* (pp. 41-55). Cincinnati, OH: Anderson Publishing Co.

Sheafor, B., C.R. Horejsi & G.A. Horejsi (1988). *Techniques and Guidelines for Social Work Practice.* Boston, MA: Allyn & Bacon.

Stuart, R.B. (ed.) (1981). *Violent Behavior: Social Learning Approaches to Prediction, Management and Treatment.* New York, NY: Brunner/Mazel.

Toch, H. & K. Adams (1989). *The Disturbed Violent Offender.* New Haven, CT: Yale University Press.

Chapter 12

The Future of Correctional Case Management

Introduction

Case management developed as the major model for correctional intervention in response to the trend toward deinstitutionalization of inmates and increasing opportunities for rehabilitation of offenders, especially in the 1960s and 1970s. Recent trends in American criminal justice (Durham, 1994) established that lay and professional groups now favor punishment (primarily incarceration) and doubt the efficacy of rehabilitation efforts. Many states and jurisdictions are increasing criminal penalties, including longer sentences and harsher conditions (e.g., the return of the chain gang in Alabama), and reducing or eliminating "good time" sentence reductions in institutional settings. Probation and parole policies have become more restrictive as the prevalent justice-oriented ideology of the present corrects some of the excesses and failed experiments of the past (Durham, 1994).

Although there are periodic shifts in correctional ideology and practice in response to changing American values and politics, both rehabilitation and punishment orientations share the goal of reducing relapse and recidivism. Related goals of correctional case management include the reintegration of offenders into their families, communities, and society at large, as well as the monitoring of individual progress and program outcome. This book has treated correctional case management as a systematic process by which the needs of offenders are matched with available resources. The dual focus upon treatment and service delivery, and offender behavior change and organizational requirements, addressed the underlying issues of effectiveness and efficiency. According to this view, rehabilitation is not offered as a basic right or humanitarian exercise. Instead, the correctional case management process is treated as the major means for attainment of meaningful, measurable outcomes.

What Works?

Since Martinson (1974) sparked the debate on "what works?" in corrections, the profession has engaged in considerable examination of the conditions required for beneficial behavior change. Assessment, classification, and intervention, as well as the other stages in correctional case management, converge eventually upon the matter of outcome evaluation. Adequate outcome evaluation is at the heart of the whole issue of effectiveness and professional accountability. Differential intervention (i.e., matching offender needs and program resources) is the key means by which effectiveness can be demonstrated (Beutler & Clarkin, 1990). Psychotherapy struggled with similar issues, best articulated in a famous question raised by Paul (1969): "What treatment, by whom, is most effective for this individual with that specific problem, under which set of circumstances, and how does it come about?" Responses to Paul's question catalyzed much integrative research on the outcomes, hence effectiveness, of psychotherapy. A similar effort is needed in corrections.

Correctional professionals have innovated, implemented, and evaluated dozens of promising interventions over the years. Contrary to the misinterpretation of Martinson's (1974) conclusions by some who would assert "nothing works," researchers and practitioners have found some good and predictable outcomes. By 1979, even Martinson acknowledged that there were group counseling programs that reduced recidivism for targeted offender populations. Yet, reviews of the field by the National Academy of Sciences, conducted in 1979 and 1981, continued the rather pessimistic position that no single correctional program had been proven unequivocally to reduce recidivism (Palmer, 1983).

Problems with demonstrating consistently the beneficial effects of correctional interventions are related to several key factors. First, there has been insufficient attention to the characteristics of offenders participating in programs. Overall size or intensity of outcomes is "diluted" when there are large numbers of true psychopaths, who have the worst prognosis among correctional populations, in the treatment group (Eysenck & Gudjonsson, 1989; Palmer, 1983). Concerns about the characteristics of program participants raise the recurrent issue of "basic treatment amenability" versus "differential intervention."

When participant selection is guided by basic treatment amenability determinations, then high-risk, poor-prognosis offenders may be excluded while highly motivated, low-risk offenders are included in an optimal program. Such programs would probably demonstrate some beneficial treatment gains; however, the outcomes may not be clinically meaningful in that low-risk offenders de facto are less likely to reoffend. On the other hand, exclusion of most psychopathic individuals could contribute to the higher crime rates. According to enlightened estimates (e.g., Blackburn, 1993; Eysenck & Gudjonsson, 1989; Wilson & Herrnstein, 1985), the sub-population of truly antisocial offenders, which may constitute only 10-30 percent of the adjudicated criminal population, produces most of the crime as they move through the "revolving door" of the criminal justice system. If one systematically excludes active criminals from treatment, then the best, most effective correctional programs may have little impact on the problem of crime.

Decisions about basic treatment amenability are not always based upon careful assessment or clinical experience. For example, currently there is a strong national movement in America to insure the incarceration of sex offenders because the prevalent popular belief is that they cannot be treated. Contrary to popular opinion, sex offender recidivism rates are not higher than other categories of offenders and can be significantly reduced through effective treatment (Becker & Hunter, 1992). When one applies the misconceptions about amenability to the treatment of sex offenders, there are few or no treatment programs available (which is frequently the case). If treatment were available, it would be reserved for sex offenders who have the best prognosis (e.g., incest perpetrators) and those who need the least treatment. In the example of rehabilitating sex offenders, there are several valuable lessons. Most importantly, the successful rehabilitation of even one sex offender could protect literally hundreds of children in the community from victimization (Abel & Rouleau, 1990). Thus, it would be beneficial to treat a group of high-risk sex offenders, even if only one or two participants realized the desired treatment outcomes. In the absence of a death penalty for sex offenders, long prison sentences can incapacitate individuals for a period of time. However, unlike other criminal populations, sex offenders may not "mature out" of their offender behavior. Therefore, they present substantial risk for community members and corresponding need for treatment when they are released from secure settings. Another lesson learned from sex offender correctional decisions is that it is much more expensive to imprison them than it is to treat them. The $15,000-$70,000 invested in each inmate per year could purchase state-of-the-art treatment, with a high probability of realizing gains from the investment (cf. Becker & Hunter, 1992; Wilson & Herrnstein, 1985).

While failure to take into account the characteristics of offenders has hampered decision-making concerning basic treatment amenability and differential intervention, another problem in demonstrating beneficial outcomes is the failure to specify the potentially effective components of treatment. Martinson's (1974) seminal review was criticized by Palmer (1983) and others for failure to take into account the particulars of the wide range of interventions subsumed under correctional treatment. Martinson included interventions ranging from plastic surgery to vocational rehabilitation. Some of the programs were short in duration while others approximated the "potency" (e.g., duration x intensity) one might expect. Many of the interventions were directed or implemented by persons of unknown educational and clinical experience. Some of the "therapists" in such programs were peers and paraprofessionals.

It is difficult to say whether or not a program is effective unless it is actually implemented for an adequate time by well-trained, experienced staff. In addition, efficacy of a particular treatment cannot be determined unless the evaluator "dismantles" the components of the treatment package. In most settings and programs, it is likely that there are some powerful, some weak or nonsignificant, and a few potentially harmful or iatrogenic treatment components. Even more importantly, the evaluator must dismantle a program in order to determine which treatment components worked for what problems and populations. Dismantling of a treatment program involves comparing the effects of implementation, not only with no-treatment or attention-only control groups, but also among the various treatment components.

The final problem in determining beneficial treatment outcomes is the overall failure to evaluate programs and follow-up participants. Outcome evaluation is an ongoing process. Initial innovations in the field are subjected to as rigorous an evaluation as possible. Potentially effective treatment components and target populations are then identified. Finally, the programs are revised and strengthened based upon the evolving understanding and accumulating data. While the aforementioned process is ideal (having seldom been realized in the behavioral sciences), corrections lags behind other fields in evaluating and revising programs.

Correctional interventions tend to be subjected to little or no evaluation or the results of outcome studies are seldom incorporated in ongoing programs. There is initial enthusiasm about a program leading to media attention and widespread diffusion of the innovation. Some potentially effective programs (e.g., community intervention and crime prevention programs) may be discontinued for lack of funding or political exigency. Other programs persist and expand even when there are data questioning the efficacy of the efforts. Two examples of questionable, yet well-received, programs shed some light on the issue.

In recent years, boot camps have been recommended with impunity for juvenile delinquents and young adult offenders. Intuitively, the boot camp experience should be beneficial for young persons and first offenders because it promises to provide needed structure and "shock incarceration." Boot camps may also function as punishment for offenders who would otherwise would have received some "light" sanction. The problem with boot camp intervention is that it may not work (Durham, 1994).

While there is generally a lack of outcome research comparing boot camp incarceration with probation and other sanctions, the available data suggest that this intervention does not reduce recidivism. Young people may complete some educational goals, learn discipline, and improve self-esteem. However, whatever process goals are realized, the intervention does not seem to be effective. One does not know if lack of efficacy results from problems in participant selection, omission of a key program component, inadequate potency, intensity of treatment, or some combination of factors. Since boot camps are usually reserved for first offenders, individuals who realized some progress, yet relapsed (and had their probation revoked), would likely be ineligible to return to their programs, where another "dose" of the intervention could raise the potency of this form of treatment above a hypothetical threshold. On the other hand, some recidivist offenders may be referred to boot camps and other intermediate sanctions due to the lack of information regarding extensive juvenile offenses. Their inclusion in the intervention may dilute the otherwise powerful beneficial effects of the boot camp experience for most program participants.

Another example of questionable efficacy is the value of intensive community supervision of adult offenders. In a nationwide study of intensive supervision with probationers and parolees (Petersilia & Turner, 1993), intensive community supervision failed to reduce recidivism and actually increased recidivism rates in some evaluation sites. For example, placing serious felons on

intensive supervision parole in Houston, Texas increased the number of technical violations and the number of persons returned to prison. That is, intensive
supervision, as an intermediate sanction, added to the prison population when
the National Institute of Justice compared intensive parole with normal parole.
Although returning felons to prison for technical violations of parole could be
an artifact of the implicit heightened surveillance of intensive supervision, such
programs nevertheless "failed" when using the evaluation criteria of reduced
imprisonment and cost-effectiveness. However, when Petersilia and Turner
(1993) dismantled the effects of treatment, they found some promising results.
Program participants who were employed or received more counseling (especially for alcohol and drug problems) were more likely to complete intensive
supervision without infraction or reoffense.

The concept of differential intervention applies to both intensive community supervision and boot camp examples. The issue of basic treatment amenability remains when one focuses upon whether serious, recidivist offenders should
be included in intermediate sanctions. However, boot camp and intensive
supervision interventions attempted to match characteristics of offenders with
available resources (i.e., differential intervention). The concept of differential
intervention (cf. Beutler & Clarkin, 1990) holds the most promise in correctional case management decisionmaking. Differential intervention addresses the
question, "What offender will benefit from which service provided where for
how long and by whom?"

The differential intervention perspective best applies the matching model
which is the foundation of our model of professional correctional case management, as well as outcome research. Treatment decisions, regarding such matters
as intermediate sanctions, are functions of adequate assessment and classification. When the characteristics of offenders are known, they can be matched
through referral and treatment planning to the most potentially effective interventions. The results of intervention are evaluated as participants are followed-
up and program innovations are modified by outcome data. When correctional
professionals are aware of what works, they can advocate program participation
and create intake policies and procedures that maximize admission and participation. In this manner, the stages in the correctional case management process
work in concert for meaningful offender behavior change and efficient delivery
of services. Having addressed the central concern of effectiveness, it is possible
to explore the characteristics of correctional programs likely to work through
differential intervention.

Promising Correctional Programs

Several correctional programs seem to be especially promising given the
results of implementation and evaluation. Alternatives to incarceration, including electronic monitoring (EM) and day reporting centers, may become widespread in the future of correctional case management. Restitution and commu-

nity service remain viable options, especially for young offenders. Group work and cognitive behavior modification are promising counseling programs. Structural family therapy and participation in self-help recovery groups have much potential for reducing relapse.

Alternative sentencing programs, including shock probation, house arrest, and restitution, represent correctional innovations designed to save money (by reducing costly incarceration) and rehabilitate offenders. Innovations such as intensive probation/parole supervision and electronic monitoring also address the public's need to incapacitate, at least temporarily, high-risk offenders. Electronic monitoring was a logical extension of house arrest. In this innovation, advances in technology (e.g., motion detection and remote computing) permit an offender to be confined in the home, rather than imprisoned. Electronically monitored clients are permitted some range of movement, such as working away from the home during designated hours, but subjected to curfews, moderately close surveillance, and enhanced detection of probation/parole violations. Electronic monitoring satisfies evaluation criteria regarding cost-effectiveness: EM costs $1-$9 per day, while incarceration ranges from $15 to $50 per day (Enos, Black, Quinn & Holman, 1992). Electronic monitoring in community supervision produced beneficial results in terms of greater likelihood of completing probation/parole without being revoked and relieving family members of the burden of responsibility for surveillance (Enos, Black, Quinn & Holman, 1992). With ongoing technological advances, electronic monitoring may become even more desirable. This case management innovation facilitates systematic structure or surveillance, as well as involvement of the client and family in counseling.

Day reporting centers represent another promising alternative in corrections. Just as in electronic monitoring, structuring of client activities can be accomplished without the massive financial and logistical concerns associated with incarceration. This type of intermediate sanction developed in Great Britain to expand the range of services available to offenders and the range of punishment options to judges (Durham, 1994). In the United States, day reporting centers evolved in response to the problem of prison overcrowding in the 1980s and 1990s. Although day reporting centers vary in their basic features, all provide surveillance, most facilitate drug testing and other screening of compliance with community supervision contracts, and some incorporate services such as group counseling and vocational rehabilitation. Day reporting centers appear to be cost effective (requiring as little as $19 daily), administratively efficient, and beneficial to program completers. One problem encountered in a National Institute of Justice survey, reported by Durham (1994) was an unacceptably high rate of persons who failed to complete the program. Dropping out and disciplinary problems may reflect lack of differential intervention.

Restitution and community service are frequent activities for juvenile and adult offenders afforded probation. Restitution focuses upon payment to actual victims or victims' assistance funds, while community service involves repayment to society for injuries and losses sustained collectively by the state. Both restitution and community service appear to especially help young offenders learn contingent consequences and some empathy.

Restitution involving in-kind contributions of work or services facilitates the moral education component of this program (Durham, 1994; Wilson & Herrnstein, 1985). Community service saves the state money when clients provide valuable public services (e.g., cleaning and maintenance at the local zoo). In addition, community service affords opportunity for naive and indecisive individuals to learn about the world of work. Participation in community service and day reporting enables offenders to work or go to school, earning stipends that can be used to make restitution. Additional research is needed to determine who benefits most from such opportunities and which treatment components are most potent.

Group work and cognitive behavior modification (also called cognitive therapy) address important skills deficits and errors in thinking presented by offenders, young and old. Group interventions are time-saving and cost-effective. However, the most attractive feature of group work may be its ability to catalyze group dynamics for healthy personal change. The skilled leader can foster cohesiveness, validation, and movement in the group such that the offender feels, perhaps for the first time, a sense of belonging and purpose. In addition, group members, who have shared in the criminal lifestyle, are in the best position to confront inconsistencies and errors in thinking.

Psychoeducational groups provide valuable information and opportunities for clarification. Skills acquisition groups afford opportunities for demonstration, modeling, and practice. Group work has always played a major role in the rehabilitation of offenders (Lester & Van Voorhis, 1992) with demonstrable efficacy (Palmer, 1983). Problem-oriented groups are offered increasingly to special populations such as sex offenders and family violence perpetrators (Salter, 1988; Stordeur & Stille, 1989).

Cognitive behavior modification is an intervention technique that targets specific distortions and errors in thinking of known groups of offenders. Each type of offender has a set of cognitive distortions that justifies offender behavior and enables the criminal lifestyle. In order for meaningful behavior change to be maintained, the client must recognize and revise these thinking errors. Knopp (1984:312-313) listed seven general mistaken beliefs of criminals (Table 12.1).

Some of the erroneous beliefs listed in Table 12.1 apply to all criminals (e.g., externalizing blame and maintaining a closed channel), while other distortions are more characteristics of some classes of offenders than others. For example, being preoccupied with power and presenting impulsivity are more common among truly antisocial offenders (Eysenck & Gudjonsson, 1989). Other specific groups of offenders (e.g., sex offenders) have their own unique mistaken beliefs, which maintain their particular offender behavior. A pedophilic sex offender may believe, "A child can make decisions about whether or not to have sex with an adult," while an incest perpetrator holds, "Having sex with my child is a good way to teach about sex and love" (Abel, Becker, Cunningham-Rathner, Kaplan & Reich, 1984). The very specific cognitive distortions held by offenders render long-lasting behavior change very

Table 12.1
Mistaken Beliefs of Offenders

1.   Love, Approval, and Respect:

It is absolutely necessary to have affection, attention, and recognition from family and friends.

This belief system is associated with *pride*, the willingness to do anything to save face, and *sentimentality*, an exaggerated image of oneself as good and caring in order to justify acting-out.

2.   Perfectionism:

One must always be competent in everything according to rigid, perfectionistic standards set for self and others.

This self-defeating perspective is related to *"zero-state"* mentality in which one must win everything or feel like an absolute zero. *"I can't"* is a similar stance in that the addict avoids responsibility and experience unless it supports the shaky, perfectionistic self-image.

3.   Awfulizing:

It is horrible when people or things are not the way the addict wants them to be.

Awfulizing is frequently based on a sense of *ownership* when people and objects are treated as personal possessions. Even differences of opinion may threaten the addict's view that things must go their way. Threats to *power or control* are seen as catastrophic.

4.   Externalizing Blame:

People and situations are responsible for my unhappiness or discomfort.

This belief system favors general *irresponsibility* as well as perpetuation of a *victim stance*, in which the addict uses outrage or self-pity to justify acting out.

5.   Avoidance:

It is better to avoid life's difficulties rather than to face up to problems.

The addict maintains avoidance through the *closed channel* of secrecy and rigidity. Externalization of blame or responsibility also involves *lack of persistence or effort*. This mistaken belief enables the co-dependent partner of the addict to assume a conflictual caretaker role.

6.   Lack of Empathy:

I must be concerned only with my safety and comfort; others must look out for themselves.

Many addicts assume this life position because they see living as survival; competing with others for scarce resources. The lack of concern for others is justified by the self-important perspective of *uniqueness*, "I'm special or superior." Naturally, the self-oriented survivalist is little concerned with keeping one's word, since negotiation is directed at maximizing selfish interests. *Failure to meet obligations* is the rule rather than the exception.

7.   Lack of Time Perspective:

All that is important is what I want now.

This attitude is based on *impulsivity*, the relief phase following a period of control in which "I want what I want and I want it now." There is also a *super optimism*, or total disregard for future possible consequences. "There's no way I'll get caught" and "One more time won't hurt" are typical examples of mistaken self-talk that lead to relapse.

difficult. In order to reduce relapse risk, it will be necessary to test and confront these errors in thinking in group and individual work.

Correctional professionals must be concerned not only with modifying the content of thought, but also the structure or rigidity. Offenders tend to present rigid and concrete thought process, which makes it very difficult to problem-solve or negotiate. However, there are promising correctional interventions based on changing decision-making strategies and enhancing creative problem-solving (Eisenman, 1991; Gendreau & Ross, 1990).

Structural family therapy, which addresses rigidity and reactivity in family systems, is another promising correctional program. Minuchin, the father of structural family therapy, developed an action-oriented model for helping families of delinquents learn better problem-solving techniques (Colapinto, 1992). Instead of focusing on the individual cognitive patterns of delinquents, Minuchin addressed offender behavior as a symptom of underlying family pathology. He helped lower-socioeconomic families organize themselves in a structured, yet flexible, manner (Minuchin, Montalvo, Guerney, Rosman & Schumer, 1967).

Structural family therapy involves improving the boundaries and rules that define a family system and create both boundaries and hierarchy. By using role-playing, directing, and other active, experiential methods, families producing offenders can learn novel, adaptive ways to interact, especially in response to the demands of daily family life. Structural family therapists work with spousal, parent-child, and sibling dyads to improve communication and teamwork. Since much relapse is precipitated by family interactional patterns, correctional case managers should become involved in some family treatment. The structural family therapy model can be readily learned and applied, even by paraprofessionals, who have no training in psychotherapy (Colapinto, 1992).

The last of the correctional programs identified as being promising is participation in a Twelve-Step, self-help group (sometimes called a "recovery group"). Since relapse prevention is an ongoing concern in correctional case management, offenders and their families need to take advantage of every resource available in the community. Given the philosophy that recovery is a lifelong phenomenon, it is useful to conceptualize crime as an addiction and treat the lifestyle accordingly. Recovery groups are ideally suited to corrections because they are available in institutional and community settings. Twelve-Step groups, such as Alcoholics Anonymous and Narcotics Anonymous, are virtually cornerstones in contemporary correctional treatment. New self-help groups, including some based on religion or ethnicity (e.g., the Nation of Islam) hold promise for the future of correctional intervention (Hamm, 1992).

In order to address the future of correctional case management, it was useful to review contemporary programs that hold promise for future application and expansion. Some of the promised programs reflect the need for close supervision during the course of rehabilitation: electronic monitoring and day reporting centers. Other promising programs directly address the need for structure, but rely upon the resources of group or family system. In general, corrections has "gone cognitive" with the rest of the mental health disciplines.

Programs that promise to facilitate cognitive development and the emergence of morality (e.g., restitution and community service) have intuitive appeal, given what we know about the limited problem-solving and decision-making repertoires of offenders. Promising programs also tend to be action-oriented, rather than verbal, self-reflective counseling.

Based upon the present review, it is possible to list the common features or charactersitics of potentially effective correctional interventions (Table 12.2).

Table 12.2
Characteristics of Effective Correctional Interventions

Characteristic	Target Group
Action-orientation	Families of delinquents
High structure	Recidivists
Coping-skills training	Concrete offenders
Restitution/service	Young/first offenders
Group work	All offenders
Electronic monitoring	First offenders
Vocational training	All offenders
Cognitive therapy	All offenders
Relapse prevention	All offenders
Recovery movement	Addicted offenders

The characteristics of effective correctional interventions can be combined as treatment components in an omnibus program. In accordance with this text's bias for the "matching model" or differential intervention, certain components, as suggested in the table, are especially promising for certain classes of offenders. Thus, it is important to carefully assess and classify clients before selecting correctional interventions.

Conclusions

Although there has been a shift in criminal justice ideology from rehabilitation to punishment, the field of corrections remains viable as long as there are effective, cost-saving programs. Correctional professionals, as well as the informed public, reject the contention that "nothing works," although concerns about recidivist offenders and the revolving door of the prison are legitimate. Correctional case management will continue to be affected by public opinion and criminal justice trends.

The response to Martinson's seminal question catalyzed the field to devote attention to outcome evaluation. There are adequate data available to assert that some interventions, conducted by skilled professionals and well-trained paraprofessionals, can be effective in some settings, when the treatment components are adequately matched with the needs and characteristics of the offender group. The present text has presented a synthesis of promising correctional approaches. The model of correctional case management emphasized the importance of matching systematically the needs of offenders with available resources. The process of correctional case management decisionmaking within this model addresses concerns about effectiveness.

The recipients of correctional case management need help with deinstitutionalization and reintegration into the home and community. There will be need for relapse prevention and rehabilitation services at the close of even the longest prison stay. By evolving a technology of correctional case management, the offender client, his or her family, the correctional professional, and the average citizen can come to understand what is needed in order to reduce the risk of reoffense.

Effective treatment decisions arise from adequate assessment and classification, as well as careful follow-up and program evaluation. As we learn more about "what works," then correctional professionals can advocate policy and procedural changes needed to reduce barriers to program participation. In this manner, professional roles and program activities throughout the stages of the correctional case management process work toward meaningful behavior change and efficiency in service delivery.

References

Abel, G.G. & J.L. Rouleau (1990). "The Nature and Extent of Sexual Assault." In W.L. Marshall, D.R. Laws & H.E. Barbaree (eds.) *Handbook of Sexual Assault* (pp. 9-21). New York, NY: Plenum.

Abel, G.G., J.V. Becker, J. Cunningham-Rathner, J.L. Rouleau, M. Kaplan & J. Reich (1984). *The Treatment of Child Molesters.* Atlanta, GA: Behavioral Medicine Laboratory, Emory University.

Becker, J.V. & J.A. Hunter (1992). "Evaluation of Treatment Outcome for Adult Perpetrators of Child Sexual Abuse." *Criminal Justice and Behavior*, 19:74-92.

Beutler, L.E. & J.F. Clarkin (1990). *Systematic Treatment Selection: Toward Targeted Therapeutic Interventions.* New York, NY: Brunner/Mazel.

Blackburn, R. (1993). *The Psychology of Criminal Conduct: Theory, Research and Practice.* Chichester, England: John Wiley & Sons.

Colapinto, J. (1991). "Structural Family Therapy." In A.S. Gurman & D.P. Kniskern (eds.) *Handbook of Family Therapy* (Vol. 2) (pp. 417-433). New York, NY: Brunner/Mazel.

Durham, A.M. (1994). *Crisis and Reform: Current Issues in American Punishment.* Boston, MA: Little, Brown & Co.

Eisenman, R. (1991). *From Crime to Creativity.* Dubuque, IA: Kendall/Hunt.

Enos, R., C.M. Black, J.F. Quinn & J.E. Holman (1992). *Alternative Sentencing: Electronically Monitored Correctional Supervision.* Bristol, IN: Wyndham Hall.

Eysenck, H.J. & G.H. Gudjonsson (1989). *The Causes and Cures of Criminality.* New York, NY: Plenum.

Gendreau, P. & R. Ross (1980). *Effective Correctional Treatment.* Toronto, CN: Butterworth.

Hamm, M.S. (1992). "The Offender Self-Help Movement as Correctional Treatment." In D. Lester, M. Braswell & P. Van Voorhis (eds.) *Correctional Counseling* (Second Edition) (pp. 211-224). Cincinnati, OH: Anderson Publishing Co.

Knopp, F.H. (1984). *Retraining Adult Sex Offenders: Methods and Models.* Syracuse, NY: Safer Society Press.

Lester, D. & P. Van Voorhis (1992). "Group and Milieu Therapy." In D. Lester, M. Braswell & P. Van Voorhis (eds.) *Correctional Counseling* (Second Edition) (pp. 175-191). Cincinnati, OH: Anderson Publishing Co.

Martinson, R. (1974). "What Works? Questions and Answers about Prison Reform." *The Public Interest*, 35:22-54.

Martinson, R. (1979). "Symposium on Sentencing." *Hofstra Law Review*, Winter:243-258.

Minuchin, S., B. Montalvo, B. Guerney, B.L. Rosman & F. Schumer (1967). *Families of the Slums.* New York, NY: Basic Books.

Palmer, T. (1983). "The 'Effectiveness' Issue Today: An Overview." *Federal Probation*, 47:3-10.

Paul, G.L. (1969). "Behavior Modification Research: Design and Tactics." In C.M. Franks (ed.) *Behavior Therapy: Appraisal and Status* (pp. 29-62). New York, NY: McGraw-Hill.

Petersilia, J. & S. Turner (1993). "Evaluating Intensive Supervision Probation/Parole: Results of a Nationwide Experiment." *National Institute of Justice Research in Brief*, May:1-11.

Salter, A. (1988). *Treating Child Sex Offenders and Victims: A Practical Guide.* Newbury Park, CA: Sage.

Stordeur, R.A. & R. Stille (1989). *Ending Men's Violence against Their Partners.* Newbury Park, CA: Sage.

Wilson, J.Q. & R.J. Herrnstein (1985). *Crime and Human Nature.* New York, NY: Simon & Schuster.

Index

Abel, 239, 243
Acceptance, 44-45, 208
Acculturation, 193
Ackerman, 7
Active criminals, 238
Adams, 226
Addictionologist, 13-14
Addictionology, 13-15
Adler, 114, 133, 137, 141
Adult Internal Management System (AIMS), 92-93
Advocacy, 2, 12, 31-32, 123
Aichorn, 139
Alcoholics Anonymous (AA), 13-14, 90, 121, 180-181, 245
Alternative sentencing, 41, 241
Ambrosino, 31, 191
American Correctional Association (ACA), 220
American Probation and Parole Association (APPA), 220
Anastasi, 77
Anderson, 195-196
Andrews, 52, 99, 102-103
Anomic suicide, 191, 211-212
Anthropological view, 25
Antisocial offenders, 101, 238
Antisocial personality, 86, 88, 117, 137-138, 227
Apter, 176
Arbuthnot, 164
Assessment, 3, 6, 8-12, 32, 57
Assimilation, 193, 196
Attention deficit, hyperactivity disorder (ADHD), 86, 102
Attitudes, 190
Attributions, 96, 137
Atwood, 172
Authenticity, 42
Aylmer, 168-170

Barbara, 43-44
Barlow, 18
Barlow strain gauge, 80
Batterers, 4
Baxter, 193
Bayles, 221-222
Beavin, 3, 136
Beck, 78, 110

Becker, 239
Behavioral classification, 79, 92-93
Behavioral observation, 79-80
Behavioral rehearsal, 48
Bellack, 66, 79
Berk, 4
Berne, 46, 52, 136
Bernstein, 232
Beutler, 9, 17, 238
Biestek, 45
Binder, 4
Biopsychosocial, 1, 23, 68-69, 81, 192
Biosocial, 189
Black, 31, 138, 142, 242
Blackburn, 72, 76, 172, 238
Bleuler, 24
Bohn, 89, 91
Boltwood, 69
Bonta, 91, 99, 102-103
Boot camps, 229, 240
Borrello, 202
Boundaries, 125, 152-153, 179, 245
Bouquet, 205
Bowlby, 69
Boyer, 203-204
Braden, 205-206
Braswell, L., 114
Braswell, M., 172
Bratter, 114
Brickman, 13, 14, 76
Brill, 209
Broderick, 165, 171, 199
Brokering, 12, 15, 122
Browne, 199
Bruhn, 221
Buzawa, C.G., 4
Buzawa, E.S., 4

Campbell, 205
Carey, 120
Carkhuff, 33
Carnes, 184
Case finding, 120-122
Case management, 23, 24, 27-28, 112, 120, 237
Case management classification (CMC), 97-98
Case management grid, 119
Case management perspective, 111-113